Introduction to
The Tarot of Awakening

T*he Tarot of Awakening: Initiation into the Western Mystery Tradition* is a series of spiritual teachings based on the Rider-Waite Tarot deck. While Tarot cards can be, and often are, used in the pursuit of our material concerns, they may also be used to help us on our spiritual quest. *The Tarot of Awakening* was written specifically as a teaching tool to aid that quest.

There is no universally accepted goal of the spiritual quest. Many spiritual systems regard the acquisition of wealth, health and personal power as appropriate spiritual goals. In *The Tarot of Awakening*, the goal is the awakening to one's true Self. This awakening, also called achieving higher consciousness, enlightenment, the Great Work, illumination or Initiation, is the experiential realization of our true identity as part of God.

Clarification of the goal is essential; clarification of language is equally important. It's the teacher's job to define terms and make the teaching as clear as possible. It's the aspirant's job to understand those terms according to the teacher's definitions for the duration of the teaching. *The Tarot of Awakening* uses the word "self" (with a small "s") to mean the sense of identity we derive from our ego and personality. The "self" is the part of ourselves that we think of as "me."

This self has opinions, ideas, preferences and goals. The term "Higher Self" is used to mean the awareness of the Divine that lies within each of us. Until the aspirant is quite far advanced on the spiritual path, the Higher Self remains conceptual, not experiential. The terms "Divine," "Grace," "God," or "the One Will" are used interchangeably to mean the Great Intelligence that appears to be the Driving Force and Master of the Universe.

A tremendous degree of confusion, drama and difficulty exist on the spiritual path because human beings perceive the *self*, the *Higher Self* and *One Will* to be different things. In the radical alteration of awareness that we call "awakening" or "enlightenment," this perception changes: the *self* is seen to be a set of ideas or beliefs rather than an independent being, while the *Higher Self* and *One Will* are revealed to be one and the same.

In the Western Mystery Tradition, awakening or enlightenment is referred to as "Initiation." This term reflects the Tradition's fabled past as an initiatory system of spiritual attainment, in which the neophyte was initiated into the Mysteries (and thereby a different mode of consciousness) by someone who had already gone through the process. The terms "aspirant" and "student" designate a person who is working toward Initiation. The term "Initiate" is used to describe a person who has undergone the Initiation.

There are also "initiations" (with a small "i"). These are lesser experiences along the way that teach the aspirant many important things. An "initiation" may start us on a path of discovery that ultimately results in Initiation.

The Tarot of Awakening is intended to help the aspirant attain Initiation by developing the aspirant's intuition and awareness of the Higher Self through the use of Tarot cards. Meditation on and use of these cards can provide important insights into the nature of our own lives and help build a bridge between the Divine and man. Aspirants are often surprised by the depth and quality of insight

The Tarot of Awakening

Initiation

into the

Kabbalistic Western Mystery Tradition

BY

Amy M. Wall

To Gary Payne—editor, boyfriend, and husband.

Without his love, support, encouragement,

sense of humor, willingness to wash dishes,

and enormous editorial talents,

this book would not exist.

Printed in the United States of America

First Printing: July 2010

ISBN 978-0-9842205-0-2

Contact the author by writing to

Desert Mystery Publishing
6890 E. Sunrise Dr., Ste 120-196
Tucson, AZ 85750

Please include a self-addressed,
stamped envelope if you wish a reply.

Book design and layout by Martha Nichols/aMuse Productions®

Contents

available through meditating on the Tarot. As Dion Fortune (1890–1946), British occultist, author, and founder of the Society of the Inner Light, explains, "It is well known to mystics that if a man meditates upon a symbol around which certain ideas have been associated by past meditation, he will obtain access to those ideas, even if the glyph has never been elucidated to him by those who have received the oral tradition 'by mouth to ear.'" [1]

The Tarot deck consists of 78 cards: 22 Major Arcana, 40 Minor Arcana, and 16 Court Cards. The 22 Major Arcana are the best-known and most widely-used cards of the deck. The 40 Minor Arcana, like ordinary playing cards, consist of four suits: Wands, Swords, Cups and Pentacles. There are ten cards in each suit. The 16 Court Cards consist of four characters in each of the four suits— King, Queen, Knight and Page.

To help students develop awareness and build the bridge, *The Tarot of Awakening* explores each of these cards in the context of the spiritual journey. To give each aspirant the greatest possible opportunity to resonate with the cards, many of the traditional correspondences to colors, gems, plants, heavenly bodies, magical equipment, deities, etc., are provided. Some of these correspondences come from the Kabbalistic tradition from which the Rider-Waite deck is derived; others come from Tarot scholars, occultists and magicians of the past few centuries. None of these correspondences are holy writ and there is absolutely no need to memorize this information. Use what works for you and disregard the rest.

A brief quote from Paul Foster Case's *Book of Tokens: Tarot Meditations* is included for each of the Major Arcana. Paul Foster Case (1884–1954) was an American member of the Golden Dawn, the creator of the Builders of the Adytum mystery school, and arguably the greatest Tarot scholar of the first half of the twentieth century.

Meditations designed specifically to lead the aspirant toward Initiation are also provided for each of the Major Arcana. Some of these meditations may touch on sensitive areas; please use your inner wisdom when deciding which meditations may be appropriate and safe for you. Certain meditations are marked for more advanced aspirants; your own self-honesty will tell you whether or not you are ready for them.

Taken as a whole, *The Tarot of Awakening* provides a model of the spiritual journey. Models must, however, be used with caution. On one hand, we all like to know where we are and where we're going. On the other hand, the process by which a person receives Initiation is little understood, fraught with difficulties, and shrouded in mystery and legend. Most of the model-making attempts have been made by mystics and spiritual leaders, and describe how the process proceeded retrospectively for these particular individuals. The advantage of these models is that we get a first-hand account of the experience; the disadvantage is that most people have different, but nevertheless valid, experiences. Other models, created by scholars and scientists, provide intellectual rather than experiential views of the process. Because these models usually derive from composite portraits distilled from a variety of experiences reported by many different people, such models have the benefit of a broader viewpoint, but the disadvantage of not having actually been experienced by the author. Both experiential and intellectual models are valuable as long as we recognize that no model can possibly be accurate for everyone.

The Kabbalistic model of spiritual development is depicted by the glyph called the *Tree of Life*. In this model, the Divine descends from the highest point to the lowest point; pure spirit becomes physical manifestation and normal consciousness. The individual soul then works its way back up the Tree to its point of origination.

When Tarot and the Tree of Life are merged, a new spiritual model is born; it is this new model that is explored in *The Tarot of Awakening*. This model begins with **The Fool,** representing the One Will beginning the descent into manifestation. The Major Arcana chart the process of creation, the role of the subconscious, contact with the inner teacher, formation of the personality, relationships, the destruction of the belief system, the intrusion of fantasy, Initiation, and finally conscious manifestation of the Divine.

The Minor Arcana have traditionally been of little value to the spiritual seeker. The standard interpretations of the Minor Arcana have little relevance to the spiritual quest. They address the everyday concerns of humankind—money, relationships, health—but not the concerns of a spiritual seeker.

However, *The Tarot of Awakening* views the Minor Arcana as stages of growth on the four major spiritual paths. The Suit of Pentacles, which corresponds to the element of earth and the physical body, is viewed as the Path of Service. The Suit of Cups, which corresponds to the element of water and the emotions, is interpreted as the Path of Devotion. The Suit of Swords, which corresponds to the element of air and the mind, is assigned to the Path of Knowledge. The Suit of Wands, which corresponds to the element of fire and the spirit, is assigned to the Mystic Path or Path of Awareness.

While we may believe ourselves to be on one particular path, the true spiritual path of our lives includes aspects of all these paths. Just as each of us has awareness, mind, heart and body, so each of us is simultaneously walking a Path of Service, Devotion, Knowledge and Will/Awareness. Each of these aspects of self influences the others: emotions are interpreted by the mind, the body experiences and reacts to them, and the spirit is oppressed or uplifted by them. No matter what Path we are on, service is performed, love blossoms, knowledge is gained and awareness arises. Further, to reach fully embodied Initiation, we must reach Initiation on *all* levels: heart, mind, body and spirit. We've all met people who seemed to have achieved a very high spiritual level, but something was lacking. Often, these people have reached Initiation on one level, but not another. The mind may have reached full awareness, but the heart has not; or the heart has fully opened to the Divine but the mental understanding of the aspirant has yet to catch up.

Ultimately, all the paths are headed in the same direction. Canadian-born mystic, philosopher, writer, and founder of the Philosophical Research Society Manly P. Hall explains, "The esoteric teachings of all religions are the same. The ends to be attained are identical in every case. The only difference between them is that each school is especially fitted to reach and work with the type of mind and body of the people among whom it is established."[2]

We all have a variety of personality characteristics that can help or hinder our progress on the spiritual path. In *The Tarot of Awakening*, these aspects are represented by the Court Cards. Since we often have difficulty seeing those parts of ourselves that make us uncomfortable, we have a tendency to paste these aspects onto other people. Only when we are willing to recognize these aspects within are the lessons of the Court Cards understood.

The Tarot of Awakening does not regard the Tarot deck as a divinatory device. It will not tell you if you will meet your mate, inherit a fortune, or develop a hangnail. If you are interested in such things, there are thousands of psychic hotlines ready to take your money and soothe your fears. Also, *The Tarot of Awakening* is not intended to be a scholarly work, and the symbols included are by no means an exhaustive study of Tarot symbolism. If you are moved to study Kabbalah and Tarot in more detail from that viewpoint, please review the Suggested Reading List at the back of the book.

It is the author's hope that *The Tarot of Awakening* will provide a little illumination on that most difficult and mysterious of all journeys that takes us deep within to find ourselves and God.

Introduction Bibliography

1   Fortune, Dion. *Mystical Qabalah*. York Beach, Maine: Samuel Weiser, Inc.,
    2000, p. 6.

2   Hall, Manly P. *What the Ancient Wisdom Expects of Its Disciples*. Los
    Angeles, CA: Philosophical Research Society, 1982, p. 36.

Chapter One

THE WESTERN MYSTERY TRADITION, KABBALAH, AND TAROT

The Western Mystery Tradition

"Western Mystery Tradition" is a catch-all term for the secret spiritual wisdom of the western world. This wisdom is not part of the teachings of religious institutions, which are available to everyone, but is hidden instead behind symbolism and analogy. Centuries ago, this wisdom may have been available through mystery schools in places such as ancient Greece and Egypt, but the details of such schools have been lost. Today, it is accessible mainly through books and private meditation.

The "mystery" referred to in the phrase "Western Mystery Tradition" is the mystery of being human. What are we? What is our purpose? What is God? The term "mystery" reflects the conviction that there is more to human life than is explained or revealed by the conventional answers to these questions. The spiritual path of the Western Mystery Tradition is the exploration of these mysteries; the treasure sought is an ever-deepening understanding of our own humanity and relationship with God. The path is walked and treasure discovered by the process of understanding and transforming our self.

Certain branches of the Western Mystery Tradition are taught within the purview of established religions. For example, many synagogues host small groups that meet during off-hours to study and discuss Kabbalistic texts. Similarly, some Christian organizations sponsor groups that study both Old and New Testaments seeking deeper meanings in the sermons attributed to Jesus. Both the small groups and the large organizations utilize the same texts, traditions and rituals; however, while the goal of the large organizations is generally to placate and worship a Creator, the goal of the small groups is to seek the esoteric truths that lie within the teachings of the exoteric host organization.

There are also a variety of mystery traditions that operate independently of established religions. There are traditions based on ancient Egyptian, Greek and Druidic mythologies. Christian mysteries are explored in Rosicrucianism and the Grail Tradition. There are schools of magic based on the teachings of the Hermetic Order of the Golden Dawn, Servants of the Light, Ordo Templi Orientis, etc. All these traditions offer paths for self-exploration and self-transformation.

The foundations and seminal ideas of today's mystery schools and teachings come from a wide variety of religious, cultural, social and historical influences. These influences are outlined in the Tree of the Mysteries[1] in Figure 1. The "Tree of the Mysteries" shows, for example, the long-reaching influence of Kabbalah, which fed the Christian and Hermetic traditions; these in turn fed into Rosicrucianism, Islam, alchemy, and anthroposophy. It should be observed that, far from polluting a pure stream, each additional source enriches the

Schools of Mystery

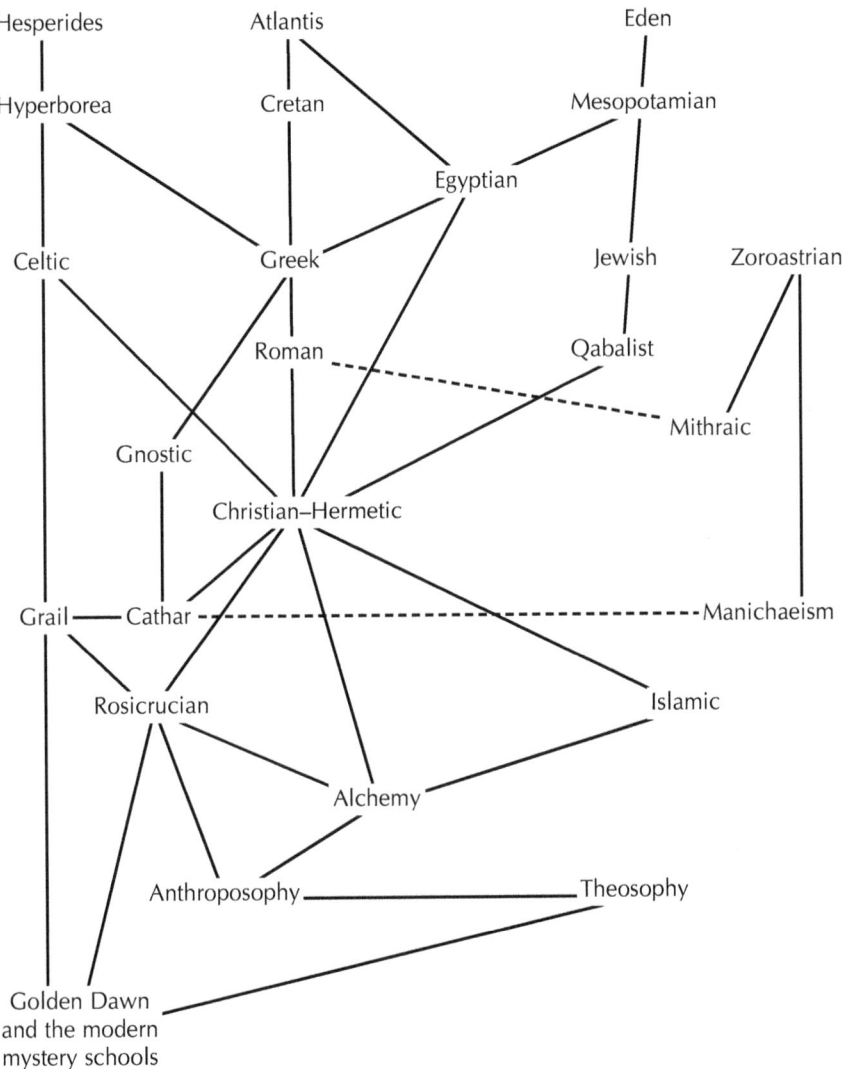

Figure 1. The Tree of the Mysteries.

waters; the Western Mystery Tradition is inclusionary, not exclusionary, and the focus is always on the exploration of the inner worlds. As authors Caitlin and John Matthews explain, "The Mystery Schools, ancient and modern, are way-showers; they possess the maps and compasses with which to explore the inner realms of creation. Through them, those seeking initiation in the temples and lodges of the Western Mystery Tradition are offered training in the use and mastery of these tools: no one is cast adrift in an open boat to sail uncharted seas, or sent forth on a highway that has not already been walked by others. The mysteries are the inner life of the people, and to discover them is to read the story of a divine spark kept burning in the temple of the human spirit." [2]

The multiplicity of options may pose a problem for incoming students. Many believe the only way to embrace the Western Mystery Tradition is to master each of its contributory disciplines. This is not only unnecessary, it's detrimental. To study all paths is to master none; the correct approach is for us to pick the one that appeals to us and delve into it deeply. None are inherently better than the others.

Manly P. Hall explains, "…the mystery schools interpret truth along the lines of the familiar, clothing wisdom in symbol and allegory familiar to those who are supposed to receive it." [3] Adherents of the Western Mystery Tradition believe that God speaks to us in the language of symbols; psychologists believe symbols to be the language of the subconscious mind. Both psychology and religion understand that symbols are a means of communicating with aspects of consciousness that are not part of our normal awareness.

It is often difficult to understand a symbol's meaning. A symbol can mean something different to different individuals, as well as to different cultures or groups. While this apparent vagueness of meaning may occasionally be frustrating, a symbol's meaning cannot and should not be pinned down. As Edith Schnapper, author of several books on religion and spirituality, points out, "Throughout the ages wherever man has sought for the meaning of life and its hidden laws he was confronted with the same obstacle. What he was seeking lay beyond the reach of conceptual thought and its language. What other tools could he use? Older than the language of concepts is the language of symbols and it is this language which alone can express the hidden, intangible and ever changing dynamics of life. Symbols are the out-flow of, and address themselves to, the whole of man, and it is that whole which, in turn is activated and responds; here lies their efficacy but also the reason why they crumble and lose all power the moment they are imprisoned in the realm of intellectual reasoning. They are then literally explained out of existence." [4]

This inexactitude must be treasured and protected. We should never feel that we fully understand our symbols. The complexity of Tarot cards, for example, allows the cards to bring different meanings to everyone who studies them; interpretations are not "right" or "wrong," only different. This is why there are hundreds of books on Tarot, each exploring another possible interpretation of its symbolism.

There is a tendency for students of the Western Mystery Tradition to place great value on ancient symbols and interpretations, while deprecating the new. It is, perhaps, a common human foible to view new teachings and interpretations with suspicion, and regard old teachings with awe. As a result, many teachers use the promise of "ancient" wisdom to get their students started. These teachers understand that until students have progressed some distance along a path of study they will continue to believe that the Divine spoke only long ago. Students eventually realize that wisdom has no expiration date, and is as readily available today as three thousand years ago. The Divine speaks now, at this and all moments; when the student recognizes this, it no longer matters whether there really was a Hermes Trismegestus or a Christian Rosencreutz.

The wisdom of the Western Mystery Tradition springs up wherever and whenever the ground is fertile and ready. The Western Mystery Tradition has adapted, endlessly, to cultures and times, surviving thousands of years of social change, religious persecution and political upheaval. Today, this spiritual path is easier to explore than ever before. Never in the history of the world has so much information been so readily available to the aspirant. With just a click of the mouse, what was once a closely-guarded secret can appear on our laptops. A few more clicks and everything that has ever been published on a subject can be brought to our doors. Blogs dedicated to every possible mythology and path are accessible through the Internet.

That same mouse click, however, can also bring a lot of nonsense to our doors. Blogs are often dominated by people with lofty titles, fantastic costumes, and no interest whatsoever in exploring the mysteries of human life. Since the odds are against finding a fully functioning mystery school in our hometown, we must be responsible for determining what is nonsense and what is not, what will lead to transformation and what will lead to a costume party.

A good metaphor for the path of the Western Mystery Tradition is that of the labyrinth. Working through the labyrinth of information and ideas, encountering blind alleys and cul-de-sacs, is not the drawback of this spiritual path—it *is* the path. At the heart of this labyrinth is the treasure we seek.

Kabbalah

Kabbalah is a mystical tradition that dates back to in the twelfth century, and is based on much older traditions and practices. The correct spelling of Kabbalah is *Kuf Bet Lamed Heh*. There isn't a one-to-one correspondence between English and Hebrew letters, so this one word can be spelled *Cabala, Cabalah, Kabala, Kabbalah, Qabala,*

Qabalah, Qabbalah, etc. My preferred spelling is Kabbalah, for no reason other than that it looks nice in print. It is pronounced Kah-BAH-lah or Kah-bah-LAH.

Kabbalah means "received" or "that which has been received." It is the best-known and most recent of the many forms of Jewish mysticism. Other forms of Jewish mysticism include *Ma'aseh Merkavah,* meaning "account of the chariot," which studies and attempts to re-create Ezekiel's vision of God enthroned on a chariot surrounded by four winged creatures; and *Ma'aseh Beresheit,* meaning "account of creation," which studies the process by which the Universe was created.

Kabbalah became widely known when its seminal text, *The Zohar,* was circulated in twelfth-century Spain. Though unquestionably Jewish in origin, Kabbalah was later adapted for other purposes. For example, Christian scholars used Kabbalistic concepts during the Renaissance to attempt to prove the truth of Christianity. Occultists and magicians found Kabbalah useful for creating magical correspondences and systems. Today, Kabbalah forms the foundation of the Western Mystery Tradition; those studying this tradition will find a basic comprehension of Kabbalistic principles invaluable. These later adaptations added a great deal to the Kabbalistic tradition; for example, since Judaism forbids the making of images, Tarot cards explore an avenue of spirituality not available to traditional Jewish Kabbalah.

From the standpoint of traditional Judaism, the practice of Kabbalah includes the study of Hebrew, sacred texts and a commitment to an orthodox Jewish lifestyle. However, Kabbalistic symbols have been used by Christians, scholars, artists and magicians since the Renaissance. It must be stated that the use of these symbols by non-Jews is not in accordance with Jewish law or custom. Nonetheless, Kabbalah has become an integral part of western spirituality; in that context, the study of Kabbalah does not require adopting Jewish customs or mastering a foreign language. Further, while traditional Jewish Kabbalah is the study of a lifetime, a basic grasp of Kabbalistic symbols and principles is well within the reach of anyone who is interested. The Suggested Reading List at the back of the book provides a list of books on Kabbalah and the Western Mystery Tradition for those interested in learning more.

Three particular Kabbalistic symbols are important to the study of the Western Mystery Tradition—the Hebrew letters, the Tree of Life and the Four Worlds.

Hebrew Letters

Kabbalists believe that Hebrew letters are the energetic building blocks of the universe. The Hebrew word for letter is *Ot*, meaning "sign, wonder or miracle." God formed creation through His Words, spoken in Hebrew. When He said, *"Yehi Or,"* meaning "Let there be light," there was light. Just as atoms combine to create molecules, so letters combine to create forms. Letters and words are holy things; this is why Kabbalists treat books containing Hebrew letters with great respect. They are never put on the floor, walked on or thrown away; they are buried when no longer useful.

In ancient times, Hebrew letters were also numbers. The first letter, *Aleph*, was the number one; the second letter, *Bet*, was the number two; and so on. In addition, a variety of words were eventually assigned to each letter. "Ox" is assigned to *Aleph*, "house" to *Bet*, "camel" to *Gimel*, and so on. In some cases, these words are the actual meaning of the letter; for example, the word *Bet* in Hebrew actually does mean "house." In other cases, meaning was assigned based on the shape of the letter or based on Hebrew words that began with that letter. Many of these associations derive not from authentic Jewish sources, but from Christian Renaissance scholars such as Athanasius Kircher (1602–1680). The numbers, words, and concepts assigned to Hebrew letters are included in our exploration of the Major Arcana in Chapters Two through Four.

The Tree of Life

The rise and fall of kingdoms, journey from birth to death, maturation of the self, process of bringing ideas to fruition, and especially the progress of our souls toward God all follow a path from one state of being to another, one that Kabbalists have observed can be mapped out ahead of time. This path has been studied for centuries; the map that describes this path, called the Tree of Life, is first referenced in the *Sefer Yetzirah*, an ancient text which may be as much as two thousand years old. The Tree of Life, shown in Figure 2, may fairly be said to lie at the very heart of Kabbalah as it is practiced today.

The symbol of the Tree is common to many spiritual traditions. In Buddhism, the tree beneath which the Buddha sat is called the Tree of Enlightenment. Nordic mythology includes Yggdrasill, the World Tree. In Shamanism, the Cosmic Tree connects the Underworld, Middle World and Upper World. However, the Kabbalistic Tree of Life, a diagram of all the processes in creation, is unique in the spiritual traditions of the world.

Diagrammatically, the Tree of Life consists of ten spheres, called *sephirot* in Hebrew (*sephirah* is the singular). The ten *sephirot* represent the structure of the universe. Kabbalah studies this structure by studying the characteristics of the various *sephirot* and the relationships between them.

The *sephirot* are arranged in three triangles and three pillars, as seen in Figure 3. Note that each triangle has a *sephirah* on the right pillar, a *sephirah* on the left pillar, and a *sephirah* in the middle. The

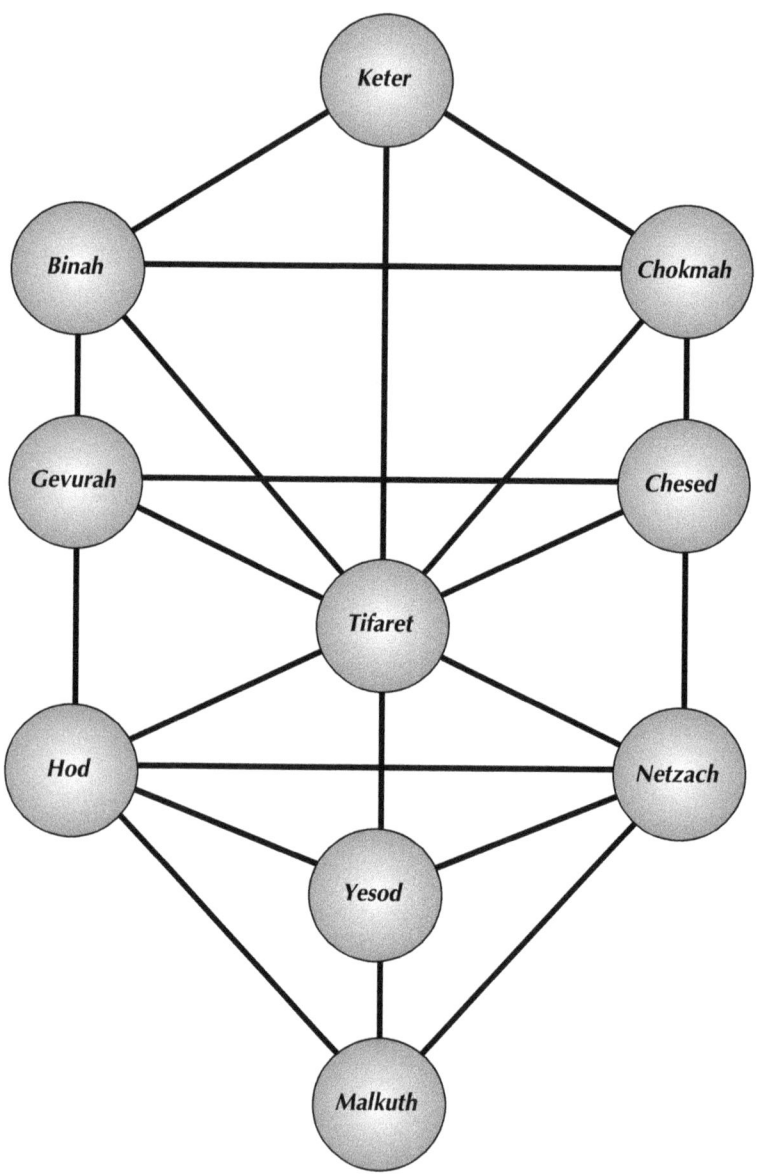

Figure 2. The Tree of Life

top triangle points up; the other two triangles point down. The upper triangle is often called the Supernal Triangle. It consists of *Keter* (meaning Crown), *Chokmah* (meaning Wisdom), and *Binah* (meaning Understanding). The middle triangle is called the Ethical Triangle, consisting of *Chesed* (Mercy), *Gevurah* (Severity) and *Tifaret* (Beauty). The lower triangle is called the Astral Triangle: *Netzach* (Glory), *Hod* (Splendor), and *Yesod* (Foundation). The last *sephirah*, called *Malkuth* (Kingdom), is on the middle column but is not part of a triangle.

The *sephirot* on the right form a vertical column called the Pillar of Mercy; it is also called the Pillar of Force or the male pillar. The *sephirot* on the left make up the Pillar of Severity, also called the Pillar of Form or the female pillar. The *sephirot* in the middle, appropriately enough, form the Middle Pillar. Note that the words "male" and "female" are used in a symbolic sense, with "male" meaning an aspect of creation that gives and "female" meaning an aspect that receives. The *sephirot* that lie on the Pillar of Mercy typically represent concepts that we think of as the warmer, kinder aspects of life; those on the Pillar of Severity are the harsher, more restrictive aspects. The *sephirot* on the Middle Pillar are the happy medium between the other two columns.

Twenty-two paths connect the *sephirot*. Early Kabbalists assigned a Hebrew letter to each of these paths. There was evidently no agreement among them as to the correct assignment of letter to path, and later Kabbalists and Tarot scholars created their own assignments. Arabic numbers were later assigned to the paths as well; the *sephirot* are numbered 1 through 10, and the interconnecting paths are numbered 11 through 32.

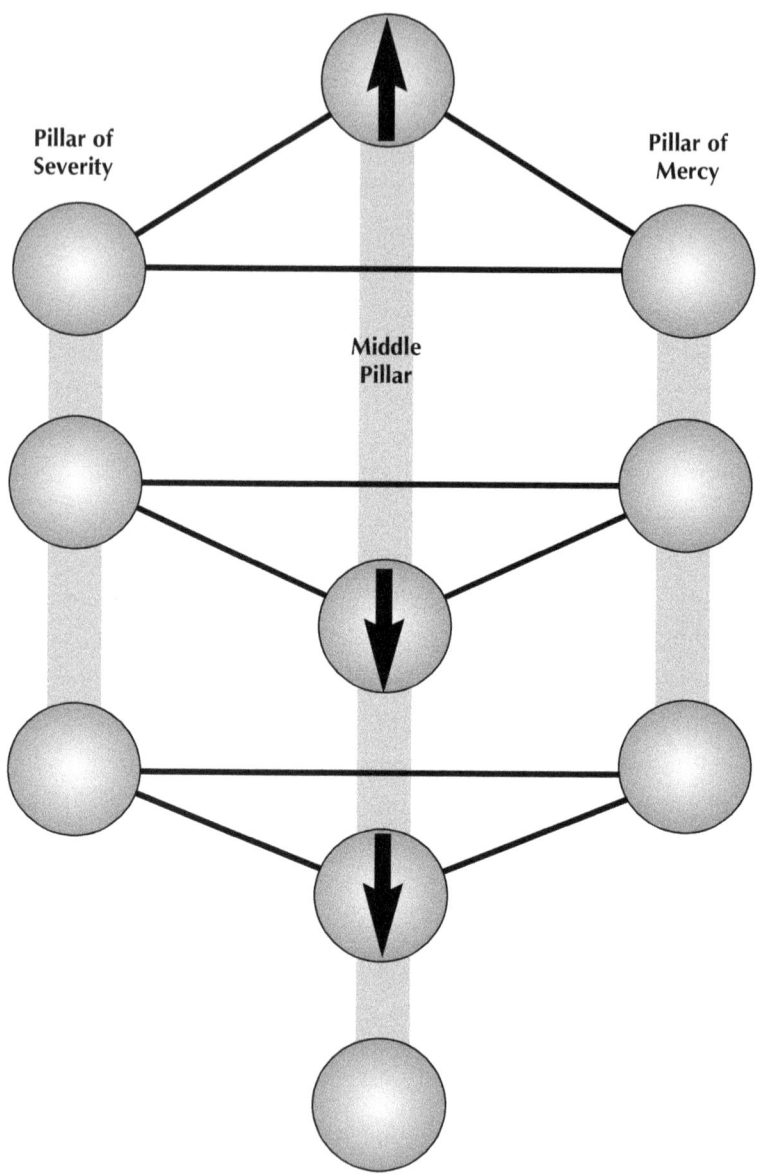

Figure 3. Triangles and Pillars

Using the Tree

The *sephirot* are like numbers—they are concepts that are useful only when applied to something. The number three, for example, doesn't mean much on its own. But when we say "three apples," we know what three means. If we say, "I have three apples and you have eight apples," we also know that one of us has five more than the other. It's the application of numbers to real life that give them meaning. This applies to the Tree of Life as well.

The Tree is often used as a diagram of the process of the Creation of the entire universe. The progress of Creation through the *sephirot* is called the Lightning Flash. It is aptly named, originating high in the unseen sky and seeking ground to discharge its energy. The Lightning Flash, shown in Figure 4, follows the *sephirot* in this order: *Keter, Chokmah, Binah, Chesed, Gevurah, Tifaret, Netzach, Hod, Yesod* and *Malkuth*.

The Tree comes from God, but is not God. God lurks behind the Tree, making Himself known to man only through His emanations. *Keter*, the first emanation, is the starting point. *Keter* contains the entire plan of Creation. Since God created the world with words, *Keter* is the in-drawn breath prior to the Divine Exhalation of Creation. *Keter* is not Creation, but it is the entire universe in seed form; not consciousness, but the raw material of consciousness. *Keter* is both nothing and everything.

The creative process begins in earnest when it moves out of *Keter* into *Chokmah*. *Chokmah*, at the head of the Pillar of Mercy, provides the energy that fuels all of Creation. The magnitude of this energy is unimaginable. However, despite *Chokmah*'s power, it cannot create form unaided; the womb of *Binah* is required to bind the energy of *Chokmah* into form.

Binah is located at the top of the Pillar of Severity. The function of this *sephirah* is to take *Chokmah*'s energy and lock it into a pattern;

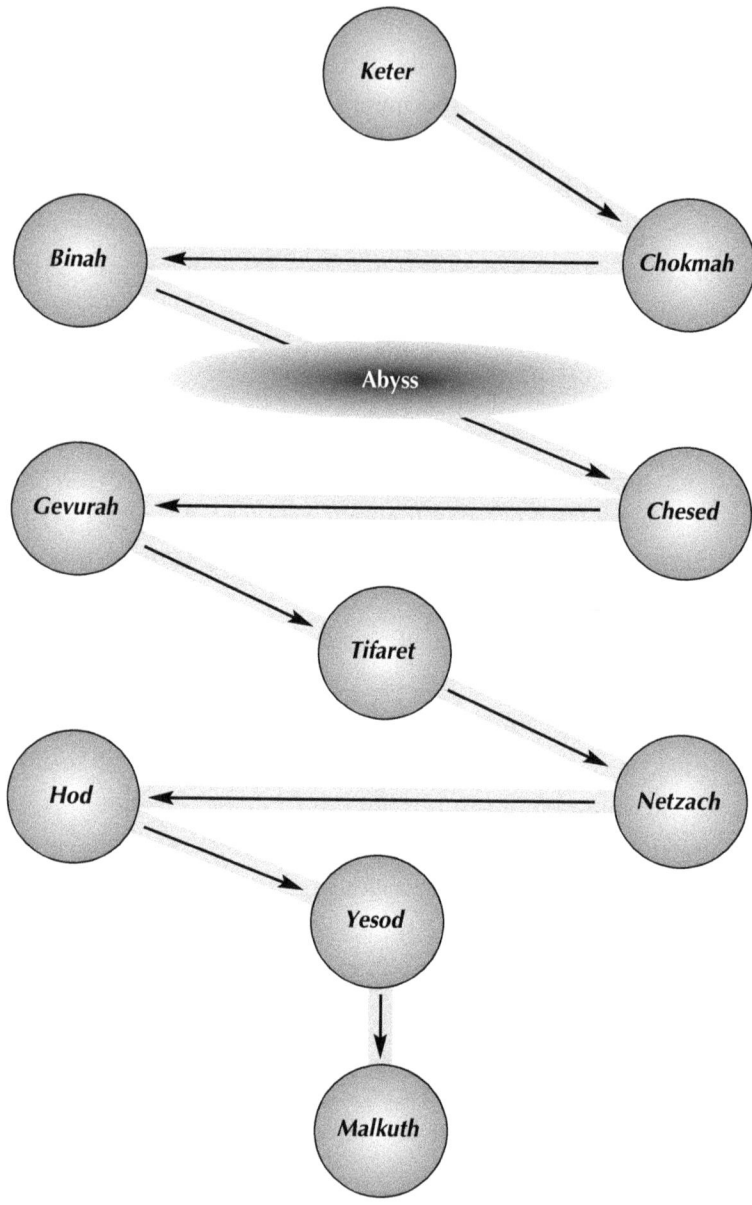

Figure 4. The Lightning Flash

this pattern solidifies as the Lightning Flash continues, eventually becoming physical matter in *Malkuth*. Since *Binah* sets the pattern for all of creation, it is often called the Great Mother. However, the creation of form leads inevitably to form's destruction; *Binah* represents time and death, as well as birth.

Moving out of *Binah*, the Lightning Flash crosses an area on the Tree known as the Abyss. The Abyss separates those *sephirot* that are beyond human comprehension—*Keter, Chokmah* and *Binah*—from those that are more accessible to our understanding.

The Lightning Flash then moves into *Chesed*, an expansive, creative energy that encourages the proliferation of a great variety of life forms, and then into *Gevurah*, a restrictive energy that allows only the fittest life forms to flourish. *Chesed* and *Gevurah* are opposing energies. *Chesed* would like everything to live; *Gevurah* favors a strict survival-of-the-fittest scenario. The energies of *Chesed* and *Gevurah* also operate in human life as archetypes. *Chesed* is peace, *Gevurah* is warfare; *Chesed* is idealistic, *Gevurah* is realistic; *Chesed* is life proliferating, *Gevurah* is the pruning knife. Both are necessary, but both may be taken to an extreme. Too much *Gevurah* is terrifying and cruel, a dictator who punishes his people needlessly. Too much *Chesed* is sentimentality and self-indulgence, a king unable to keep order because he will not enforce his own laws.

The creative energy of the Lightning Flash leaves *Gevurah* and moves into *Tifaret*, the mid-point of the Tree. *Tifaret* is a perfect balance of life and death, war and peace. *Tifaret* also represents the spiritual experience—awakened consciousness, mystical experiences, illumination and sacrifice. Many spiritual aspirants long to reside entirely and permanently in *Tifaret*, but this is not possible. The human experience takes place in all of the five lower *sephirot*—*Tifaret, Netzach, Hod, Yesod* and *Malkuth*.

The Lightning Flash then moves into *Netzach*, which resides at the bottom of the Pillar of Mercy and partakes of that Pillar's open, expansive energy. Here the creative energy takes the form of emotions, instincts, sexuality and the arts. Next is *Hod*, which includes all mental processes—medicine, science, communication, ceremonial magic and mystery. Mental processes are restrictive, so it is appropriate that *Hod* resides at the foot of the Pillar of Restriction.

As with *Chesed* and *Gevurah*, *Netzach* and *Hod* have the potential to be dangerous when out of balance. Too much *Netzach* results in emotion without intellect, hysterical reactions unchecked by reason. Conversely, too much *Hod* is intellect without emotion. Human growth and development depend on balancing emotion and intellect.

The Lightning Flash continues into *Yesod*, where the astral, akashic, or dream plane is created. This is the *sephirah* of sleep, dreams, imagination, fantasy and psychic visions.

At the very bottom of the Tree, *Malkuth* coalesces out of this astral world, becoming fire, water, air and earth. *Malkuth* represents the everyday world of normal human consciousness, our bodies, and the entire physical world. This is the final destination of the Lightning Flash and the ultimate end of the process that started in *Keter*.

The Four Worlds

Kabbalah also interprets the universe through a symbolic model comprising four planes or "worlds." Each world is represented by a letter of the Divine Name (*Yod Heh Vav Heh*), an element (fire, air, water, earth) and a suit of Tarot cards (Wands, Swords, Cups, Pentacles).

The first world is the Archetypal World, called *Atziluth* in Hebrew. It is represented by the *Yod* of the Divine Name. The corresponding element is fire, symbolizing desire and awareness in humankind; the corresponding Tarot suit is the Suit of Wands. *Atziluth* is the world of ideas, the root-notions inherent in the innermost nature of the universal Conscious Energy. For example, the pure idea of a shoe is the idea of protecting the feet. This idea of protecting the feet is at the root of every shoe ever created (though it has been embellished by the root idea of fashion).

The next world is the Creative World, called *Briah* in Hebrew. It is represented by the first *Heh* of the Divine Name. The corresponding element is air, symbolizing the intellect, and the corresponding Tarot suit is the Suit of Swords. In *Briah*, the ideas of *Atziluth* become particular patterns. The idea of protecting the feet evolves here into patterns for particular shoes—boots, slippers, loafers, and so on.

Next is the Formative World, called *Yetzirah* in Hebrew. It is represented by the *Vav* of the Divine Name. The corresponding element is water, symbolizing the emotions, and the corresponding Tarot suit is the Suit of Cups. In *Yetzirah*, the ideas from *Atziluth* which became patterns in *Briah* are brought into more concrete expression. A design for the shoe is made and discussed. Materials are considered. This is the plane of creative processes and actions that will eventually culminate in an actual shoe.

Finally, the Material World is called *Assiah* in Hebrew. It is represented by the final *Heh* of the Divine Name. The corresponding element is earth, symbolizing the body, and the corresponding Tarot suit is the Suit of Pentacles. This is the plane of physical forms which are apparent to our physical senses; here a shoe is actually produced.

Some Kabbalists think of these four worlds as flat surfaces, one on top of another, and the *sephirot* as three-dimensional spheres containing all four worlds. Others think of the Supernal Triangle as *Atziluth*, the Ethical Triangle as *Briah*, the Astral Triangle as *Yetzirah* and *Malkuth* as *Assiah*. Others view the four worlds as four Trees, one above the other, so that the *Malkuth* of *Atziluth* is the *Keter* of *Briah*, the *Malkuth* of *Briah* is the *Keter* of *Yetzirah*, the

Malkuth of *Yetzirah* is the *Keter* of *Assiah*. And still others see these worlds as interconnected, so that the *Tifaret* of *Atziluth* is the *Keter* of *Briah*, the *Tifaret* of *Briah* is the *Keter* of *Yetzirah*, and so on.

Tarot

Tarot is the most recent element of the Western Mystery Tradition. The study of Tarot cards is immensely popular, even among people with no other connection to the Western Mystery Tradition. There are hundreds of Tarot decks available, with new ones appearing all the time.

The history of Tarot is not well-documented; what is known about its history has been obscured, deliberately or otherwise, by occultists. This has resulted in the creation of various Tarot myths. One such myth claims the deck was created by a group of adepts who met periodically at some undisclosed location to discuss philosophy, magic, natural science, etc. Hampered by the lack of a common language, they created the Tarot deck to serve as a means of communication. Other myths place the origin of the cards in Egypt, India, China, Morocco or Mount Sinai. The word *Tarot* is thought to be Egyptian, Latin, Greek, Hebrew or, best of all, a mysterious anagram, whose meaning has yet to be discovered.

Unromantically enough, however, Tarot almost certainly originated as a set of playing cards created by various artists in northern Italy sometime during the early fifteenth century. The oldest Tarot cards still in existence today are lavishly hand-painted decks from the courts of the Italian nobility. They employ images familiar to Medieval and Renaissance European court life—popes, knights, fools, jugglers, etc. The word *Tarot* "…is simply the French version of the Italian word *tarocco* (*tarocchi* in the plural): in the XVI century, it was frequently spelled *tarau*, *tarault* or the like. It went into

German as *tarock*, into Hungarian as *tarokk*, into Czech as *taroky* into Swiss German as *trogge*, and so on. French is the only language in which the final guttural disappeared...." [5]

Tarot cards and Kabbalah were apparently united for the first time by the Comte de Mellet, who wrote a short essay about a connection between the 22 Hebrew letters and the 22 Major Arcana. The essay was published in Court de Gébelin's *Le Monde Primitif* in 1781. Later, French author and occultist Eliphas Lévi (1810–1875) pursued the connection, assigning a card to each Hebrew letter and path on the Tree of Life. Lévi believed that there was an ancient connection between Kabbalah and Tarot, though, as contemporary writer and religious philosophy scholar Stephan Hoeller comments, "The critics observe with possible justification that the worthy Frenchman, being a romanticist, had simply mistaken a matter of coincidence for an organic and historical connection. To this objection the mystical and magical scholars of France as well as their English counterparts replied that the connection between Kabbalah and Tarot was always known to certain initiates of the Hermetic and magical mysteries, but that it was simply not publicly revealed until the days of Eliphas Lévi." [6]

The Hermetic Order of the Golden Dawn (founded in 1888) eventually changed Lévi's order and assignments, creating the correspondence between cards and paths in common use today. Arthur Edward Waite (1857–1942), author, occultist and member of the Golden Dawn, worked with artist and fellow member of the Golden Dawn Pamela Coleman Smith (1878–1951) to create the now classic Rider-Waite Tarot deck. The deck and accompanying *Key to the Tarot* were published by Wm. Rider and Sons in London in 1909. Many Tarot scholars now call the deck the Waite-Smith deck, honoring the gifted artist who created the cards rather than the publisher.

A good part of this deck's success as a spiritual teaching tool is due to the simple, direct, archetypal and iconic power of Coleman-Smith's pictures. Arthur Edward Waite noted the importance of these images. "The Tarot embodies symbolical presentations of universal ideas, behind which lie all the implicits of the human mind, and it is in this sense that they contain secret doctrine, which is the realisation [sic] by the few of the truths imbedded in the consciousness of all, though they have not passed into the express recognition by ordinary men." [7] Waite understood that pictures appeal directly to the unconscious mind, teaching us on a level that words alone cannot reach.

Because these cards carry universal ideas, each and every card offers insights appropriate to our personal situations. As contemporary author Pamela Eakins explains, "*Any card of the tarot applies equally to any human problem or endeavor. Each card gives you an angle on your subject matter. Each card gives you a specific vantage point. It is as if you are a photographer and the subject of your photograph is standing in the middle of an open field. From each point around the field's perimeter, you get a different view or backdrop. Some angles might be prettier than others, but each is just as real. The tarot cards are like vantage points around the perimeter of the field. They give you 78 different angles on any given subject. Some angles might be prettier than others, but each is just as real.*" [8]

Another reason for the Rider-Waite deck's success is its link to Kabbalah. Riding piggy-back on the shoulders of a giant, Tarot acquires a depth and relevance that is impossible to overstate. While there is no scholarly evidence to support the idea of an ancient connection between Tarot and Kabbalah, there is nevertheless a real and powerful outcome within the aspirant's consciousness when these two symbolic systems are studied together. Some aspirants believe this outcome to be the result of exterior forces; others believe it to be entirely psychological. This is a matter of personal preference and ultimately not relevant: the perceived differences between within and without eventually vanish on this path.

Figure 5 shows how the Major Arcana are most commonly placed on the Tree of Life according to today's Western Mystery Tradition. Being linked to the Tree, these cards partake of a mature, refined, complex symbolism that has been developed over centuries. This association deepens our understanding of each card's meaning. For example, **The Fool** might originally have been viewed as an image depicting a thoughtless, light-hearted youth gone wandering. But its assignment to the path from *Keter* to *Chokmah*, at the beginning of Creation, reveals the sense of a new beginning. These meanings were not the original intent of the cards; they are supplied by our own inner wisdom.

Note that Major Arcana are assigned to the paths between the *sephirot*. The forty Minor Arcana are assigned to the ten *sephirot*: the four Aces (Wands, Swords, Cups and Pentacles) to *Keter*, the first *sephirah*; the four Twos to *Chokmah*, the second *sephirah*, etc. The Court Cards are also placed on the Tree; in some Tarot systems, the Pages are assigned to *Malkuth,* the Knights to *Chokmah*, the Queens to *Binah*, and the Kings to *Tifaret*. In other Tarot systems, these sixteen Court Cards are assigned instead to the so-called "invisible" paths. An invisible path is a path between *sephirot* that is not one of the twenty-two paths assigned to the twenty-two Hebrew letters. For example, the path between *Binah* and *Chesed* is not one of the twenty-two paths shown in Figure 5; it is assigned to the **Knight of Cups**. This path is shown in Figure 6 in Chapter Ten (page 262), where we will discuss the positioning of the Court Cards on the Tree of Life in greater detail.

The Tree of Life is such a complex symbol that it is often difficult for aspirants to relate Tarot cards to the *sephirot* or the paths between the *sephirot*. To help the aspirant master the relationship between the Tree and the cards, Table 1 provides a list of attributes for each *sephirah*; this "cheat-sheet" may be used as a reference until the student has attained some level of mastery of the Tree.

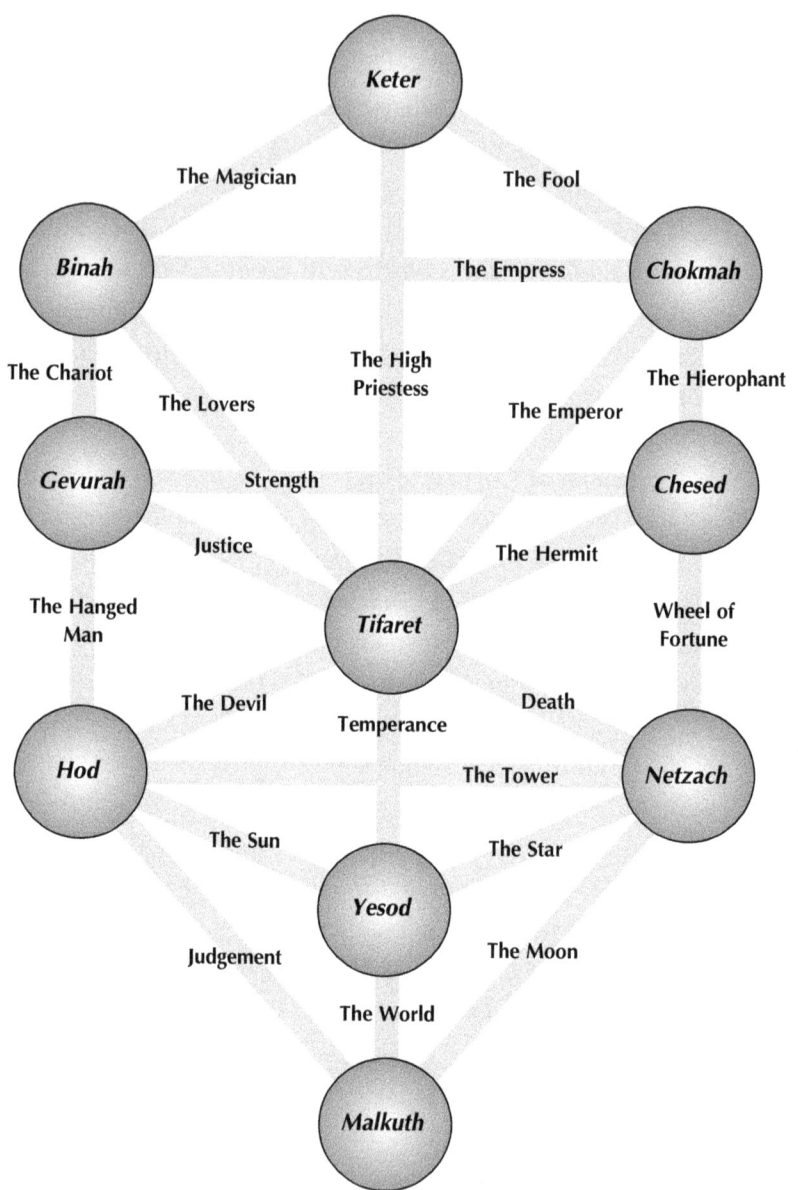

Figure 5. Tarot Cards on the Tree of Life

Table 1. Attributes of the *Sephirot*

Keter	Beginning, will, desire, awareness, holiness, divinity
Chokmah	Father, male, force
Binah	Mother, female, water, birth, death, time, form, patterns, Saturn
Chesed	Mercy, love, compassion, peace, expansion, plenty, devotion, growth, Jupiter
Gevurah	Fear, pain, suffering, lack, severity, war, restriction, Mars
Tifaret	Spirituality, essence, higher self, truth, heart, Sun
Netzach	Nature, instincts, emotions, sexuality, fertility, Venus
Hod	Intellect, structure, container, magic, ritual, messages, Mercury
Yesod	Astral, subconscious, water, imagination, dreams, sleep, ego, personality, Moon
Malkuth	End, final result, manifestation, physical, Initiation, realization, Earth

There are always three different numbers assigned to each card. This is sometimes confusing. The first of these numbers corresponds to the card itself; the second corresponds to the number of the path on the Tree to which the card has been assigned; and the third to the matching number of the assigned Hebrew letter. The card number is usually written as a roman numeral; both the path number and number of the Hebrew letter are written as arabic numerals. For example, **The Fool** has a card number of 0* and a path number of 11 (since the path numbers 1 through 10 are assigned to the *sephirot*). The corresponding Hebrew letter is *Aleph*, which is assigned to the number 1. So **The Fool** is associated with the numbers 0, 11, and 1. Similarly,

---

* Technically, zero is not a roman numeral; however, Tarot tradition assigns zero to The Fool.

The Magician is card number I (a roman numeral), path number 12 and Hebrew number 2.

The *Sefer Yetzirah* is the source of many Tarot correspondences, providing associations to both the paths on the Tree and the Hebrew letters. For example, Aryeh Kaplan's translation of the *Sefer Yetzirah* refers to the eleventh path as Glaring Consciousness and assigns the Hebrew letter *Aleph* to the element of air. Thus, **The Fool**, which is assigned to the eleventh path and the Hebrew letter *Aleph*, is also called the Glaring Consciousness and is associated with the element of air. These correspondences are occasionally germane to their corresponding Tarot cards, but are more often apparently unrelated. This is no surprise, as the *Sefer Yetzirah* was not written with Tarot cards in mind. Nonetheless, the *Sefer Yetzirah*'s correspondences are included in this book in order to give the student yet another glimpse of the complex Kabbalistic structure that lies behind the cards. Also, attempting to discover the ways in which the Kabbalistic correspondences apply to Tarot cards helps uncover truths that might otherwise remain hidden. A spiritual mystery will frequently draw us closer to the Source than an obvious truth.

Chapter One Bibliography

1   Matthews, Caitlin, and Matthews, John. *The Western Way: A Practical Guide to the Western Mystery Tradition. Volume 2, The Hermetic Tradition.* London, England: Arkana Paperbacks, 1986, p. 18.

2   Matthews, Caitlin, and Matthews, John. *The Western Way: A Practical Guide to the Western Mystery Tradition. Volume 2, The Hermetic Tradition.* London, England: Arkana Paperbacks, 1986, p. 16.

3   Hall, Manly P. *What the Ancient Wisdom Expects of Its Disciples.* Los Angeles, CA: Philosophical Research Society, 1982, p. 36.

4   Schnapper, Edith B. *The Inward Odyssey: The Concept of the Way in the Great Religions of the World*. London, UK: George Allen & Unwin, 1980, p. 36.

5   Decker, Depaulis and Dummett. *A Wicked Pack of Cards: The Origin of the Occult Tarot*. London: Gerald Duckworth & Co., 2002, p. 38.

6   Hoeller, Stephen. *The Royal Road*. London, England: Arkana Paperbacks, 1986, p. 26.

7   Waite, Arthur Edward. *The Pictorial Key to the Tarot*. Mineola, New York: Dover Publications, 2005, p. 29.

8   Eakins, Pamela. *Tarot of the Spirit*. York Beach, ME: Weiser Books, 1992, p. 17.

THE CARDS OF
THE SUPERNAL TRIANGLE

Card 0: The Fool.

"I AM,
Without beginning, without end,
Older than night or day,
Younger than the babe new-born,
Brighter than light,
Darker than darkness,
Beyond all things and creatures,
Yet fixed in the heart of every one." [1]

THE FOOL.

The Fool is a youth who is about to walk off a cliff. In one hand, The Fool holds a stick from which a bag hangs; in the other hand, he holds a white rose. A white dog frolics at his feet. Ice-capped mountains tower in the background and the sun shines overhead.

The Fool is assigned to the path from *Keter* to *Chokmah*. In the context of the spiritual journey, this card may be seen as our Higher Self at the beginning of an incarnation. The bag hanging from The Fool's stick represents past experience, whether from this life, past lives, or humanity's overall subconscious. The rose represents earthly desire —beautiful, but painful if carelessly grasped. The white color of the rose implies that our true desire is for learning and experience, not sex, drugs, and rock 'n roll. The white dog symbolizes intellect and instincts, both intended to be our servants, not our masters.

The Fool may also be seen as the beginning of the Divine creative process. He carries the Divine intent-to-create in his bag as he begins his journey. **The Fool** is not God, but he is God's emissary. Preparing to walk off the cliff into incarnation, he isn't peering down at the bottom or trying to angle his fall so he lands *here*, not *there*. In fact, he isn't looking at all. He's about to take a hard fall, but it's all right. Knowing that nothing can truly harm him, he is unafraid of the abyss before him. **The Fool** says YES to all of Creation. His blithe acceptance of all that life presents is what the aspirant seeks for himself.

Among native peoples, a fool was believed to have been touched by the gods; but the term "fool" has negative implications in our culture. Few of us want to be regarded as foolish, though many people who make the spiritual path their life's work are regarded as foolish by neighbors and family.

Many of the questions **The Fool** invites us to consider seem pretty foolish, simply because they are unanswerable. What's the purpose of this journey? Where am I going? Though these questions have no definite answers, attempts to answer them are informative and important.

One such foolish, unanswerable question is this: Why did God create the universe? The Kabbalistic tradition sometimes describes creation as God's mirror. Z'ev ben Shimon Halevi, contemporary author of many books on Kabbalah and founding member of the Kabbalah Society, writes, "According to tradition, once there was only God. Nothing else existed. Kabbalah perceives the Godhead as AYIN or

Absolute Nothing and AYIN SOF or Absolute All. Little else can be said because God is God and therefore totally alone, and beyond human comprehension. Because of this, the oral tradition tells us, God wished to behold God and be known, and so the mirror of Existence was called forth and man the image of God placed within it." [2]

This concept gives purpose to both the human and Divine journeys. Since most of us spend a great deal of time and effort trying to know ourselves and be known by others, the idea that we exist because God wants to know Himself rings a deep and familiar chord.

An alternate Kabbalistic view is that the physical world was created because it is only in physical manifestation that good can fight evil. Aryeh Kaplan (1934–1983), American Kabbalist, physicist and author, comments on this belief in his translation of the *Sefer Yetzirah*. "The main difference between the material and spiritual involves space. Physical space only exists in the physical world. In the spiritual, there is no space as we know it." In the spiritual world, Kaplan explains, closeness is dependent upon resemblance. Things that are alike are close; things that are different are far apart. As a result, good and evil cannot approach one another in the spiritual realm. The physical realm, however, operates differently. "Two opposites can then be brought together by being bound to physical objects. In the physical world, space exists, and two opposites can literally be pushed together. Furthermore, two spiritual opposites can even be bound to the same material object." Kaplan concludes, "The fact that good and evil can exist in the same physical space also allows good to overcome evil in this world. Here again, this is only possible in a physical world. In a purely spiritual arena, good could never come close enough to evil to have any influence over it. In the physical world, however, good and evil can exist together, and good can therefore overcome evil." [3] The belief in a war between good and evil is deeply ingrained in the human psyche, so this concept feels right to us on an archetypal level.

However, *The Kybalion,* an anonymously written occult handbook, cautions us to beware of ascribing human motivations to what it calls THE ALL. "And still more presumptuous are those who attempt to ascribe to THE ALL the personality, qualities, properties, characteristics and attributes of themselves, ascribing to THE ALL the human emotions, feelings, and characteristics, even down to the pettiest qualities of mankind, such as jealousy and praise, desire for offerings and worship, and all the other survivals from the days of the childhood of the race." [4] (*The Kybalion* is believed to have been written by Paul Foster Case and William Walker Atkinson aka Yoga Ramacharaka.)

Thomas Troward (1847–1916), an English author whose work heavily influenced the New Thought movement, believed that we cannot know the motivations of the One Will. "How do we know what the intention of the Universal Mind may be? Here comes in the element of impersonality. It has no intention, because it is impersonal." [5] If the Divine is indeed impersonal, even such lofty motivations as the One Will wanting to know Itself or good winning out against evil are likely to be just human conceptions, exactly what *The Kybalion* warns us against.

Israel Regardie (1907–1985), author of many texts on Kabbalah and magic, agrees that we cannot understand the Divine. He explains, "All that can be said with truth of this Absolute and Supreme Reality is that IT IS. This must suffice. Omnipresent, eternal, and self-existent—these are ideas which transcend even the loftiest flights of the trained imagination, abstractions beyond the grasp of mortal minds." [6]

But knowing that the purpose of Creation is beyond our grasp does not satisfy us. Carl Jung, with his deep understanding of the human psyche, acknowledged both our desire to know why God created the universe and the impossibility of ever achieving that knowledge. In his *Memories, Dreams, Reflections*, he writes "...I do not know for what reason the universe has come into being, and shall never know. Therefore I must drop this question as a scientific or intellectual problem. But if an idea about it is offered to me—in dreams or in mythic traditions—I ought to take note of it. I even ought to build up a conception on the basis of such hints, even though it will forever remain a hypothesis which I know cannot be proved." [7]

As we explore the Western Mystery Tradition, it is important that we build our own conception of the Divine and the Divine Purpose. By attempting to understand the Divine Purpose we begin to understand our own purpose, and our conception of the Divine forms the ground beneath our feet as we walk our path. But there is a paradox here: we need to create solid footing for our journey while simultaneously holding our concepts lightly enough that we can let them go when we encounter clearer or more meaningful ideas.

Achieving Initiation answers our questions about the Divine Purpose by making them irrelevant. A question such as "Why am I here?" implies a separation that cannot exist when we finally realize that we are one with the Divine.

This realization is not as easy to grasp as it sounds. We nod and smile, yes, we are one with God. But most of us have at least one unspoken exception to the concept of "everything." Perhaps we feel that evil can't be part of God, or the perishable body can't be part of God, or that people who don't believe as we believe can't be part of God (or that they are a lesser part of God). Whatever our belief system considers wrong, bad, or unholy is the exception that we hold dear, and it is that very exception which prevents us from achieving Initiation.

The Fool is assigned to the Hebrew letter *Aleph*, meaning "ox." As the ox was the driving force behind early civilization, **The Fool** is the driving force behind creation. Further, the *Sefer Yetzirah* assigns the element of air to the letter *Aleph*. Interestingly, the word "fool" comes from the Latin word *follis*, meaning "a bag or sack, a large inflated ball, a pair of bellows." A person who might resemble the bellows or any inflated object was also called a "windbag" or "airhead." So "fool" and "air" are, unexpectedly, related concepts.

Western Mystery Tradition Correspondences

Roman numeral: 0*
Path number: 11
Hebrew letter: *Aleph*
Hebrew number: 1
Astrological or planetary correspondence: Aquarius
Color: Yellow
Deities: Jupiter and Zeus
Gem: Topaz and chalcedony
Plant: Aspen
Perfume: Galbanum
Magical Equipment: Fan
Sefer Yetzirah Path Name: Glaring Consciousness

Sefer Yetzirah Hebrew Letter Description: "He made the letter Alef king over breath, bound a crown to it, permuted one with another, and with them formed air in the Universe, the temperate in the Year, and the chest in the Soul, male and female." [8]

The ancient idea of the Primum Mobile is also assigned to this path. The Primum Mobile has no cause but is the cause of all things; its assignment to the first path and the beginning of creation is axiomatic. The Primum Mobile concept comes from Ptolemaic or geocentric (earth-centered) astronomy, which was the accepted view of the solar system from the time of ancient Greece until the sixteenth century, when it was gradually superseded by the heliocentric, or sun-centered, astronomy of Copernicus, Galileo and Kepler. Today, the Primum Mobile is a conceptual, but not a scientific, device.

---

* Technically, zero is not a roman numeral; however, Tarot tradition assigns zero to The Fool.

Meditations

Bag Meditation: Withdraw from your personal concerns and sit quietly. Take a deep, slow breath and discover that you are holding a bag that contains something you need in this phase of your life. Feel the bag gently and notice that there is an odd shape here that you don't recognize. Open the bag, reach inside and pull out this object. What is it? What does it mean to you? Is there a reason that it was concealed? What might you do to bring it out of hiding? When you have understood what this object means in your life, return to normal consciousness.

Rose Meditation: Withdraw from your personal concerns and sit quietly. Take a deep, slow breath and realize that you hold a rose in your hand. You selected this rose for your own particular enjoyment in this part of your life. What does the rose represent for you? Are there thorns on the rose? What do the thorns represent? When you have finished exploring your rose, return to normal consciousness.

Little Dog Meditation: Withdraw from your personal concerns and sit quietly. Take a deep, slow breath and picture the little dog at **The Fool**'s heels. In fairy tales, there is often an "animal helper" that appears at just the right moment to offer aid to the hero. In our own lives, this helper is usually a person, not an animal, though these helpers may have particular qualities that are represented by animals—the courage of a lion, the wisdom of an owl, the ferocity of a hawk, etc. Who are the people in your life whose special qualities helped you when you most needed them? When you have identified these helpers, return to normal consciousness.

Creation Meditation: This meditation is suitable for more advanced aspirants. Withdraw from your personal concerns and sit quietly. Take a deep, slow breath and find yourself standing on the edge of a cliff. Realize that you are experiencing your own Higher Self prior to this life. Look below and see this life laid out before you. You can't see all the twists and turns from where you're standing, but you can see the overall pattern of this life. A small creature sits at your feet; it has one last thing to tell you before you step off the cliff into the new body that awaits you. Stoop down and let the creature whisper in your ear. When you have understood the message, return to normal consciousness.

Card 1. The Magician

"Happy art thou if thou canst grasp this truth.
For then, understanding that not thy weak self,
But my all-knowing Mind,
Looketh out upon the world through thine eyes,
Shalt thou have faith to let me see." [9]

THE MAGICIAN.

The Magician stands before a table holding a Cup, a Pentacle, a Sword and a Wand. The Magician wears a white tunic, cinched at the waist by a serpent devouring its own tail, and a red outer robe. A white band encircles his head and an infinity sign hovers above. His right hand holds a small white Wand and is raised toward heaven; his left hand points toward earth. Red roses and white lilies flourish on the ground and overhead.

This card is the path from *Keter* to *Binah*; it represents the process by which *Keter*'s "intent-to-create" becomes the patterns of *Binah*. These patterns form the physical reality of *Malkuth*. **The Magician** represents God's creation of the universe and our creation of our own lives.

The Magician's assigned Hebrew letter is *Bet*, meaning "house." Creation is the house of God. *Bet* is also the first letter of *Beresheit*, the Hebrew name for the Book of Genesis. *Beresheit* means "in the beginning." In the beginning, God created the world from the unformed, bringing order from chaos with words. The idea that God

35

created the world with words is a very old one and is the foundation upon which the western magical tradition is built. The famous all-purpose magical word *Abracadabra* comes from two Aramaic words that literally mean "I create as I speak." The relationship between magic and words is further reflected in the similarity of certain words that pertain to both, such as grimoire (a book of magical rituals) and grammar; spelling (of words) and (magical) spell.

The Western Mystery Tradition sees man as a miniature of God; God's creation of the world and man's creation of his own world are essentially the same process. As God creates manifestation with the four physical elements and Divine words, we create our personal reality with our four elements (body, heart, mind and spirit) and our words. The implements on **The Magician**'s table symbolize both physical elements and human elements. The Wand represents the physical element of fire and the human element of awareness; the Sword represents air and intellect; the Cup represents water and emotion; the Pentacle represents earth and body.

Humanity as a whole creates a reality as well. Kabbalists use the term *Adam Kadmon*, Primordial Man, to refer to all of humankind. While each of us creates a personal world, *Adam Kadmon* creates the world in which we all live, the consensual world of humanity. *Adam Kadmon* is creating art, literature, and symphonies as well as foul waters, dead forests, and a poisonous atmosphere. The challenge faced by *Adam Kadmon* is to create with wisdom (*Chokmah*) and understanding (*Binah*).

The Magician's posture is evocative. The upraised right hand and downward-pointing left hand symbolize the movement of Divine creative energy from *Keter* above, through *Binah* to *Malkuth* below. This posture suggests that **The Magician** acts as a clear channel for the Divine Will. In order to become that clear channel, we must learn to recognize and set aside our personal will. This is not even remotely as easy as it sounds and many aspirants are not as advanced in this area as they believe; it is very common to mistake personal will for that of the Divine.

As we learn to distinguish personal will from Divine Will, we bump inevitably into the paradox of free will. To the extent that we have free will, our free will creates our world. To the extent that our free will is an expression of the Divine Will, it is only Divine Will that creates our world. There is no one correct way to view this difficulty. It is our responsibility to meditate on this issue and resolve it in a way that allows us to move forward on our path. An unsuccessful resolution might impel us to sit on a park bench and wait for the Divine Will to drop food into our mouths. A successful resolution might allow us to conclude that there is nothing but Divine Will, and what the Divine Will desires is for us to behave as if we did have free will. We will encounter the paradox of free will again during our examination of **The Devil**.

Both the infinity sign and the serpent belt represent eternity; the infinity sign also symbolizes the caduceus and healing through the reconciliation of opposites. The red robe, easily removed, is the outer shell of **The Magician**'s self-awareness; the white robe underneath symbolizes Divine awareness. The white band around **The Magician**'s head symbolizes his willingness to focus his self-awareness on the Divine.

Roses represent desire and lilies represent thought; these flowers also appear in **The Hierophant**, **Ace of Pentacles** and **Two of Wands**. Their inclusion in Tarot imagery probably derives from the Song of Solomon 2:1, "I am the rose of Sharon, and the lily of the valleys."

Western Mystery Tradition Correspondences

Roman numeral: I
Path number: 12
Hebrew letter: *Bet*
Hebrew number: 2
Astrological or planetary correspondence: Mercury
Color: Yellow
Deities: Mercury, Hermes and Thoth
Gem: Agate and opal
Perfume: Mastic, mace and storax
Creature: Ibis and baboon
Magical Equipment: Caduceus
Sefer Yetzirah Path Name: Glowing Consciousness

Sefer Yetzirah Hebrew Letter Description: "He made the letter Bet king over wisdom, bound a crown to it, permuted one with another, and with them He formed Saturn in the Universe; Sunday in the Year, and the mouth in the Soul, male and female." [10] Tarot tradition assigns **The Magician** to Mercury, the planet traditionally associated with magic, and Saturn to **The Devil**.

Meditations

Balanced Elements Meditation: Withdraw from your personal concerns and sit quietly. Take a deep, slow breath and discover that the elements of your being sit on a table before you, represented by the symbols of your choice. Your life at this moment is a perfect mirror of how you have used these elements so far. Which element is bigger than the others? Which shows the most development? Which is under-developed? Sit for a while and absorb what the nature, size and condition of these elements can tell you. The advanced aspirant may wish to transform this meditation into a magical practice by mentally adjusting the size of the elemental symbols to help bring about a more balanced psyche. When you are ready, return to normal consciousness.

Magical Creation Meditation: Withdraw from your personal concerns and sit quietly. Take a deep, slow breath and discover that you have become **The Magician**. In this vision you are standing erect, right hand raised to *Keter*, left pointed down to *Malkuth*. You have the opportunity now to create your world anew. Picture your desired life in as much detail as possible. When you are ready, feel a lightning bolt of energy enter your right hand from above, pass through your body, and streak out through your left hand. Your new world has just been created. What does it look like? What do you see? Is it what you wanted? Do not pass judgment on yourself—simply observe this new world. When you are ready, return to normal consciousness.

Clear Channel Meditation: This meditation is suitable for more advanced aspirants. Withdraw from your personal concerns and sit quietly. Take a deep, slow breath. Find an area in your life about which you are unhappy or that you believe needs a bit more work on your part. Now recognize that your world, as it is right now, is the Divine Will in action. There is nothing in your world that has not been given a Divine Stamp of Approval. Allow your discontent to gaze on that Divine Stamp. When you are ready, return to normal consciousness.

Card II.
The High Priestess

THE HIGH PRIESTESS.

"Creation is the record of mine
ever-changing manifestation.
All things bear the imprint of the history
of the universe.
Nothing of mine activity escapeth this record.
In it do men share, because they, too,
Are parts of mine inferior nature.
Thus are they partakers in my
perfect recollection,
Which is the source of all memories,
And the root of all the wisdom of mankind." [11]

The High Priestess sits on a throne. Behind her is a canopy stretched between two flanking pillars; one is black, marked with a "B" and one is white, marked with a "J." The canopy is decorated with palms and pomegranates. A lunar crescent rests at The High Priestess' feet, slightly submerged in the waters of her silver-blue robe, which flows down her body and pools at her feet. Her silver crown consists of two crescents and a round ball. She wears a cross on her breast and holds a scroll marked with the letters TORA.

The High Priestess is assigned to the Hebrew letter *Gimel*, which corresponds to the word "camel" (the actual Hebrew word for camel is *Gamal*). This suggests the long, harsh journey of this path that begins in *Keter*, the Divine Will, crosses the Abyss and continues into *Tifaret*, the spiritual heart of the Tree.

The scroll on **The High Priestess'** lap is the record of everything that has been, is and will be. The term "Akashic Records" is sometimes used for the contents of this scroll. It is half-hidden by the robe, indicating that not everything will be revealed. The letters on the scroll, TORA, may be intended to mean "Torah" (the Old Testament), "Rota" (the Latin world for wheel), or "Tarot." These same letters appear again on The **Wheel of Fortune** card.

The pillars represent the pillars of the Tree of Life and all pairs of opposites. "B" and "J" are the initials of the names of the pillars of Solomon's Temple—Boaz and Jachin. **The High Priestess'** position between the pillars indicates that she is in perfect balance between opposites. Appropriately, this card is assigned to the path from *Keter* to *Tifaret*, which lies entirely on the Middle Pillar. **The High Priestess** communicates *Keter*'s will-to-create directly to our Higher Self in *Tifaret*.

The color and flow of **The High Priestess'** robe reveals it to be a water symbol. Her crown consists of two crescent moons and one full moon, and is made of silver, the metal assigned to the moon. The moon and water are symbols both of the individual subconscious and the Great Unconscious, which is the sum total of all humanity's subconscious, as well as the subconscious of all animals, plants, rocks, even the earth herself. The presence of the tapestry behind **The High Priestess** teaches us that the Great Unconscious is hidden from our view. The pomegranates and palms on the tapestry are symbols of fertility, indicating that the reproductive drive comes from subconscious levels of our being.

The importance of the subconscious and the Great Unconscious is shown by the placement of **The High Priestess** in the Tarot progression. As we discussed earlier in this chapter, **The Fool** represents the start of creation, carrying the intent-to-create in a bag.

The Magician represents the process of Creation, manifesting through the spoken Word of the Creator. As the next step in this progression, **The High Priestess** teaches us that Creation is made manifest through the subconscious. Students of the Western Mystery Tradition understand that while most of us think of our conscious minds as our "true" selves, the subconscious is the enormous iceberg submerged beneath the surface of the water. The work of **The Magician** is made possible only through the hidden action of **The High Priestess**.

Paul Foster Case says, "What is even more important for the occultist and the psychologist is that our personal definitions of the meaning of our experiences constitute suggestions which are accepted, without reservation, by our subconscious. Thus, in a sense, every man makes his own law, writes the constitution of his own personal world, and finds that his life-experience is the reproduction of that constitution through the working of subconscious responses." [12]

However, this does not always go well. Many of the difficulties experienced by individuals and humanity at large may be attributed to our failure to properly understand and work with the subconscious. Case further explains, "The number 2 [card number of **The High Priestess**] also suggests the ideas of duplicity, deception, untruth, illusion, error and delusion. This is correct, because subconsciousness repeats and elaborates the mistaken results of faulty, superficial self-conscious observation. Being at all times uncritically amenable to suggestion, and at the same time the channel of telepathic communication, subconsciousness is the source of most of the foolish notions which lie behind our maladjustments." [13]

We often believe our subconscious to be somehow less important than our normal consciousness or Higher Self. Our mental picture often places the subconscious in the basement, conscious awareness in the lobby, and the Higher Self in the penthouse. In reality, our subconscious is very important; learning to communicate with it is crucial to achieving Initiation. The subconscious is a reservoir of ideas and values that create our sense of self; this "self" is who we believe we really are. The power of these subconscious concepts lies in the very fact that we are unaware of them. When we bring these ideas and values to the attention of our waking consciousness, we begin to see the falseness inherent in them. This weakens our belief in the "self" they have created, and helps clear the path to Initiation.

Communicating with our subconscious is not easy. **The High Priestess** speaks to us in the language of symbols. There are some people who appear to have a natural ability to understand the language of **The High Priestess**, but the remaining 99% of us must learn it. One of the tasks of the Western Mystery Tradition is to provide a set of symbols with which to communicate with our subconscious. The Tarot cards are one such set of symbols. By immersing ourselves in the symbols, meditating on them and dreaming about them, we teach the symbols to both our conscious and subconscious minds; this forms a bridge between them.

Western Mystery Tradition Correspondences

Roman numeral: II

Path number: 13

Hebrew letter: *Gimel*

Hebrew number: 3

Astrological or planetary correspondence: Moon

Color: Blue

Deities: Lunar goddesses, virgin goddesses and prophetesses
such as Artemis, Hecate and Diana

Gem: Moonstone and pearl

Perfume: Camphor and aloes

Plant: Hazel, moonwort and ranunculis
Creature: Dog
Magical Equipment: Bow and arrow
Sefer Yetzirah Path Name: Unity Directing Consciousness

Sefer Yetzirah Hebrew Letter Description: "He made the letter Gimel king over wealth, bound a crown to it, permuted one with another, and with them He formed Jupiter in the Universe, Sunday in the Year, and the right eye in the Soul, male and female." [14] The Tarot tradition assigns the Moon to **The High Priestess** and Jupiter to **Wheel of Fortune**.

Meditations

The Scroll Meditation: Withdraw from your personal concerns and sit quietly. Take a deep, slow breath and discover that your High Priestess has written a message for you in her scroll. As the scroll slowly unrolls, what do you see written there? If you have trouble reading the words, ask **The High Priestess** to tell you what she has written. When she has responded, thank her and return to normal consciousness.

Language Meditation: Withdraw from your personal concerns and sit quietly. Take a deep, slow breath and consider new ways of communicating with **The High Priestess**. Possibilities include dreamwork, skrying (gazing into a mirror, pool of water or crystal ball), Tarot cards, artwork, writing with your non-dominant hand or any other method that occurs to you. Watch for a sign of **The High Priestess'** approval, such as a "click" or a warm feeling. When you are ready, thank her and return to normal consciousness.

The Iceberg Meditation: This meditation is suitable for more advanced aspirants. Withdraw from your personal concerns and sit quietly. Take a deep, slow breath and realize that an enormous but unseen iceberg is creating some havoc in your life. This iceberg may be hard to find, because it's usually something that your subconscious believes but your conscious mind does not. You can detect this iceberg by recognizing a pattern in your life that you don't seem to be able to change. This may involve relationships, work, family or anything that seems to be operating according to an agenda you don't understand. Uncovering these subconscious beliefs is the first step to changing them. When you feel you have identified an iceberg, return to normal consciousness.

Card III. The Empress

THE EMPRESS.

"I am the Door of Life,
The passage from the world of ideas
Into the world of form.
Expressing myself, I take form in substance,
But the power which worketh in that substance
Is the sovereign force of mine outflowing
ideas." [15]

The Empress reclines on a throne covered with soft, comfortable pillows. She wears a crown of stars and holds an orb-tipped scepter. Her dress is decorated with pomegranates and her hair is bound with a wreath of myrtle. Leaning against the foot of her throne is a heart-shaped shield inscribed with the symbol of Venus: a circle with a cross below it. The world around her is lush; wheat or corn grows in the foreground, and trees thrive around a waterfall.

The Empress is the path from *Chokmah* to *Binah*, the first of three horizontal paths on the Tree. These horizontal paths are stabilizing forces, connecting the Pillar of Force with the Pillar of Form. The Hebrew letter of this card is *Daleth*, meaning "door;" by linking *Chokmah* (male force) and *Binah* (female womb), **The Empress** serves as the door through which creation emerges.

Fertility is the theme of **The Empress**. The many-seeded pomegranate on her dress is a symbol associated with Persephone, Greek goddess of fertility; the myrtle wreath and grain are sacred to Venus,

Roman goddess of fertility. **The Empress'** crown holds twelve stars, indicating that she has dominion over the entire year. The scepter she holds is a symbol of power. As we spend time with **The Empress**, we sense the magnitude of this power. The flower that grows from an invisible crack in the pavement, the mold that springs to life from just a hint of moisture under the sink—this is the power of **The Empress**.

This card also represents the creative ability of humankind. Every one of us has a bit of **The Empress** within us, which serves as a doorway through which force becomes form. We create homes, even if it's just by picking out the paint colors or arranging the furniture. We create meals several times a day. We even create the stories of our lives. Each of us embodies the creative principle in action.

As we create throughout our lives, we discover that creation requires both force—meaning energy—*and* form. However, we usually have a tendency to prefer force over form, based on the mistaken belief that the non-physical is "more spiritual." Form and physical manifestation (as personified by **The Empress**) is therefore given short shrift. In exploring this idea, British occultist and author Gareth Knight says, "There is a natural tendency in those who seek spiritual development to fail to realise [sic] the importance of the Earth pole in all of this. At one level this is a disguised or unconscious form of Earth denial, not so much branding it as evil as trying to pretend it is of no importance and to be left far behind at the earliest possible moment. This is not so much high spirituality as mental and emotional immaturity. It is often marked by a gross failure to come to terms with ordinary life." [16]

This denial of **The Empress** is mirrored in our culture's long-held beliefs that humankind is superior to the earth and male is superior to female. Bill Devall and George Sessions, professors, lecturers and authors of works on deep ecology, explicate these beliefs. "Ecological consciousness and deep ecology are in sharp contrast with the dominant worldview of technocratic–industrial societies which regards humans as isolated and fundamentally separate from Nature, as superior to, and in charge of the rest of creation. But the view of humans as separate and superior to the rest of Nature is only part of larger cultural patterns. For thousands of years, Western culture has become increasingly obsessed with the idea of dominance: with dominance of humans over nonhuman Nature, masculine over feminine, wealthy and powerful over the poor, with the dominance of the West over non-Western cultures. Deep ecological consciousness allows us to see through these erroneous and dangerous illusions." [17]

The term "deep ecology" originated with Arne Dekke Eide Naess, the foremost Norwegian philosopher of the twentieth century. The core principle of deep ecology is that the entire living environment has a right to flourish. It views ecology as a spiritual practice, rather than as a branch of biological science, embracing the worldview offered by **The Empress**.

Unfortunately, the Western preference for the non-physical over the physical has been reinforced by Eastern spiritual traditions that believe physical manifestation is only illusion. Contemporary transpersonal psychologist Ken Wilber agrees. "There is no doubt in my mind that the purely Ascending (or Gnostic) Traditions, which see the manifest merely and only as illusion, have indeed contributed to a set of cultural prejudices that have allowed a despoliation of the Earth." [18] The idea that physical manifestation is inferior or illusory may rise from a very simple root: our own fear of decline and death. Unable to accept this inevitability, we imagine some sort of perfect world in which sickness and death don't exist. This perfect world is everything the physical world isn't: eternal, happy, good, moral, etc. This imaginary place is the perfect place, the place we'd like to be, the place we could be if only we could be good enough (meaning spiritual enough) to deserve it.

By perpetuating the duality of a perfect heaven opposed to an imperfect world, we keep ourselves separate from God. God is pain and suffering as much as joy and happiness. This is the truth that most people are trying to avoid by seeking a spiritual wonderland. We approach Initiation only when we realize that all the so-called ills of the world are actually the perfect mirror of God.

Western Mystery Tradition Correspondences

Roman numeral: III
Path number: 14
Hebrew letter: *Daleth*
Hebrew number: 4
Astrological or planetary correspondence: Earth
Color: Emerald green
Deities: Earth goddesses such as Venus,
Aphrodite, Maia, Cybele and Freya
Gem: Emerald
Perfume: Sandalwood and rose
Plant: Myrtle and rose
Creature: Sparrow, dove and swan
Magical Equipment: Girdle
Sefer Yetzirah Path Name: Illuminating Consciousness

Sefer Yetzirah Hebrew Letter Description: "He made the letter Dalet king over seed, bound a crown to it, permuted one with another, and with them He formed Mars in the Universe, Monday in the Year, and the left eye in the Soul, male and female." [19] The Tarot tradition assigns Venus to this card and Mars to **The Tower**.

Meditations

Life Power Meditation: Withdraw from your personal concerns and sit quietly. Take a deep, slow breath and discover that you are in a meadow sitting at the feet of **The Empress**. You look around the field and realize that time is moving very quickly here. Everything is growing so fast that as you watch you see plants decay and die in moments, replaced by small green shoots that grow up from the soil, flower, then droop, decay and start the process again. As you watch the meadow change, you realize that this is happening in the world around you at every moment. Thank **The Empress** for showing you her power and return to normal consciousness.

The Wish Meditation: Withdraw from your personal concerns and sit quietly. Take a deep, slow breath and discover that you are in a meadow sitting at the feet of **The Empress**. In her quiet, calm voice she informs you that she has the power to give you a gift in the physical world. The gift must not violate her fundamental law that everything must decay and die. Think long and hard, as you get only one gift. What does your soul most long for, here in the world? When you are ready, make your wish. Thank **The Empress** and return to normal consciousness. Reflect on the wish you made. Why did you ask for this? What benefit would you receive from this?

The No-Wish Meditation: This meditation is suitable for more advanced aspirants. Withdraw from your personal concerns and sit quietly. Take a deep, slow breath and discover that you are in a meadow sitting at the feet of **The Empress**. In her quiet, calm voice she informs you that she has the power to give you a gift in the physical world. Sit quietly at her feet, sink deep within yourself until you have access to your Higher Self and realize that nothing is lacking. Feel what it is like to want nothing; then thank **The Empress** for her kindness and tell her that everything is perfect, just as it is. (She knows that, of course, but it's always nice to be told.) Return to normal consciousness.

Card IV. The Emperor

"All this am I.
Therefore, though none may capture me
In the net of thought,
He shall speak truly who shall say,
Laying his hand on anything soever,
(Whether men prize it, or scorn it
as of no worth),
"Dost ask me to show thee the Lord?
Verily, in this shall thou find Him,
If thou hast eyes to see." [20]

THE EMPEROR.

The Emperor *is a gray-bearded man who sits on a throne decorated with ram's heads. He holds a scepter in the shape of an Egyptian ankh in his right hand. Beneath his red robe he wears armor. A stream and mountains are seen in the background.*

The Emperor represents normal waking consciousness, the rational mind and self-awareness. The card is assigned to the Hebrew letter *Heh*, meaning "window;" **The Emperor** functions as the window through which we view the world. The assignment of this card to the path from *Chokmah* to *Tifaret* suggests that the aspects represented by **The Emperor** are balanced by, or are necessary to, the spiritual experience of *Tifaret*.

Self-awareness and ability to reason are a good part of what we believe separates humans from the other animals. The Western Mystery Tradition holds that these aspects are actually necessary for humankind to fulfill its purpose in the Universe. Paul Foster Case says, "Man is the synthesis of all cosmic activities. Human intelligence gathers together all the various threads of the Life Power's self-manifestation and carries that manifestation beyond anything that could come into existence apart from Man and human intelligence."[21]

However, if we don't learn to use these abilities wisely, we will find that we are separated not just from other animals, but from awareness of God. **The Emperor** believes that his rational faculty is in charge of the entire human experience, not just one level of existence. The armor he wears represents self-importance, which turns the blessing of self-awareness and rationality into the curse of ego and narcissism. **The Emperor**, while an important part of being human, cannot bring us to Initiation by himself. We cannot perceive God through rational thought; the more we rely upon our rational processes, the more likely we are to turn *Heh*'s windows into walls that separate us from God.

Of course, few of us want (or have the ability) to completely switch off our self-awareness and rational mind. In addition, if man is a microcosm of God, then this means that God, too, is self-aware and able to reason. Our goal should be not to shut down the rational mind, but to limit **The Emperor**'s influence to its proper domain.

The concept of man as a microcosm of God makes many people uncomfortable. Isn't this just more human ego and self-centeredness? Even more discomfiting is the Western Mystery Tradition's view of humankind as greater than the angels; as Dion Fortune explains, "Man is a perfect Microcosm of the Macrocosm; none other creature, so it is taught, shares this development. To the angels, the lower aspects are lacking; to the Elementals, the higher. In consequence of his manifold nature, man is in magnetic relationship with the cosmos as a whole, not merely with a limited or selected presentation of it. There is a flow and return between every aspect of our beings and characters and the corresponding aspect in the cosmos." [22] Fortune's belief that angels lack the lower aspects is supported by Kabbalist Aryeh Kaplan. "The archetype of the spiritual being is the angel. Since an angel has no body, it can never contain both good and evil in its being." [23]

While recognizing the anthropocentricity inherent in a human-as-microcosm philosophy, let us acknowledge that it is impossible for humans to consider the Divine from anything other than a human point of view; all other perspectives are simply the products of imagination. Every creature in the universe understands God in the particular way available to that species. It would be downright presumptuous of any species to believe it can understand God from the perspective of a species other than its own. It is impossible for man to understand his Creator as anything other than a Person: a Super Person, a Perfect Person, but a Person nonetheless. Even those traditions that use animal figures as deities still view those animals from a human perspective and focus primarily on those attributes that we consider important and relevant to the human experience.

Western Mystery Tradition Correspondences

Roman numeral: IV

Path number: 15

Hebrew letter: *Heh*

Hebrew number: 5

Astrological or planetary correspondence: Aries

Color: Scarlet

Deities: War gods and goddesses such as Mars, Tyr, Mentu, Minerva and Athena

Gem: Ruby

Perfume: Cinnamon and patchouli

Plant: Tiger lily and geranium

Creature: Owl, ram and hawk

Magical Equipment: Spear and the burin, a
steel-cutting tool used in engraving
Sefer Yetzirah Path Name: Stabilizing Consciousness
Sefer Yetzirah Hebrew Letter Description: "He made the letter Heh king over
speech, bound a crown to it, permuted them one with another, and with them He
formed Aries in the Universe, Nissan in the Year, and the liver in the Soul,
male and female." [24] *Nissan* is the first month of the Jewish calendar.

Meditations

Symbols on the Throne Meditation: Withdraw from your personal
concerns and sit quietly. Take a deep, slow breath and discover that
you are the ruler of all you survey. You are seated on a throne with
many images carved into it; this throne and the images it bears tell
everyone who you are and what you are about. What does the throne
look like? What are these images? What do they mean? Are these the
images you want associated with your reign? If there are changes
you would like to make to the throne and its images, you can do so
by just thinking about it. Watch the throne and images change
according to your direction. When you find something that pleases
you, state that this will be your throne from now on. Return to ordinary consciousness. If you are so moved, draw and color the throne
and images you chose.

Wearing Armor Meditation: Withdraw from your personal concerns and sit quietly. Take a deep, slow breath and discover that you
are wearing a suit of armor. The armor is heavy and constrictive, but
it makes you feel safe. What habits, beliefs and ideas make up this
armor? How might it feel to remove just one piece? Spend some
time discovering what these various pieces of armor mean in your
life. When you are ready, return to ordinary consciousness.

Card V. The Hierophant

"The Creator is myself,
And I am the Nail which joineth thee to me.
In thee am I ever present,
And thou hast only to turn within to
find me." [25]

THE HIEROPHANT.

The Hierophant *sits on a throne between two pillars. His religious regalia, ornate crown, and the crosses upon his robe and slippers attest to his important religious status. He makes a sign with his hand— two fingers are shown, three are hidden. Two disciples kneel at his feet, one dressed in a pattern of red roses and the other in a pattern of white lilies. Two crossed keys, one gold and one silver, are placed in front of the dais, and two lines of alternating black-and-white tiles are embedded on top.*

This is the path of the Inner Teacher. The card shows us a picture of the teaching process, which comes from the interaction of the Teacher (symbolized by **The Hierophant**) with desire (the figure wearing roses) and with thought (the figure wearing lilies). Gold represents awakened consciousness and silver represents the subconscious; these crossed keys tell us that both awakened consciousness and the subconscious participate in the teaching process. The crossed keys are also an alchemical device, as David Allen Hulse explains: "The exponents of Alchemy identified the Qabalah as the sole key to their Hermetic Art by various pictorial devices...a pair of crossed keys over a tree growing inside the alchemical vessel..." [26]

The black and white tiles symbolize the ignorance of darkness and the wisdom of the light; this tile pattern was used on the floor of the temples of the Hermetic Order of the Golden Dawn. The sign **The Hierophant** makes with his hand suggests that there will always be things that are known and things that are hidden.

Three cards—**The High Priestess**, **The Hierophant**, and **Justice** —show a figure between two columns. Each of these cards depicts a place of balance between pairs of opposites. **The High Priestess**, as the Great Unconscious, is not male or female, good or evil. **The Hierophant**'s teachings come to us from the Great Unconscious and are always geared towards helping us reach a place of balance. **Justice**, as we shall see in the next chapter, also comes from this place of perfect balance and represents the eternal balancing of positive and negative energies.

The Hebrew letter assigned to this path is *Vav*, meaning "nail" or "hook." The concept of *Vav* is that of joining two things together. **The Hierophant** is assigned to the path from *Chokmah* to *Chesed*, joining the Supernal Triangle to the Ethical Triangle. **The Hierophant** also joins the Inner Teacher to waking consciousness. The yellow yokes on the backs of the kneeling figures are a symbol of joining or "yoking" the teacher with the student, and inner knowledge with waking consciousness.

The search for a teacher is a natural part of the spiritual path. We all hope to find someone who can understand what we're going through, hear our inner longings, see the good in us, point us in the right direction, and make sure we don't get lost or side-tracked. In addition to "teacher," the Western Mystery Tradition uses the terms "adept" and "Master." Though these terms are often used interchangeably, they do not carry quite the same meaning. A good analogy might be the difference between a "Ph.D." and a "Professor." A

"Ph.D." is someone who has attained an advanced graduate degree. A "Professor" is (usually) someone who has a "Ph.D." but is also a teacher. An adept is a Ph.D.; a Master is a Professor.

However, not all authors use these terms consistently; so it's helpful when teachers and authors tell us exactly what they mean by the terms adept or Master. For example, in his *Occultism and Christianity: A Restatement of Faith*, occultist Hugh Roscoe states, "Owing to the different senses in which the word 'adept' is used by different writers, it is necessary to explain that I do not use it in the sense of an exalted Being whose human evolution is completed, which is the sense usually adopted by theosophical writers. In this book 'adept' means simply a man or woman who after a lengthy training in some definite school of occult development has reached a level at which he or she can safely continue to study and experiment without further supervision. Even in this lower sense of the word the ranks of the adepts are not overcrowded!" [27]

In studying the Western Mystery Tradition, it's easy to get confused about whether or not Masters and adepts are real, physical beings. For example, the unknown authors of *The Kybalion* believed such people were real. "As a matter of fact, none but advanced Mental Alchemists have been able to attain the degree of power necessary to control the grosser physical conditions, such as the control of the elements of Nature; the production or cessation of tempests, the production and cessation of earthquakes and other great physical phenomena. But that such men have existed, and do exist to-day, is a matter of earnest belief to all advanced occultists of all schools." [28]

Actually, it's not a matter of earnest belief to all advanced occultists. Manly P. Hall, for example, holds that adepts exist not as persons, but as aspects of the inner spiritual self. "Within each of us is the adept Self, the rose diamond. On rare occasions, we glimpse for an instant the tremendous implication of the Self, and we become aware that the personality is indeed merely a shadow of the real.

57

These infrequent mystical experiences, these rare occasions when the sincere seeker feels himself to be in the presence of his own divine nature, were described in the old books as a visit from one of the adepts." [29]

Dion Fortune claimed to have met her Master (Jesus) in a dream and, in her book *The Cosmic Doctrine,* describes the meeting in detail. Moving a little further up the "hard-to-believe" scale, Paul Foster Case claimed to have spent several days alone in a room with the incarnation of a Master who had previously spoken to him only in his mind. During this meeting, Case received the teachings that were later to become the material for his Builders of the Adytum organization.

After comparing the accounts and opinions of a number of Western Mystery Tradition adherents, it becomes apparent that people who were fortunate enough to have a flesh and blood teacher tend to believe that Masters and adepts are real. People who teach themselves—through books, sincere effort, and the strictest self-honesty—tend to believe that Masters and adepts are just allegorical figures.

Either way, we should never abrogate responsibility for the course of our own journey. Accepting guidance is one thing; allowing someone else to determine the nature and direction of our spiritual path is another. If we hand the reins over to someone else, we'll doubtless end up following a path of some kind, but it is unlikely to be a spiritual one. Happily, the ready accessibility of books and teachings makes it unnecessary for us to abandon self-responsibility and autonomy in exchange for instruction. As Manly P. Hall points out, "Evolution has brought to the average man the power to analyze and estimate his own character. It is no longer necessary for the priestcraft to show him the forces of right and wrong. Each man is now his own high priest, his own initiator, the master of his own metaphysical life. Having realized this, your own integrity must strengthen you for the path of discipleship." [30]

We stay on the right track by winding our way not outward, but inward, always inward. This inward journey leads us to the Inner Teacher. Contemporary Christian mystic Bernadette Roberts says, "Another invaluable lesson was the imperative to always follow God's interior direction, and to be wary of all direction coming from the outside. Since the nature of the contemplative movement is the intimate revelation of God's mysterious ways in the soul, it is totally a One-to-one situation." [31]

Many of us fail because we listen to voices other than that of our own Inner Teacher. The cries of ego, self-importance, acquisition, vanity, fear, lust, regret, worry and anger are all louder than the still, small voice of the Inner Teacher. Learning to mute these other voices is part of our work on the spiritual journey. (Note that the term "voice" is not necessarily a literal description of how our Inner Teacher manifests. While some people actually do hear a voice, others are guided by an inner knowledge or certainty.)

Western Mystery Tradition Correspondences

Roman numeral: V
Path number: 16
Hebrew letter: *Vav*
Hebrew number: 6
Astrological or planetary correspondence: Taurus
Color: Red-orange
Deities: Apis, Mithras, Hera and Hathor
Gem: Topaz
Perfume: Storax
Plant: Mallow
Creature: Bull and peacock
Magical Equipment: Labor of preparation
Sefer Yetzirah Path Name: Enduring Consciousness
Sefer Yetzirah Hebrew Letter Description: "He made the letter Vav king over thought, bound a crown to it, permuted them one with another, and with them He

59

formed Taurus in the Universe, Iyar in the Year, and the gall bladder in the Soul, male and female." [32] *Iyar* is the second month of the Jewish calendar.

Meditations

Meditation on the Master: Withdraw from your personal concerns and sit quietly. Take a deep, slow breath and discover that you have been contacted by a Master of your tradition. He sits on a chair between two pillars. You approach him and kneel at his feet. He indicates that you may ask him for a favor. What is it that you want from this Master? Are you looking for a particular gift? A certain relationship? He is not interested in a generic response like "enlightenment" or "world peace." He is looking for a particular response from you as an individual. (And, as you may have surmised, he already knows what you want—he wants to know if you know.) When you have made your request, back away from the Master respectfully and return to normal consciousness.

The Hierophant's Pillars Meditation: Withdraw from your personal concerns and sit quietly. Take a deep, slow breath and discover that you are standing in a large temple. Your Inner Teacher is sitting between two pillars; two figures kneel at his feet. He motions you to approach. He explains that the two pillars are the two extremes he wants you to avoid; the kneeling figures are two qualities you possess that will help you avoid these extremes. Spend some time thinking about what these pillars and kneeling figures might mean to you. When you are ready, thank **The Hierophant** and return to normal consciousness.

Card VI. The Lovers

"This name is the sharp sword
Whereby the One that I am
Divideth itself into the Many." [33]

THE LOVERS.

A naked man and woman stand in the foreground. Above them floats an archangel dressed in violet robes; his skin is yellow, his wings are red, and his hair is made of red and green flames. Behind the woman stands a tree bearing apples; a snake is wrapped around its trunk. Behind the man stands a tree whose twelve branches are tipped with burning flames. In the background is a single mountain peak and a giant yellow sun dominates the sky.

The apple tree and snake obviously refer to the Garden of Eden, where human and divine consciousness were first separated. There are four archangels in the Major Arcana; the one in **The Lovers** is identifiable as Rafael, Archangel of Air, because of his yellow skin and violet robes. The twelve flames on the tree behind the man represent the twelve astrological signs; looking closely, we see that each flame is divided into three smaller flames, indicating the decanates of each sign.

The Lovers is assigned to the path from *Binah* to *Tifaret. Binah* is the *sephirah* of the womb and the creation of multiplicity; in *Tifaret*, the spiritual heart of the Tree, multiplicity becomes one.

The Hebrew letter assigned to this path is *Zayin*, meaning "sword." The sword is a symbol of air, confirming that the archangel pictured in this card is Rafael. This card depicts the drama underlying all of Creation: separation and reunion. *Zayin* is the sword that cuts one into two.

The first separation, according to the Old Testament, occurred when God created man. The Book of Genesis contains two different accounts of the creation of man: one visible and one concealed. The visible account, contained in verses 2:18–24, teaches that Adam was created first and Eve second. The hidden account is found earlier, in Genesis 1:27: "And God created man in His image, in the image of God He created him; male and female He created them." Kabbalists teach that God created Adam as an androgynous creature in God's own image—God is both male and female. God thereafter cut Adam in half, creating two out of what was once one.

The end of separation is symbolized by the reunion of male and female. This is spoken of in the *Zohar*, one of the foundational texts of Kabbalah:

> "'Male and female He created them.'
> From here we learn:
> Any image not embracing male and female
> is not a supernal, true image.
> Come and see:
> The blessed Holy One does not place His abode
> anywhere male and female are not found together." [34]

The "supernal, true image" embracing male and female means that a true image of God contains both male and female. On the mystical level of the *Zohar*, "male" refers to a particular aspect of God—the out-pouring energy of creation and divine awareness. "Female" refers to the aspect of God that transforms energy into physical form and is manifested as human awareness. Therefore, a true image of God embraces both the physical and divine worlds.

This coming together of the archetypal male and female is sometimes called the "Mystical Marriage." In writing about this marriage, Thom Cavalli, contemporary psychologist, writer and lecturer, says, "The royal marriage of the Solar King and the Luna Queen is one example of this great coniunctio experience. In many traditions it is called the mystical marriage. In fact, this symbolic marriage is the cornerstone of all the great religions. It is the yin–yang of Tao, the Shakti-Shiva of Hinduism, Father Sky and Mother Moon of Native Americans, the union of *Sephirot* Tif'eret and Malkhut of Kabbala, the heirosgamos of alchemy, and the crucifixion of Christ. Each religion has a symbol that functions something like a doorway to this transpersonal experience." [35]

The Mystical Marriage theme is suggested by two other cards— **The Devil** and **Judgement**. With **The Lovers**, these three cards form a path that leads from *Binah* to *Tifaret*, *Tifaret* to *Hod*, and *Hod* to *Malkuth*, suggesting a progression in the unfolding of the Mystical Marriage concept. We will explore this progression during our explication of **The Devil** and **Judgement** cards.

This card also concerns relationships, which can be a confusing area for aspirants. Relationships become an important aspect of the spiritual practice because they highlight areas of unconsciousness; they can also hinder our spiritual practice by locking us into our unconsciousness. Cyril Scott, author of *The Initiate* series published in the 1920s, sums the situation up nicely. "As to marriage, it brings bondage to fools and spiritual progress to wise men; it is a playground with many dangers for children, and a school for the enlightened. It is that fertile ground on which may be grown the beautiful flowers of a hundred virtues, or the noisome weeds of a hundred vices." [36]

One aspect of relationships that may inhibit our spiritual progress is the fact that many relationships are based on little more than projections of our own inner reality onto an apparent outer reality. Jung speaks of this in *Memories, Dreams, Reflections*. "In general, emotional ties are very important to human beings. But they still contain projections, and it is essential to withdraw these projections in order to attain to oneself and to objectivity. Emotional relationships are relationships of desire, tainted coercion and constraint; something is expected from the other person, and that makes him and ourselves unfree. Objective cognition lies hidden behind the attraction of the emotional relationships; it seems to be the central secret. Only through objective cognition is the real coniunctio possible." [37]

It is a rare relationship in which both parties are committed to the process of becoming free of projections. Generally, when one person begins to look for their own truth, the other person feels threatened and the battles intensify. It isn't always easy for us to continue on our path if we're in a relationship like this. There may be a choice between endangering the relationship by continuing on the path or keeping the relationship intact by abandoning the journey. However, before assuming that this choice is necessary, we must make sure our own projections about relationships aren't coloring our worldview. It may be that our partner is also ready for a change.

Some aspirants choose to avoid relationships entirely rather than risk any interference with spiritual goals. Others enter into relationships the same way one might take on a mortgage or commit to employment—just another thing one "does" in life. And yet other aspirants equate "relationship-with-others" as "relationship-with-God," and focus on service, love and devotion in the context of the relationship.

After Initiation, relationships can become even more challenging. Some Initiates feel obliged to awaken those around them; they are surprised when their offers of assistance are not met with gratitude and appreciation. This is a common reaction during the first flush of Initiation, and most Initiates eventually get over it.

While most Initiates retain something close to their normal personality, some experience such dramatic personality changes that there's no hiding the changes they've undergone. This may create problems in their relationships; no one likes to have the music changed in the middle of the dance. Some people will therefore leave pieces of their old personality in place, even if they no longer fit, just to keep their family, friends, or lovers happy.

It's important to remember that no one solution is right for everyone. Each personality and life situation is different. Some Initiates find their old lives and relationships impossible to maintain; others have no such problem. Some Initiates are bored to tears by the concerns and conversation of less-aware people; others continue to find people interesting and important. What works for someone else may not work for us; what works for us now may not work for us later. Ignore all books, gurus, theories, teachers, traditions, etc., that dictate how we're "supposed" to live post-awakened life. There's no rule that says we must teach others, help everyone, become a vegetarian, save the world, become a hermit, change our relationships, etc. After Initiation, we make our own choices and follow our own path.

Note that the man is looking at the woman but the woman is looking at the archangel; this reminds us that the Western Mystery Tradition believes that normal consciousness (the man) communicates with the Higher Self (the archangel) through the agency of subconsciousness (the woman).

Western Mystery Tradition Correspondences

Roman numeral: VI

Path number: 17

Hebrew letter: *Zayin*

Hebrew number: 7

Astrological or planetary correspondence: Gemini

Color: Orange

Deities: Castor and Pollux, Janus with his two faces

Gem: Tourmaline and alexandrite

Perfume: Wormwood

Plant: Orchid

Creature: Magpie

Magical Equipment: Tripod

Sefer Yetzirah Path Name: Consciousness of the Senses

Sefer Yetzirah Hebrew Letter Description: "He made the letter Zayin king over motion, bound a crown to it, permuted them one with another, and with them He formed Gemini in the Universe, Sivan in the Year, and the spleen in the Soul, male and female." [38] *Sivan* is the third month of the Jewish calendar.

Meditations

The Meditation Mirror: Withdraw from your personal concerns and sit quietly. Take a deep, slow breath and discover that standing opposite you is someone with whom you are currently having relationship issues. This need not be a romantic relationship—it may be a parent, a friend, a colleague, etc. Think about what it is in this person that you most dislike. What annoys you? What sets your teeth on edge? Now look more closely. Discover that there is not another person standing opposite you at all—you're actually looking in a mirror. The characteristic you dislike so much is now pasted on your own reflection. What is your reaction to seeing this characteristic on your own face? When you have seen enough, return to normal consciousness.

Mystical Marriage Meditation: This meditation is more suitable for more advanced aspirants. Withdraw from your personal concerns and sit quietly. Take a deep, slow breath and discover that standing beside you is your subconscious; hovering above you is your Higher Self. Your subconscious volunteers to act as a liaison between you and your Higher Self. Remember that your subconscious speaks in images. Consider carefully what message you wish to send and then give that message—in images—to your subconscious. Wait as your subconscious silently delivers these images to your Higher Self and receives a reply, also in images; these images are then relayed back to you. This may take some time, so be patient. When you believe you understand the message you have received, return to normal consciousness.

Card VII. The Chariot

THE CHARIOT.

"If thou canst grasp it,
That liberation consisteth in the breaking down
And utter destruction of the hedge of
protection
Which encircleth thee, and guardeth thee
From the terror of the Darkness which is
without." [39]

Outside a walled city a man stands in a chariot before which rest two sphinxes, one black and one white. **The Chariot's** *front panel is adorned with a yoni-lingam and a winged globe; a starry canopy forms the top. The charioteer's shoulders are decorated with lunar symbols and he wields a scepter in his right hand.*

In **The Chariot** card, the chariot itself represents the personality. The charioteer represents the Higher Self, which uses the personality as a vehicle. The starry canopy symbolizes the astrological forces that may influence our personality and experience. The card may give the impression of movement, but **The Chariot** isn't going anywhere; there are no reins connecting the sphinxes to **The Chariot** and, in any case, the sphinxes lie motionless on the ground. This immovability is, as the Initiate knows, quite apropos—ultimately, there is nowhere to go and nothing to do.

This path is assigned to the Hebrew letter *Chet*, meaning "fence;" as a fence encloses the city (seen in the background of this card), so does the personality enclose the Higher Self. The placement of this card on the path between *Binah* and *Gevurah* on the Pillar of Severity reinforces the idea of restriction, which is the function of a fence.

A myriad of important issues on the spiritual path revolve around the issue of personality. The everyday point of view maintains that our personalities are what make us special and distinct. In the Western Mystery Tradition, our changing, malleable personalities are seen as masks or vehicles for the Higher Self. Commenting on this, Raymund Andrea, Britain's Rosicrucian Grand Master from 1921 to 1946 and author of several books on spirituality, says, "The form of personality is a self-erected structure of being and doing in accordance with a relative standard of correctitude and expression; a structure of opinion, belief, and living built up mainly from family, religious, professional, or other human contacts, and conforming to an accepted ritual of respectability and good report." Andrea adds that, by comparison, "The soul is formless, knows nothing of respectability or conformity, and heaves opinions, beliefs, and formalities headlong. The mystical scripture says that the disciples must renounce the idea of individual rights and the pleasant consciousness of self-respect and virtue." [40]

Since the soul, or Higher Self, is a silent, impersonal awareness, it must express itself through the vehicle of personality. Perhaps a silent, impersonal awareness can live without this vehicle while ensconced in an isolation chamber high in the Himalayas, but here, in the pandemonium of the real world, decisions must be made, preferences stated, actions taken. Something as simple as ordering ice cream requires the intervention of the personality. When the kid at the ice cream parlor asks what flavor you'd prefer, the only response the Higher Self would be able to give is silence. If pressed to respond, the best it might come up with is "What does it matter?" At that rate, you'd be at the ice cream parlor all day. It is the personality that comes up with an appropriate response: "One scoop of cherry vanilla, one scoop of mint chocolate chip, hot fudge and a cherry, hold the whipped cream." A personality is required to function in the world.

There is, however, a commonly held belief in spiritual circles that while the personality is a vehicle for the Higher Self, it nonetheless can and should reflect the attributes of the Higher Self. Gareth Knight, in his commentary on Dion Fortune's *Principles of Hermetic Philosophy*, describes this relationship symbolically. "The six-pointed star is composed of two interlaced triangles, and the grade of the initiate is symbolised by the degree to which these triangles are superimposed, the upper triangle representing the individuality [Knight's term for Higher Self], and the lower one the personality. In the unillumined man, the triangles are represented as point to point, and the process of initiation in the Mysteries consists in preparing the personality to be a vehicle for the manifestation of the individuality. This is done by bringing the aim of the personal life into alignment with the aim of the higher self, and making the personality a miniature replica of the higher self." [41]

It's rare to find a personality that is a miniature replica of the Higher Self. Georg Feuerstein, contemporary author of several books on mysticism and eastern religions, establishes this with telling simplicity. "That the personality of enlightened beings and advanced mystics remain largely intact is obvious when one examines biographies and autobiographies of adepts, past and present. Each one manifests specific psychological qualities, as determined by his or her genetics and life history. Some are inclined toward passivity, others are spectacularly dynamic. Some are gentle, others fierce. Some have no interest in learning, others are great scholars. What these awakened beings have in common is that they no longer identify with the personality complex, however it may be configured, but live out of the identity of the Self. Enlightenment, then, consists in the transcendence of the ego-habit, but enlightenment does not obliterate the personality."[42]

What does it mean to transcend the ego-habit? It means that Initiates no longer think of their personalities as who they really are. Their belief in the reality of the personality's injuries and wounds changes; this may allow them to alter their automatic reactions to their personalities' demands if they so desire. For example, we may have struggled for years with feelings of inadequacy; after Initiation, we realize that this epic struggle with inadequacy was little more than a collection of ideas and mental and emotional habits that we had acquired during our lives. We were chained to these ideas and habits by the belief that they were real. After Initiation, these feelings of inadequacy may simply dissolve. As Raymund Andrea explains, "A multitude of anxieties and perturbations which hitherto held undisputed sway in the soul lose their tyranny and pass away. Not that we forsake the arena of personality and deny the constant interplay of forces therein, but that we stand at a remove and survey these from a point of ascension, with a new power of self-direction and insight, and have the ability to harmonize opposing vibrations." [43]

Much of the symbolism in **The Chariot** reflects this idea of harmonizing opposing vibrations in the personality, or healing those conflicting aspects of personality that, though not "evil" or "bad," can simply make life a little difficult. These conflicts can make us feel like one wheel of our chariot is bigger than the others. Our chariot still functions, but it doesn't provide the smoothest ride.

Ideally, a balanced personality is unaffected by the ebb and flow of our emotions, which are symbolized by the lunar crescents on the charioteer's shoulders. Sexuality and male/female energies are also brought into balance, as is symbolized by the yoni-lingam. The scepter in the charioteer's hand symbolizes will and purpose, which are important tools for balancing the personality. The sphinxes symbolize constructive and destructive forces, which are definitely not under the control of either chariot (personality), or charioteer (Higher Self), as is demonstrated by the fact that the sphinxes are not connected to the chariot or charioteer in any fashion.

It's best to take this idea of an ideal, balanced, Higher-Self-reflecting personality with a liberal dash of salt. Remember that the Higher Self is a silent, impersonal awareness; the real hallmark of the Initiate is not warmth and love, but, as Andrea maintains, impersonality. "The attainment of self-knowledge is mainly the demonstration of an increasing measure of impersonality. Impersonality is the secret doctrine of practically all of the occult classics." [44]

Impersonality does not mean that we shut off all our emotions; it means we now recognize that the personality and its emotions are not who we are. Thus, a more useful approach may be to accept our personalities as they are, right now, warts and all. If we can make personality adjustments in order to get a smoother ride, fine; but realize that a good part of our personality's difficulties have to do with our own negative self-judgment. This is completely unnecessary; it is possible and acceptable for a person to Initiate, look at the personality it wears, shrug and say, "Sure, why not?"

The personality may be regarded as another body. Just as the best-looking dude in the room isn't necessarily the enlightened guy, the best personality in the room probably isn't the enlightened guy, either. That's disappointing news to the many aspirants who are searching for a "Disney" guru. Disney gurus, whether by nature, nurture, or design, are endlessly loving, kind and compassionate—at least while they're in public. What they're like when they're not on stage is a matter for speculation.

Western Mystery Tradition Correspondences

Roman numeral: VII
Path number: 18
Hebrew letter: *Chet*
Hebrew number: 8
Astrological or planetary correspondence: Cancer
Color: Amber or orange-yellow
Deities: Apollo and Kephra
Gem: Amber
Perfume: Onycha
Plant: Lotus
Creature: Crab and turtle
Magical Equipment: Fiery furnace
Sefer Yetzirah Path Name: Consciousness of the House of Influx
Sefer Yetzirah Hebrew Letter Description: "He made the letter Chet king over sight, bound a crown to it, permuted them one with another, and with them He formed Cancer in the Universe, Tamuz in the Year, and the *hemsess* in the Soul, male and female."[45] *Tamuz* is the fourth month of the Jewish calendar; *hemsess* is believed to be the small intestines.

Meditations

Chariot of the Spirit Meditation: Withdraw from your personal concerns and sit quietly. Take a deep, slow breath and discover that you are the charioteer in **The Chariot**. As you get your bearings, observe the sphinxes crouched on the ground. In this meditation, these sphinxes represent certain of your spiritual beliefs or practices that are not actually getting you anywhere. Spend some time identifying these beliefs and practices; recall all the places you thought they could take you. Perhaps you hoped to become healthier or more loved. Examine to what extent you engaged in these practices because you wanted to be someone other than who you are, or because you wanted something in your life that wasn't there. See that the sphinxes are not connected to your journey; these practices are not going to take you anywhere. Rest for a time with this new understanding; when you are ready, return to normal consciousness.

Meditation on Going Nowhere: This meditation is suitable for more advanced aspirants. Withdraw from your personal concerns and sit quietly. Take a deep, slow breath and discover that you are the charioteer in **The Chariot**. Realize that you want this chariot to move, to get somewhere. We all have the impression that we are "going somewhere." We use this language constantly: "Where do you think this will end up?" "Where does he think he's going with this?" "Where will that get you?" In reality, none of us are going anywhere. **The Chariot** is a perfect picture of what's really going on. There's a chariot, there are sphinxes to pull it, and there's a driver. But the chariot is made of stone, there are no reins, and the sphinxes are at rest. Experience what it is like to sit in this chariot that is not moving and is never going to move. Understand that this motionlessness tells you that who and where you are, in this instant, is exactly right. Properly performed, this is a very restful meditation. When you are ready, return to normal consciousness.

Chapter Two Bibliography

1   Case, Paul Foster. *Book of Tokens: Tarot Meditations.* Los Angeles, CA: Builders of the Adytum, 1968, p. 7.

2   Halevi, Z'ev ben Shimon. *Kabbalah and Exodus.* Boulder, Colorado: Shambala Publications, 1980, p. 15.

3   Kaplan, Aryeh (Trans.). *Sefer Yetzirah.* York Beach, Maine: Samuel Weiser, Inc., 1997, pp. 59-60.

4   Three Initiates. *The Kybalion*. Chicago, Illinois: Yogi Publication Society, 1940, pp. 56-57.

5   Troward, Thomas. *Edinburgh Lectures on Mental Science*. Charleston, South Carolina: Biblio Bazaar, 2007, p. 50.

6   Regardie, Israel. *The Tree of Life: An Illustrated Study in Magic*. Woodbury, Minnesota: Llewellyn Publications, 2006, p. 46.

7   Jung, Carl. *Memories, Dreams, Reflections*. New York, NY: Random House, 1965, p. 301.

8   Kaplan, Aryeh (Trans.). *Sefer Yetzirah*. York Beach, Maine: Samuel Weiser, Inc., 1997, p. 274.

9   Case, Paul Foster. *Book of Tokens: Tarot Meditations*. Los Angeles, CA: Builders of the Adytum, 1968, p. 23.

10 Kaplan, Aryeh (Trans.). *Sefer Yetzirah*. York Beach, Maine: Samuel Weiser, Inc., 1997, p. 275.

11 Case, Paul Foster. *Book of Tokens: Tarot Meditations*. Los Angeles, CA: Builders of the Adytum, 1968, p. 34.

12 Case, Paul Foster. *The Tarot: A Key to the Wisdom of the Ages*. Richmond, Virginia: Macoy Publishing Company, 1947, p. 66.

13 Case, Paul Foster. *The Tarot: A Key to the Wisdom of the Ages*. Richmond, Virginia: Macoy Publishing Company, 1947, p. 51.

14 Kaplan, Aryeh (Trans.). *Sefer Yetzirah*. York Beach, Maine: Samuel Weiser, Inc., 1997, p. 275.

15 Case, Paul Foster. *Book of Tokens: Tarot Meditations*. Los Angeles, CA: Builders of the Adytum, 1968, p. 41.

16 Fortune, Dion (commentary by Knight, Gareth). *Principles of Hermetic Philosophy*. Loughborough, UK: Thoth Publications, 1999, p. 56.

17 Devall, Bill and George Sessions. "Deep Ecology: Living as if Nature Mattered" in Walsh, R. and Vaughan, F. (Eds.), *Paths Beyond Ego*. New York, New York: Penguin Putnam, Inc., 1993, p. 242.

18 Wilber, Ken. "Paths Beyond Ego in the Coming Decade" in Walsh, R. and Vaughan, F. (Eds.), *Paths Beyond Ego*. New York, New York: Penguin Putnam, Inc., 1993, p. 264.

19 Kaplan, Aryeh (Trans.). *Sefer Yetzirah*. York Beach, Maine: Samuel Weiser, Inc., 1997, p. 275.

20 Case, Paul Foster. *Book of Tokens: Tarot Meditations*. Los Angeles, CA: Builders of the Adytum, 1968, p. 58.

21 Case, Paul Foster. *The True and Invisible Rosicrucian Order*. York Beach, ME: Samuel Weiser, Inc., 1985, p. 179.

22 Fortune, Dion. *Applied Magic*. York Beach, ME: Samuel Weiser, Inc., 2000, pp. 27-28.

23 Kaplan, Aryeh (Trans.). *Sefer Yetzirah*. York Beach, Maine: Samuel Weiser, Inc., 1997, p. 60.

24 Kaplan, Aryeh (Trans.). *Sefer Yetzirah*. York Beach, Maine: Samuel Weiser, Inc., 1997, p. 277.

25 Case, Paul Foster. *Book of Tokens: Tarot Meditations*. Los Angeles, CA: Builders of the Adytum, 1968, p. 68.

26 Hulse, David Allen. *The Key of It All: An Encyclopedic Guide to the Sacred Languages & Magickal Systems of the World. Book One: The Eastern Mysteries*. St. Paul, MN: Llewellyn Publications, 1996, p. 54.

27 Roscoe, Hugh. *Occultism and Christianity: A Restatement of Faith*. London, UK: Rider & Co., 2004, p. 47.

28 Three Initiates. *The Kybalion*. Chicago, IL: Yogi Publication Society, 1940, p. 47.

29 Hall, Manly P. *Self-Unfoldment by Disciplines of Realization*. Los Angeles, CA: Philosophical Research Society, 1995, p. 116.

30 Hall, Manly P. *Self-Unfoldment by Disciplines of Realization*. Los Angeles, CA: Philosophical Research Society, 1995, pp. 16-17.

31 Roberts, Bernadette. *Path to No-Self*. Albany, NY: State University of New York Press, 1991, p. 59.

32 Kaplan, Aryeh (Trans.). *Sefer Yetzirah*. York Beach, Maine: Samuel Weiser, Inc., 1997, p. 278.

33 Case, Paul Foster. *Book of Tokens: Tarot Meditations*. Los Angeles, CA: Builders of the Adytum, 1968, p. 76.

34 Matt, Daniel. *Zohar: Annotated & Explained*. Woodstock, VT: Skylight Paths Publishing, 2003, p. 21.

35 Cavalli, Thom. *Alchemical Psychology.* New York, NY: Penguin Putnam, Inc.,
    2002, p. 153.

36 Scott, Cyril. *The Initiate in the New World.* York Beach, ME: Samuel Weiser,
    Inc., 1991, p. 146.

37 Jung, Carl. *Memories, Dreams, Reflections.* New York, NY: Random House,
    1965, p. 296.

38 Kaplan, Aryeh (Trans.). *Sefer Yetzirah.* York Beach, Maine: Samuel Weiser,
    Inc., 1997, p. 278.

39 Case, Paul Foster. *Book of Tokens: Tarot Meditations.* Los Angeles, CA:
    Builders of the Adytum, 1968, p. 85.

40 Andrea, Raymund. *The Mystic Path.* San Jose, CA: Grand Lodge of the English
    Language Jurisdiction, 1999, pp. 39-40.

41 Fortune, Dion (commentary by Knight, Gareth). *Principles of Hermetic
    Philosophy.* Loughborough, UK: Thoth Publications, 1999, p. 175.

42 Feuerstein, Georg. "The Shadow of the Enlightened Guru" in Walsh, R. and
    Vaughan, F. (Eds.) *Paths Beyond Ego: The Transpersonal Vision.* New York,
    NY: Penguin Putnam, Inc., 1993, p. 147.

43 Andrea, Raymund. *The Technique of the Master.* Kingsport, TN: Kingsport
    Press, 1979, pp. 62-63.

44 Andrea, Raymund. *The Technique of the Master.* Kingsport, TN: Kingsport
    Press, 1979, p. 61.

45 Kaplan, Aryeh (Trans.). *Sefer Yetzirah.* York Beach, Maine: Samuel Weiser,
    Inc., 1997, p. 278.

CARDS OF THE ETHICAL TRIANGLE

Card VIII. Strength

"For the Serpent is the first appearance of the
Anointed One,
And that which casteth Adam out from the
garden of the East,
Even that shall bring him back once more
to Paradise." [1]

STRENGTH.

A woman dressed in white appears to be either opening or closing the jaws of a red lion with her bare hands. She wears roses around her head and waist, and an infinity sign hovers above her head. A mountain is seen in the background.

The Western Mystery Tradition views humankind as composed of both animal and angel. In **Strength** we see these two aspects together; this joining is accomplished via personal transformation. **Strength** occupies the second horizontal path that crosses the Tree, from *Chesed* on the Pillar of Mercy to *Gevurah* on the Pillar of Severity, reinforcing the concept of combining animal and angel, restrictive and expansive, energies.

The serpent is a traditional symbol for transformation, and the *Sefer Yetzirah* assigns the Hebrew letter *Tet* or "snake" to this path. But in alchemy, transformative power is symbolized not by the snake, but by the lion. Contemporary medieval art historian and Tarot scholar Robert Wang explains, "In the symbolism of Alchemy, the lion takes three separate forms. First, there is the *Green Lion*, the energy of nature before it is purified and subjected to the will. Next is the *Red Lion*, represented on the card of *Strength*. This is the force of nature under perfect control, what the Alchemists would describe as the Sulphur (solar energy) combined with Mercury (will). Waite underscores this meaning by showing the infinity sign of *The Magician* above the woman's head; this is the directing willpower of the twelfth Path, what Mathers calls the *Philosophic Mercury*. Finally, there is the *Old Lion*, meaning the completely purified consciousness, the linking of all the components of the soul with the Highest Spiritual Self which is 'older than time itself.'"[2]

There are three important components to this card—the red lion, the woman and the roses. The red lion, as Wang says, symbolizes nature under control. Nature in this case is not Mother Nature, but our own animal nature. This includes the so-called animal instincts, such as the drive to eat and reproduce, as well as the less obvious animalistic traits such as ambition, greed, the urge to follow the rest of the herd, etc.

The woman represents the spiritual aspirant. Her white robe signifies the purity of her intention. The roses signify her desire for self-mastery, which she seeks not because she wants power or material gain, but because it advances her on the spiritual path. The title of the card tells us that it requires strength to conquer the lion, and that this woman has become stronger as a result of her efforts. The infinity sign above her head symbolizes eternity and the caduceus, healing through the resolution of opposites. It also links her with **The Magician**, representing the development of the will; we thereby understand that mastering the animal self requires this same effort of will.

However, we must remember that the goal is to bring our animal self under our conscious control, not to kill it. As Raymund Andrea notes, "...I have known students who no doubt felt much elevation because they had accomplished so arduous a task as a short period of novitiate, and their quiescence and profound calm have been disconcerting. They had attained a condition of peace and repose through mental concentration and there they remained, self-hypnotized, awaiting the contact of a live soul to awaken them.

"The trouble with these students is that they have read the scripture literally instead of spiritually and have made a heroic attempt to kill out ambition and cease from sensation before they had measured themselves against the force of the one or sounded the depths of the other. Their quiescence and peace arose from absence of experience instead of from the knowledge and use of it."[3] Tempting as it is to attain peace and repose through any means available, the goal of the Western Mystery Tradition is to facilitate the evolution of a complete human being living everyday life; killing off important aspects of ourselves is not part of the program.

Further, we should remember that the energy that fuels transformation, called "kundalini" in the eastern tradition, must be handled with the greatest caution. Aspirants are therefore encouraged to walk their path, not run it. Progress made too quickly can result in a form of disaster called "spiritual emergency," which will be examined in more detail in **The Tower**.

Western Mystery Tradition Correspondences

Roman numeral: VIII
Path number: 19
Hebrew letter: *Tet*
Hebrew number: 9
Astrological or planetary correspondence: Leo
Color: Yellow
Deities: Venus, Demeter, Pasht, Sekht and Mau
Gem: Cat's-eye
Perfume: Olibanum
Plant: Sunflower
Creature: Lion
Magical Equipment: Discipline
Sefer Yetzirah Path Name: Consciousness of the
Mystery of All Spiritual Activities

Sefer Yetzirah Hebrew Letter Description: "He made the letter Tet king over hearing, bound a crown to it, permuted them one with another, and with them He formed Leo in the Universe, Av in the Year, and the right kidney in the Soul, male and female."[4] *Av* is the fifth month of the Jewish calendar.

Meditations

The Lion Meditation: Withdraw from your personal concerns and sit quietly. Take a deep, slow breath and discover that you are holding onto a lion with your bare hands. The lion is standing quietly, but you feel certain it is dangerous. The beast represents something within you, something that you are working to control but fear you cannot. Engage the lion in conversation; tell him what you fear and why. Describe these fears in as much detail as you can, so that you and the lion will both understand them well. Ask the lion to give you some ideas on how to master and then integrate the characteristic he represents. When you have finished your conversation, thank the lion, and return to normal consciousness.

The Flowers Meditation: Withdraw from your personal concerns and sit quietly. Take a deep, slow breath and discover that you are holding a lion with a leash made of flowers. Obviously, these are no ordinary flowers. They represent your own hidden strengths, ones that you might not have fully recognized or appreciated. Consider these hidden strengths. What are they? Realize that what looks delicate and lovely may also be quite powerful. When you have spent some time appreciating these flowers, return to normal consciousness.

Card IX. The Hermit

THE HERMIT.

"I AM the creative Hand,
Which fashioneth the worlds
And establisheth the spheres,
While yet the primal FIRE
Circleth untrammeled in the womb of space.
That fashioning is not as the handiwork
of man." [5]

*The **Hermit** is an old bearded man in a long, dark cloak. He stands on the uppermost peak of a snow-covered mountain. In one hand he holds a staff; in the other, a brightly-lit lantern containing a six-pointed star. His head is bowed and his eyes are closed.*

The cloak indicates that **The Hermit** is hidden from the world. We see virtually nothing of his body. In fact, cloak and background blend together. This teaches us that **The Hermit** himself is no longer important; what matters now is the light he carries. The star in the lantern is six-pointed, formed by one triangle pointing up and a second triangle pointing down. This is a symbol of the reconciliation of opposites: love/fear, masculine/feminine, fire/water, spiritual/physical, etc. From this, we learn that **The Hermit** has reconciled these opposites within his own being and has reached his calm center; as a result, he is now able to light the way for others.

The assignment of this card to the path between *Chesed* and *Tifaret* hints that **The Hermit**'s activities originate in the spiritual center of *Tifaret*, but it is the compassion of *Chesed* that lights his lantern. The letter *Yod* is assigned to this path; *Yod* means "hand" and often refers to the Hand of God, which helps us along our path. David Allan Hulse says that *Yod* refers specifically to the right hand; it is **The Hermit**'s right hand that holds the lantern. [6]

Though **The Hermit**'s lantern is lit for others, **The Hermit** himself is a solitary being. He stands alone on the mountain peak. This card teaches us the role of solitude in the spiritual journey and challenges us to examine the fears we have about being alone, lonely, or cut off from the company of humankind.

In elaborating upon this, Manly P. Hall observes, "There must first be the courage and dedication to depart from the errors of other men and to devote the life to a reality which is beyond the understanding of associates and friends."[7] It is not easy to deliberately move away from our circle of friends and relatives. In some cases, it is not a deliberate movement; many aspirants feel they have been pushed away from others by the *Yod*, the hand of the One Will, and had no real choice in the matter.

Actual physical solitude can be a powerful spiritual teacher. Bernadette Roberts comments, "Few people realize that a great change takes place after spending time alone, and the longer the period of time, the greater the change."[8] The idea of the solitary journey, of withdrawing from the world in order to focus on one's inner being, is archetypal. Jesus went into the wilderness for forty days in preparation for his mission. Buddha wandered alone throughout India. Nuns enter cloisters, monks enter monasteries, and acolytes enter ashrams.

There are many people who long for solitude's teachings. But while they might dream of walking into the desert to lose their names and find their souls, their concern for the welfare of those left behind often makes this impossible. The Buddha, for example, abandoned his wife and child to seek enlightenment. We may admire him for this—and Yasodhara probably didn't need child support in the palace—but few of us would like to be the abandoned spouse or child.

Deciding whether we are best served by solitude or ordinary life is very much an individual decision that is based on our particular responsibilities, preferences and values. Contemporary spiritual writer Ernest Boyer, Jr., notes, "Judged against the values of the desert, families can seem uncommitted to God or to deeper issues. They seem materialistic, lethargic, caught up in minor details. And yet judged according to the values of the family, life lived on the edge appears unconcerned with human need, irresponsible, and self-absorbed."[9]

The happy news (if it can be called happy) is that we don't have to leave our homes and families to experience the loneliness of the spiritual journey. The emotional isolation experienced by those who pursue their spiritual quest while staying in the world is just as difficult as physical isolation. This emotional isolation results from the necessary monomaniacal focus on one's own process. It can be difficult to juggle the needs of those we love with the needs of our inner journey. It helps to have a mate who is willing to at least try to understand what we're going through, though few aspirants are so blessed.

Ultimately, it doesn't matter whether we choose solitude or an ordinary life. The alchemy of transformation occurs on an individual level; the Self manifests in the cauldron of the self. The location of the cauldron—desert, mountaintop, ashram, family—is irrelevant. No matter where or what our life circumstances, the difficulties we require for full Initiation will find us. As researcher and author Murry Hope promises, "What happens is, we are hit where it hurts the most, and the fact that we exist in a modern world in which there would appear to be no obvious transcendental realities, in no way precludes us from being subjected to the rigours of initiation through those channels of suffering afforded by the conditions rampant in the world."[10]

When these difficulties find us and we begin our struggle, we soon learn that it's not just our families who have trouble with our transformation. Society as a whole is resistant to spiritual development. Roger Walsh, author and professor of psychiatry, believes that our relationship to society moves through three stages—preconventional, conventional and postconventional. Preconventional is the stage commonly found in childhood; the focus at this stage is primarily on self. During the conventional stage of adulthood, this focus expands outward to include other people, primarily those in our community. Our spiritual interests are generally confined to organized religion. The postconventional stage is marked by a further expansion that includes the world beyond our immediate community; it is during this stage of development that our interest in spirituality moves beyond organized religion. Walsh explains the problem. "...postconventional wisdom can seriously undermine conventional assumptions and ways of life, the innumerable shared myths (such as that money can guarantee happiness or that our nation is superior) that lull individuals and societies asleep and maintain the social status quo. Though these myths may comfort, they do so at considerable cost. A person attempting to grow beyond the usual conventional level cannot expect much support from society."[11]

It's a shame. Duane Elgin, author, educator and speaker, reveals the strange paradox of our times—we have all the resources for spiritual development, but little incentive. "Our cultural conditioning has rendered us perceptually deaf to our own higher human possibilities even though Western culture provides a more fertile ground for exploring these potentials than perhaps any in history."[12] A great many of us have the time and money to read spiritual books, attend workshops, and pursue spiritual practices. Our government guarantees us the religious freedom to practice almost anything we want, as long as no one gets hurt in the process. Few nations on this earth can boast such a happy combination of time, money and political freedom.

But our society rests on a foundation of conventional understanding. For example, our economic well-being depends on consumerism. From the standpoint of our society, spending money on cars, computers and cell phones brings value to the community. People who have moved into the postconventional stage are typically less interested in consumerism, and so do not contribute to society's well-being in this way. In general, conventional understanding serves the society we now have; as a result, those trying to move to the next level should not count on the support and understanding of their fellow citizens.

In fact, as our experience deepens, we may find that our inability to even discuss our deepest thoughts and experiences with those fellow citizens becomes more profound. Manly P. Hall notes, "As enlightenment increases, the desire to share it increases; but with this desire comes the realization that it is impossible to share the Real. Realization is an inward experience which can come only to those who have won it in their own right. It cannot be conferred." [13]

Bernadette Roberts sees the differences between the spiritually awakened and the unawakened as an unbridgeable gap. In her view, the unawakened are caterpillars and the awakened are butterflies. They are members of the same species, but inhabit vastly different regions of the world. "Another dissatisfying situation exists in the relationship between the butterfly and the caterpillar, because there can be no even exchange between them. Neither wants what the other has and, therefore, sharing is limited to a superficial, non-gratifying level. Put this together with the fact that, due to a different level of seeing and knowing, the butterfly's insights are not understood or valued, and we can see why the butterfly is a destined loner.

Because there is no personal gratification on a purely human level, this is a very solitary state, and over a period of time this solitude can become a difficult cross to bear. Though never without deep joy at the center, at the level of the human heart there is indeed a deficit of joy, a deficit that becomes so weighty it eventually breaks the heart in two." [14]

It is natural for butterflies to seek other butterflies, whether in the ashram or in spiritual groups in the marketplace. This is not just to assuage loneliness, which may be considerable, but also to seek support during the frequent and inevitable periods of difficulty and confusion. This doesn't always go well; while some find the presence of a live teacher and the extra motivation provided by group work helpful, others discover that nothing in the benefits of fellowship can compensate for the back-stabbing and bickering that occurs within even the highest-minded group of spiritual seekers. Despite what we might expect from a spiritual group, the reality is far different from the vision. As Manly P. Hall remarks, "Religious communities have failed consistently ever since a disgruntled disciple burned the Pythagorean Institute at Crotona over the heads of Pythagoras and his followers. The Pythagorean community was the first religious community in history, and its fate has been reflected in the fate of all those that have followed it. It is very difficult for spiritual-minded people to live together." [15]

Thomas Moore, writer, lecturer and ex-monk, confirms this. "The Renaissance humanist Erasmus says in his book, *In Praise of Folly*, that people are joined in friendship through their foolishness. Community cannot be sustained at too high a level. It thrives in valleys of soul rather than in the heights of spirit." [16]

Western Mystery Tradition Correspondences

Roman numeral: IX
Path number: 20
Hebrew letter: *Yod*
Hebrew number: 10
Astrological or planetary correspondence: Virgo
Color: Greenish-yellow
Deities: Attis the eunuch, unmarried Isis and Nephthys
Gem: Peridot
Perfume: Narcissus
Plant: Snowdrop and lily
Creature: Rhinoceros
Magical Equipment: Lantern
Sefer Yetzirah Path Name: Consciousness of Will

Sefer Yetzirah Hebrew Letter Description: "He made the letter Yud king over action, bound a crown to it, permuted them one with another, and with them He formed Virgo in the Universe, Elul in the Year, and the left kidney in the Soul, male and female." [17] *Elul* is the sixth month of the Jewish calendar.

Meditations

Meditation on The Hermit: Withdraw from your personal concerns and sit quietly. Take a deep, slow breath and discover that you are walking alone up a steep mountain path. Realize that you will never meet another human being on this path and you will be walking alone for the rest of your life. How does this realization feel? Is it frightening? Is it a relief? Resist the temptation to feel noble or special about being alone; up here on the mountaintop, there's no one to impress. When you are ready, return to normal consciousness.

Meditation on the Lantern and the Staff: Withdraw from your personal concerns and sit quietly. Take a deep, slow breath and discover that you are walking alone up a steep mountain path with a staff in one hand and a lantern in the other. The staff and the lantern are gifts given to you by the One Will to enable you to walk this particular path. What serves as the staff in your life, supporting you when the way becomes difficult? What is the lantern in your life, providing you with illumination in the darkness? When you have recognized these gifts, spend some time looking at the ways in which you use them. Perhaps there is something you can do to utilize them more effectively. When you are ready, return to normal consciousness.

Card X. Wheel of Fortune

WHEEL of FORTUNE.

"IN my grasp are all things
Held in perfect equilibrium.
I bind all opposites together,
Each to its complement.
One by another do I mitigate,
So that nowhere in the universe
Is there any real want or failure.
Neither is there anywhere injustice,
For the semblance of it
Is one of the manifold aspects
Of the delusion of separateness."[18]

Occupying the center of the card is a large Wheel upon which appear the letters R O T A, the Hebrew letters Yod Heh Vav Heh, and the alchemical symbols for mercury, sulphur, salt, and transformation. A sphinx sits on top of the Wheel. The Wheel is carried on the back of Hermanubis, a figure that combines the attributes of Hermes, from Greek mythology, and Anubis, from Egyptian mythology. A snake appears to the left of the Wheel opposite the Hermanubis. Four winged creatures occupy the corners of the card—an eagle, a man, a lion and a bull, each reading a book.

These four creatures are the astrological symbols for the four elements. The lion represents Leo, assigned to fire and the first letter of the Divine Name, *Yod.* The man represents Aquarius, assigned to air and the second letter of the Divine Name, *Heh.* The eagle represents Scorpio, assigned to water and the third letter of the Divine

Name, *Vav*. The bull represents Taurus, assigned to earth and the fourth letter of the Divine Name, *Heh*. The elements are further symbolized by the alchemical symbols for salt, mercury, water and sulfur shown on the middle Wheel. The four wheels represent the four Kabbalistic worlds—the inner pivot point is *Atziluth*, the inner circle is *Briah*, the middle circle is *Yetzirah*, and the outer rim is *Assiah*. The **Wheel of Fortune** thus represents the many aspects and levels of the universe. As the Wheel turns, so the moon circles the earth and the earth circles the sun. The entire universe is in motion.

The primary teaching of **Wheel of Fortune** is that the operation of the universe is based on law. This concept is basic to the Western Mystery Tradition. Paul Foster Case maintains, "The Universe is an orderly, rhythmic manifestation of life, determined by fixed laws."[19] Manly P. Hall agrees. "Metaphysics is based upon law. Law is the will of the universe for itself and its creations. Law is absolute and immutable."[20] Hugh Roscoe writes, "It will, I think, be conceded at the present day by all thoughtful persons, of whatever shade of belief, that God is a God of LAW, and that all things that happen throughout the Universe happen in accordance with Law."[21]

But not all Laws are known; many Laws remain hidden from our gaze, resulting in the appearance of chance or fortune as random as the spin of a wheel. The sphinx holding the sword teaches us that these Laws may be discovered by the power of the mind. That each of the four creatures is engrossed in a book reinforces the idea that our mind is the primary tool by which we may understand these Laws, as well as the idea that the created universe is itself a book that the wise may read.

The importance of Law in the Western Mystery Tradition may seem a little odd to today's spiritual seekers, who often see science and spirituality as diametrically opposed in methods and goals. It is only during the past few centuries, however, that we have experienced a separation in the study of the spiritual and natural worlds.

Prior to that time, the study of the natural world, that which we today call science, was an integral part of the Western Mystery Tradition's quest for knowledge and wisdom.

The Hebrew letter assigned to the **Wheel of Fortune** is *Kaph*, meaning "fist." This suggests that the universe in which we live is a closed system: nothing may escape. However, most aspirants would very much like to escape, and the image of the **Wheel of Fortune** shows why. Life on the outer rim of the Wheel is a life of constant motion. A ride on the Wheel going up eventually guarantees a ride going down. Up and down, up and down, without surcease throughout the life of the created universe, and, therefore, throughout the life of each individual. For some of us, the desire to escape this Wheel becomes a pressure that builds up and forces us to move inward, to the only place on the Wheel that is motionless—the center, representing the Higher Self. This is the meaning of the figure of the Hermanubis and of the serpent. The Hermanubis, with the body of a jackal and the head of a man, is a picture of humanity's current state of evolution. It is red, showing that this creature's primary emotional state is anger, rage and a tendency toward violence. The serpent, hard on the Hermanubis' heels, represents the pressure to move, change, and evolve.

This card is assigned to the path from *Chesed* to *Netzach*, entirely on the Pillar of Mercy. This indicates that our desire for the good things—mercy, compassion and love—helps keep the Wheel in motion. Recognizing the true nature of the Wheel and releasing this desire will help us move away from the outer rim.

Many students get **Wheel of Fortune** confused with the next card, **Justice**. Both cards are concerned with Law. The **Wheel of Fortune**, however, symbolizes the universal application of Law. **Justice** symbolizes one particular Law—the Law of Cause and Effect.

Western Mystery Tradition Correspondences

Roman numeral: X
Path number: 21
Hebrew letter: *Kaph*
Hebrew number: 20
Astrological or planetary correspondence: Jupiter
Color: Blue
Deities: Jupiter, Zeus, Brahma, Indra and Pluto
Gem: Lapis lazuli and amethyst
Perfume: Saffron
Plant: Hyssop and oak
Sefer Yetzirah Path Name: Desired and Sought Consciousness

Sefer Yetzirah Hebrew Letter Description: "He made the letter Kaf king over life, bound a crown to it, permuted one with another, and with them He formed the Sun in the Universe, Tuesday in the Year, and the right nostril in the Soul, male and female."[22] The Tarot tradition assigns Jupiter to **The Wheel of Fortune** and the Sun to **The Sun**.

Meditations

Evolutionary Meditation: Withdraw from your personal concerns and sit quietly. Take a deep, slow breath and think about your life just now. Are you feeling disturbance or pressure? This pressure is the serpent of transformation nibbling at your heels, urging you to change. What would this transformation look like? If you are uncertain, address the snake and ask him directly; he's more approachable than his reputation suggests. When you have understood his advice, thank him and return to normal consciousness.

Life at the Hub Meditation: Withdraw from your personal concerns and sit quietly. Take a deep, slow breath and discover that you are dealing with a situation right now in which you have experienced a significant downturn. Your personality may be sad, worried or angry; but what is your Higher Self's experience of this situation? What would your personality need to surrender in order to help you move a little closer to your Higher Self's experience? When you have some idea of what needs to be released, return to normal consciousness.

Accepting the Wheel Meditation: Withdraw from your personal concerns and sit quietly. Take a deep, slow breath and discover that you are strapped to the Wheel. Sometimes the Wheel is turning the way you'd like it to and sometimes it isn't. Recognize that even if your awareness moves to the hub, the circumstances of your life are still ever-changing. This is the nature of the Wheel. Struggling against the Wheel accomplishes nothing; instead, let the Wheel carry you. Realize that you cannot alter its course or make it stop. For the duration of the meditation, relax into the Wheel's motion. When you are ready, return to normal consciousness.

Card XI. Justice

" 'Have I not free will?' saith the fool;
But the wise know that in all the
chains of worlds
There is no creature
That hath any will apart from
my One Will."[23]

*The **Justice** card shows a crowned figure sitting on a throne. The throne is flanked by two high pillars; a drapery or veil is stretched between them. The crowned figure wears a red robe and a red cape with green trimming, and holds a sword and a set of scales.*

Justice focuses on the application of one particular Law in our lawful universe—the Law of Cause and Effect. This Law simply states that nothing happens without a reason. There is no bad luck, good luck, or any luck at all. Everything happens as a result of something else. On the Tree of Life, this card is appropriately placed on the path between *Gevurah*, a *sephirah* of justice, and *Tifaret*, a *sephirah* of perfect balance.

The sword held by the figure has two edges, meaning that it cuts both ways. The goal of **Justice** is to move into *Tifaret* by achieving balance; both positive and negative must be cut away to attain that balance. The sword in one hand and empty scales in the other suggest the possibility that when our balance has been achieved and the scales are empty, **Justice**'s sword will metaphorically cut off our head, removing the perception of individuality and allowing us to achieve Initiation.

The Law of Cause and Effect precludes the possibility of chance occurrences. *The Kybalion* states, "Every Cause has its Effect; every Effect has its Cause; everything happens according to Law; Chance is but a name for Law not recognized; there are many planes of causation, but nothing escapes the Law." [24]

Many people, particularly those who participate in eastern traditions, equate the Law of Cause and Effect with karma. While karma is indeed based on the Law of Cause and Effect, not everyone shares the same understanding of the concept of karma. The most commonly held belief is that we each earn our individual karma by our past actions. Others believe there is a giant collective melting-pot of karma in which each soul participates, and we are each responsible for the total karma of the race. This means none of us get off the Wheel until everyone gets off the Wheel, thereby making bodhisattvas of us all.

As Dion Fortune explains, accepting the idea of karma and law can change the way we lead our lives. "Students must accept the concept of the absolute rule of law—that nothing is fortuitous, accidental or incidental. Whatever happens is the result of a cause; whatever is going to happen is also the result of a cause. Being aware of this law, the initiate never grumbles or repines, but accepts calmly and unresentfully whatever may befall him, knowing that nothing comes to him which is not his due.

"The initiate may accept his lot with a calmness which amazes men whose impulse it is to curse or pray according to their nature, but his acceptance does not necessarily imply passivity. To accept one's fate without murmuring does not pledge one to make no effort to better it. Knowing the power of concentrated thought, the initiate makes use of it in all the problems of his life. His method, however, is not that of direct attack in which he 'wills' the change of the unpleasant condition, but is directed to bring about certain changes in his own consciousness, for he knows that it is his own temperament which is the real instrument of karma. It is only through those factors in his own nature which react that karma can affect him. He knows that certain conditions come to him in order that they may provoke certain reactions in his own nature, and according to his handling of these reactions will be his karma, even in the present life. When he has harmonized these reactions, he has worked out his karma."[25]

Paul Foster Case agrees with Fortune; our own temperament is the instrument of karma. He ties karma to the subconscious, the secret pattern that determines our lives. "Our subconscious deductions from experience are the seeds of karma and are actually the basis of all our activities. From them we gain instruction and knowledge."[26] The importance of the subconscious is often not recognized by the aspirant. Many of life's difficulties have their origin in our subconscious material; they must be addressed on that same level.

When we interpret the events of our lives as random chance, it's hard to cope with repeated ill fortune. We feel ill-used and downtrodden. If we believe that we are "unlucky," then there's nothing for us to do but endure it. However, when the aspirant understands that it is within his power to change his life by changing himself, he feels encouraged to place responsibility for his life firmly upon his own shoulders.

The assigned Hebrew letter, *Lamed*, means "ox-goad." An ox-goad drives an ox in a certain direction. The ox is assigned to **The Fool**, which symbolizes the beginning of a new incarnation; karma is the goad that guides the ox. But while it is important for us to take responsibility for our actions and our karma, we should be careful not to take it personally. As Raymund Andrea cautions us, "Unconsciously, the man has become the centre of a new sphere of higher mentation which attracts to him a new order of experience necessary for the expression of the vibration which has now become stabilized in his vehicles; and these experiences will have the profoundest significance for him as related to his further advancement. Should he interpret them from the narrow and limited standpoint of the personal self, they will often appear meaningless and cruelly retarding; whereas if they are regarded as the inevitable concomitants of benignant law working for strength and wisdom, he will willingly and expertly make continually fresh adjustment which the higher life-rhythms demand." [27]

David Allen Hulse suggests that *Lamed* also means to train, chastise or discipline. [28] Many of us remember how it felt to be punished in childhood; all too often, we carry that feeling and expectation into adulthood. As a result, we may misinterpret the events of our lives as being similarly punitive, only this time the punishment comes from God or karma, instead of our parents. Once we've released our habitual fears and expectations of punishment, we can see that there is neither punishment nor reward; the events of our lives are just the automatic responses of the system that keeps everything in balance.

Western Mystery Tradition Correspondences

Roman numeral: XI
Path number: 22
Hebrew letter: *Lamed*
Hebrew number: 30
Astrological or planetary correspondence: Libra
Color: Green
Deities: Vulcan, Themis and Maat
Gem: Emerald
Perfume: Olibanum
Plant: Aloe

Creature: Spider and elephant
Sefer Yetzirah Path Name: Faithful Consciousness
Sefer Yetzirah Hebrew Letter Description: "He made the letter Lamed king over coition, bound a crown to it, permuted them one with another, and with them He formed Libra in the Universe, Tishrei in the Year, and the *korkeban* in the Soul, male and female." [29] *Tishrei* is the seventh month of the Jewish calendar; *korkeban* is believed to be a part of the stomach.

Meditations

Assigned Karma Meditation: Withdraw from your personal concerns and sit quietly. Take a deep, slow breath and think of a particularly difficult situation occurring in your life right now. Imagine, for a moment, that this difficult situation derives not from your karma, but from karma that was assigned to you simply because you are someone who can handle it. You didn't create it, but you are the person who has been asked to take it on. Does this change your experience of this particular situation? Return to normal consciousness.

Conversation with Justice: Withdraw from your personal concerns and sit quietly. Take a deep, slow breath and discover that you stand before **Justice**, who sits regally, sword in one hand and scales in the other. As you consider this imposing figure, realize there is something you've done in your life for which you believe you will be punished. **Justice** motions you to speak; describe what you believe you've done and what you fear will come of it. When you are finished, **Justice** explains that what you did was simply part of the world's karma and not something you chose as an individual. Feel a burden being lifted from your shoulders and spend some time appreciating how much lighter you feel. When you are ready, thank **Justice**, bow respectfully and back away. Then return to normal consciousness.

Card XII. The Hanged Man

THE HANGED MAN.

"Absorb thyself in this Great Sea of the Waters of Life.
Dive deep in it until thou hast lost thyself.
And having lost thyself,
Then shalt thou find thyself again,
And shalt be one with me,
Thy Lord and King." [30]

The Hanged Man *is suspended upside-down from a T-shaped cross made of living wood. He is dressed in a blue shirt, red leggings and yellow shoes. A rope is tied around one ankle and his hands are bound behind his back. His face is calm and a nimbus surrounds his head.*

A. E. Waite alludes rather mysteriously to a hidden meaning within the **The Hanged Man**. "It is a card of profound significance, but all the significance is veiled. One of his editors suggests that Eliphas Lévi himself did not know the meaning, which is unquestionable—nor did the editor himself. It has been called falsely a card of martyrdom, a card of prudence, a card of the Great Work, a card of duty; but we may exhaust all published interpretations and find only vanity. I will say very simply on my own part that it expresses the relation, in one of its aspects, between the Divine and the Universe." [31]

The relation Waite refers to may be one of complete, utter and conscious dependence. **The Hanged Man** knows he can do nothing: after all, he is hanging upside-down with his hands tied behind his back, ripening like a piece of fruit. This "ripening," which brings us closer to the Divine, occurs only when we surrender our belief that we as individuals make decisions and take action. **The Hanged Man** encourages us to learn how to live upside-down, without foundation, blowing to and fro in the wind. As Paul Foster Case states, "The greater the adept, the more complete his personal self-surrender." [32]

However, hanging in space does not mean being inactive. **The Hanged Man** has given up the idea of personal action, but he still acts. The need to be active and to work is an important part of the human experience. Surrender does not preclude us from getting up early to go to work, cleaning the house, cooking the dinner and yelling at the kids.

How do we live in surrender while still remaining active? How do we remain active while remembering that there is nothing to do and nowhere to go? The answer is that we must learn to live on multiple levels of awareness—the levels of self and Self—simultaneously. This is not an easy task. It is appropriate that **The Hanged Man** is assigned to the path from *Gevurah* to *Hod*, entirely on the Pillar of Severity. Learning to live on two levels is a harsh, difficult task; our personality has a tough time relinquishing its belief that it alone controls our life experience. In fact, the urge to control the experience is so powerful that our personality will even attempt to co-opt the spiritual experience of the Self for its own purposes. Bernadette Roberts writes of the personality's desire to control the spiritual experience. "It was from this silence that a new life emerged, a new energy that, without any sweetness or delight, was the powerful flame of love, a flame that would never be extinguished until it had consumed its unitive partner, the self. I call this flame an energy because this is its experience. Initially I made the mistake of thinking this flame or energy belonged as equally to me as it did to God, but went on to make the bewildering discovery that I could never use it, tap into it, control it, increase or decrease it, express it in any way to the outside and, in the end, discovered it was not mine and never had been." [33]

At some point—a week, month, year, or lifetime into the transformative process—our personality realizes that it cannot control the life experience; worse, it never did. This realization is crucial, but it can be difficult. It is often accompanied by pain, rage and sorrow. Eventually, in the wake of helplessness and hopelessness, comes peace.

The Hanged Man may also be seen as the pendulum of the student's awareness, swinging back and forth between poles of desires, thoughts and emotions. The goal is to stop the pendulum's motion, as *The Kybalion* explains. "The advanced Hermetist polarizes himself at the Positive Pole of his Being—the 'I am' pole rather than the pole of personality, and by 'refusing' and 'denying' the operation of Rhythm, raises himself above its plane of consciousness, and standing firm in his Statement of Being he allows the pendulum to swing back on the Lower Plane without changing his Polarity. This is accomplished by all individuals who have attained any degree of self-mastery, whether they understand the law or not. Such persons simply 'refuse' to allow themselves to be swung back by the pendulum of mood and emotion, and by steadfastly affirming the superiority, they remain polarized on the Positive pole. The master, of course, attains a far greater degree of proficiency, because he understands the law, and by the use of his Will he attains a degree of Poise and Mental Steadfastness almost impossible of belief on the part of those who allow themselves to be swung backward and forward by the mental pendulum of moods and feelings." [34]

Willing one's desires, thoughts and emotions out of existence requires a high degree of self-mastery. Raymund Andrea admits, perhaps a little ruefully, "It is not a simple matter to put aside the physical, emotional and mental vehicles of expression, to remain apart and unhampered by their vibration, poised in the clean and undivided consciousness of the Self." [35] In fact, most aspirants find it impossible to stop the pendulum until they have accomplished a great deal of preliminary healing work. People on the spiritual path who have significant emotional injuries from childhood or adult trauma usually find they must resolve these issues before much progress can be made; otherwise, their attempts to stop the pendulum result in emotional repression and unfortunate consequences. Many aspirants choose not to attempt to master their emotions with a will of titanium, but instead to utilize a continual process of examining their emotional wounds and then rising above the emotional conflict. This ongoing decision to rise above the conflict is key— fighting anything on the lower level condemns us to remain on that lower level, forever engaged in the fracas.

The *Sefer Yetzirah* assigns the letter *Mem* to this card. Paul Foster Case explains the relevance of this letter. "Water, the element represented by Mem, is the first mirror. Water reflects images upside-down, and this idea is carried out by the symbolism and title of Card 12, which is a symbol of reflected life, of life in image, of life in the forms taken by the occult 'water,' or cosmic substance." [36] David Allen Hulse gives *Mem* the meaning of the juice of fruits,[37] which accords perfectly with the ripening aspect of **The Hanged Man**.

Western Mystery Tradition Correspondences

Roman numeral: XII
Path number: 23
Hebrew letter: *Mem*
Hebrew number: 40
Astrological or planetary correspondence: Neptune
Color: Blue
Deities: Neptune and Poseidon

Gem: Beryl
Perfume: Onycha and myrrh
Plant: Lotus and other water plants
Creature: Eagle and scorpion
Magical Equipment: Cup and sacramental wine
Sefer Yetzirah Path Name: Sustaining Consciousness
Sefer Yetzirah Hebrew Letter Description: "He made the letter Mem king over water, bound a crown to it, permuted one with another, and with them formed the earth in the Universe, the cold in the Year, and the belly in the Soul, male and female." [38]

Meditations

The Wind Meditation: Withdraw from your personal concerns and sit quietly. Take a deep, slow breath and discover that you are hanging upside-down from a tree. You are buffeted by winds that blow you back and forth. How do these winds manifest in your life? What are their names? Recognize your fear that you will be torn from your tree and dashed to the ground, unripe and unready. Now realize that you are so securely attached to this tree there is no chance you will fall or be plucked before you are ready. Allow this feeling of trust to build up in your being. When you are ready, return to normal consciousness.

Meditation on Expectations: Withdraw from your personal concerns and sit quietly. Take a deep, slow breath and discover that you are hanging upside-down and swaying gently back and forth. Consider the expectations that shape your life: the expectations of others, the expectations of society, and the expectations you have for yourself. As you consider each expectation, notice that you begin to swing a bit harder. Try to release one of these expectations and notice that your motion slows down. Release more if you are comfortable doing so. When you are done, return to normal consciousness.

Chapter Three Bibliography

1   Case, Paul Foster. *Book of Tokens: Tarot Meditations.* Los Angeles, CA: Builders of the Adytum, 1968, p. 92.

2   Wang, Robert. *The Qabalistic Tarot: A Textbook of Mystical Philosophy.* Canada: Marcus Aurelius Press, 2004, p. 205.

3   Andrea, Raymund. *The Technique of the Disciple.* San Jose, CA: Grand Lodge of the English Language Jurisdiction, 1999, p. 58.

4   Kaplan, Aryeh (Trans.). *Sefer Yetzirah.* York Beach, Maine: Samuel Weiser, Inc., 1997, p. 278.

5   Case, Paul Foster. *Book of Tokens: Tarot Meditations.* Los Angeles, CA: Builders of the Adytum, 1968, p. 99.

6   Hulse, David Allen. *The Key of It All: An Encyclopedic Guide to the Sacred Languages & Magickal Systems of the World. Book One: The Eastern Mysteries.* St. Paul, MN: Llewellyn Publications, 1996, p. 26.

7   Hall, Manly P. *Self-Unfoldment by Disciplines of Realization.* Los Angeles, CA: Philosophical Research Society, 1995, p. 198.

8   Roberts, Bernadette. *Path to No-Self.* Albany, NY: State University of New York Press, 1991, p. 175.

9   Boyer, Ernest, Jr. *A Way in the World: Family Life as Spiritual Discipline.* San Francisco: Harper & Row, 1984, p. 29.

10 Hope, Murry. *The Psychology of Ritual.* Longmead, Shaftesbury, Dorset, UK: Element Books, 1988, p. 216.

11 Walsh, Roger. *Essential Spirituality: The 7 Central Practices to Awaken Heart and Mind.* New York, NY: John Wiley & Sons, 1999, p. 27.

12 Elgin, Duane. "The Tao of Personal and Social Transformation" in Walsh, R. and Vaughan, F. (Eds.), *Paths Beyond Ego: The Transpersonal Vision.* New York, NY: Penguin Putnam, Inc., 1993, p. 249.

13 Hall, Manly P. *Self-Unfoldment by Disciplines of Realization.* Los Angeles, CA: Philosophical Research Society, 1995, p. 199.

14 Roberts, Bernadette. *Path to No-Self.* Albany, NY: State University of New York Press, 1991, pp. 130–131.

15 Hall, Manly P. *Self-Unfoldment by Disciplines of Realization.* Los Angeles, CA: Philosophical Research Society, 1995, p. 43.

16 Moore, Thomas. *Care of the Soul: A Guide for Cultivating Depth and Sacredness in Everyday Life.* New York, NY: Harper Perennial, 1992, p. 94.

17 Kaplan, Aryeh (Trans.). *Sefer Yetzirah.* York Beach, Maine: Samuel Weiser, Inc., 1997, p. 278.

18 Case, Paul Foster. *Book of Tokens: Tarot Meditations.* Los Angeles, CA: Builders of the Adytum, 1968, p. 107.

19 Case, Paul Foster. *The True and Invisible Rosicrucian Order.* York Beach, ME: Samuel Weiser, Inc., 1985, p. 166.

20 Hall, Manly P. *Self-Unfoldment by Disciplines of Realization.* Los Angeles, CA: Philosophical Research Society, 1995, p. 29.

21 Roscoe, Hugh. *Occultism and Christianity: A Restatement of Faith.* London, UK: Rider & Co., 2004, p. 29.

22 Kaplan, Aryeh (Trans.). *Sefer Yetzirah.* York Beach, Maine: Samuel Weiser, Inc., 1997, p. 275.

23 Case, Paul Foster. *Book of Tokens: Tarot Meditations.* Los Angeles, CA: Builders of the Adytum, 1968, p. 116.

24 Three Initiates. *The Kybalion.* Chicago, Illinois: Yogi Publication Society, 1940, p. 38.

25 Fortune, Dion. *Training and Work of an Initiate.* York Beach, Maine: Samuel Weiser, Inc., 2000, pp. 54–55.

26 Case, Paul Foster. *Tarot: A Key to the Wisdom of the Ages.* Richmond, VA: Macoy Publishing Company, 1947, p. 126.

27 Andrea, Raymund. *The Technique of the Master.* Kingsport, TN: Kingsport Press, 1979, pp. 74-75.

28 Hulse, David Allen. *The Key of It All: An Encyclopedic Guide to the Sacred Languages & Magickal Systems of the World. Book One: The Eastern Mysteries.* St. Paul, MN: Llewellyn Publications, 1996, p. 27.

29 Kaplan, Aryeh (Trans.). *Sefer Yetzirah.* York Beach, Maine: Samuel Weiser, Inc., 1997, p. 278.

30 Case, Paul Foster. *Book of Tokens: Tarot Meditations.* Los Angeles, CA: Builders of the Adytum, 1968, p. 122.

31   Waite, Arthur Edward. *The Pictorial Key to the Tarot.* Mineola, New York: Dover Publications, 2005, p. 58.

32   Case, Paul Foster. *Tarot: A Key to the Wisdom of the Ages.* Richmond, VA: Macoy Publishing Company, 1947, p. 135.

33   Roberts, Bernadette. *Path to No-Self.* Albany, NY: State University of New York Press, 1991, p. 88.

34   Three Initiates. *The Kybalion.* Chicago, Illinois: Yogi Publication Society, 1940, pp. 218–219.

35   Andrea, Raymund. *The Technique of the Master.* Kingsport, TN: Kingsport Press, 1979, pp. 65–66.

36   Case, Paul Foster. *Tarot: A Key to the Wisdom of the Ages.* Richmond, VA: Macoy Publishing Company, 1947, p. 131.

37   Hulse, David Allen. *The Key of It All: An Encyclopedic Guide to the Sacred Languages & Magickal Systems of the World. Book One: The Eastern Mysteries.* St. Paul, MN: Llewellyn Publications, 1996, p. 27.

38   Kaplan, Aryeh (Trans.). *Sefer Yetzirah.* York Beach, Maine: Samuel Weiser, Inc., 1997, p. 274.

CARDS OF THE ASTRAL TRIANGLE

Card XIII. Death

"For know ye, O Israel,
That what men call life and death
Are as beads of white and black
strung upon a thread;
And this thread of perpetual change
Is mine own changeless Life,
Which bindeth together the unending series
Of little lives and deaths." [1]

DEATH.

Death *is depicted as a yellow skeleton clad in black armor riding a white horse.* **Death** *carries a banner emblazoned with the Mystic Rose. His horse has red eyes and a bridle decorated with skulls and crossed bones. On the ground lie an adult figure, a crown and a scepter. A child and a woman are kneeling, evidently about to expire; a figure dressed in clerical garb holds his hands before him in prayer as the horse approaches. In the background is a river; a sun is seen between two towers.*

Most of the symbolism in this card relates to our customary view of death—the skeleton, scythe, and people falling down on the ground. However, there is more here. The Mystic Rose with its five petals symbolizes life. The scepter, crown, hands, feet and heads on the ground symbolize the end of old ways of doing and being. The towers in the background represent a gateway to another world. The sun is both setting on an old life and rising on a new one.

On one level, this card is about our fear of physical death. Intellectually, we understand that the dissolution of the physical is an essential part of nature. Without it, life could not exist; if everything that ever lived was still alive today the entire surface of the earth would be miles deep in teeming, living bodies. However, this intellectual understanding of death's necessity is rarely enough to counter our terror of death. It is appropriate that **Death** follows **The Hanged Man** in the Tarot progression. **The Hanged Man** teaches us the importance of surrender; **Death** puts our fledgling awareness of surrender to the acid test, requiring us to release our darkest fears and overcome our terror.

Jung expresses both our usual view of death as well as an alternative viewpoint. "…death is indeed a fearful piece of brutality, there is no sense pretending otherwise. It is brutal not only as a physical event, but far more so psychically: a human being is torn away from us, and what remains is the icy stillness of death. There no longer exists any hope of a relationship, for all the bridges have been smashed at one blow. Those who deserve a long life are cut off in the prime of their years, and good-for-nothings live to a ripe old age. This is a cruel reality which we have no right to sidestep. The actual experience of the cruelty and wantonness of death can so embitter us that we conclude there is no merciful God, no justice, and no kindness.

"From another point of view, however, death appears as a joyful event. In the light of eternity, it is a wedding, a mysterium coiunctionis. On Greek sarcophagi the joyous element was represented by dancing girls, on Etruscan tombs by banquets. When the pious Cabbalist Rabbi Simon ben Jochai came to die, his friends said that he was celebrating his wedding. To this day, it is the custom in many regions to hold a picnic on the graves on All Souls' Day. Such customs express the feeling that death is really a festive occasion."[2]

On another level, **Death** symbolizes not physical death, but the death of old ways of being. Paul Foster Case describes this. "Thus, little by little, there comes a complete readjustment of one's personal conceptions of life and its values. The change from the personal to the universal viewpoint is so radical that mystics often compare it to death."[3]

What Case refers to as our personal viewpoint is an accretion of the many identities we use throughout our lives—Mom, daughter, husband, worker, addict, engineer and all the other ideas and self-descriptions that constitute who we think we are. Replacing our personal viewpoint with an impersonal, universal viewpoint is not achieved by becoming a better Mom, better husband or better worker. It is achieved only by finding the Self that is not a mom, husband or worker. Once the Self behind these identities is found, we realize that these identities existed only on a surface level. Realizing the limited nature of these identities, and learning to live from a place that does not include them, feels very much like a series of painful and traumatic deaths. But the doorway to death is also the doorway to life—the more of ourselves we allow to die, the more we are able to live.

The assignment of this card to the path from *Tifaret* to *Netzach* suggests that the metaphoric death symbolized by this card comes about as a result of the spiritual experience of *Tifaret*. The Hebrew letter *Nun* is assigned to this path; *Nun* is generally translated as "fish," which is a well-known symbol of Christ. **Death** is a card of voluntary death, of the god or king who gives his life for the purification of the kingdom. Also, Robert Wang teaches that *Nun* has a verb form meaning to sprout or to grow. "In this we can view the skeleton as a symbolic and perpetual seed." [4] The seed, like death, is the beginning of new life.

Western Mystery Tradition Correspondences

Roman numeral: XIII

Path number: 24

Hebrew letter: *Nun*

Hebrew number: 50

Astrological or planetary correspondence: Scorpio

Color: Green-blue

Deities: Mars, Ares, and Kephra

Gem: Snake-stone

Perfume: Opoponax

Plant: Cacti and all poisonous plants

Creature: Scorpion and wolf

Sefer Yetzirah Path Name: Apparitive Consciousness

Sefer Yetzirah Hebrew Letter Description: "He made the letter Nun king over smell, bound a crown to it, permuted them one with another, and with them He formed Scorpio in the Universe, Cheshvan in the Year, and the *kivah* in the Soul, male and female." [5] *Cheshvan* is the eighth month of the Jewish calendar; the *kivah* is believed to be the spleen.

Meditations

Letting Go Meditation: Withdraw from your personal concerns and sit quietly. Take a deep, slow breath and discover that the figure of **Death** stands before you. **Death** has come not for your physical body, but for one particular aspect of you that you are now ready to release. This might be a fear, an old identity, anything that has served its purpose. Name this aspect of yourself and thank it for the lessons it has brought you. Watch as it separates itself from your body in whatever form it chooses to take, steps up to **Death** and announces that it is ready to leave. **Death**'s skeletal hand reaches out and touches this aspect, which promptly vanishes. **Death** nods at you and vanishes as well. What does it mean to you that this part was ready to go? What feels different inside your being? There may be a feeling of openness; but it's also common to feel grief and sorrow. When you are ready, return to normal consciousness.

Going Home Meditation: Withdraw from your personal concerns and sit quietly. Take a deep, slow breath and discover that you have advanced into the future and today is the day of your death. You find that you are part of a vast stream of beings, each making this same transition at this same moment—old people, young people, animals, insects, fish and plants. Ahead of you are beings that died moments before you did; behind you are beings that died moments afterward. At the same time, going in the opposite direction, you see a vast stream of beings moving down to enter life. You find yourself moving faster and faster; with a sudden leap of joy, you realize you are going home. All that is required for you to get there is to visualize what home looks like. Spend some time allowing your vision of "home" to build up. Does it include your family and friends? A particular way of life? A deity? Do not impose judgment on yourself; visualize whatever "home "appeals to you. Once you have created a firm vision of home, experience yourself entering into this home at last. Stay as long as you like before returning to normal consciousness.

Card XIV. Temperance

TEMPERANCE.

"Behold, I am he who tryeth thee
With many subtle tests.
Wise art thou if thou knowest
That the subtle serpent of temptation
Is in truth the Anointed One
Who bringeth Thee to liberation."[6]

Temperance *shows a red-winged, white-robed archangel with one foot in the water and one on land, pouring water from one cup into another. Upon his robe are displayed the Hebrew letters that spell the name of God, Yod Heh Vav Heh, and the upward-pointing triangular symbol for fire. A sun disk is displayed on his head. Two flowering yellow irises rise from the greenery in the right foreground; a path winds up into the mountains towards a rising sun.*

The archangel shown is Michael, the Archangel of Fire. With one foot on dry land and one in water, the archangel demonstrates balance between different levels of existence. The word "temperance" comes from the verb "to temper." The purpose of tempering is to harden or strengthen material by adding another material. Iron and steel, for example, are tempered by the addition of elements such as manganese or molybdenum. The Hebrew letter assigned to this card, *Samech*, means "to prop up." Further, this card is assigned to the path between *Tifaret* and *Yesod*, entirely on the Middle Pillar. The card title, its corresponding Hebrew letter, and its position on the Tree all indicate the importance of strength and balance, which prepare us to be suitable vehicles for the coming influx of Divine energy.

This preparation takes the form of such practices as meditation, ritual, self-inquiry, prayer, ascetic practices, creative expression, therapy, etc. However, while spiritual practice is essential, many aspirants place too much importance on the practice itself and make the mistake of believing that a particular practice is the one and only path to truth. As Manly P. Hall explains, "Student Number One destroys Truth by declaring that one must practice yoga to discover it. Student Number Two destroys Truth by affirming he can discover the Real through the intensive study of chemistry. Student Number Three destroys Truth by taking mathematics as the key to universal knowledge. Student Number Four destroys Truth by maintaining that it can be discovered by the practice of austerities. Student Number Five destroys Truth by insisting that Reality can be achieved through pilgrimage. Student Number Six destroys Truth by declaring that understanding can be won through contact with holy relics. Student Number Seven destroys Truth by maintaining that it can be discovered in books. And Student Number Eight destroys Truth by denying that it can be discovered in books.

"Each in his own way follows along the lines of his own endeavors and tries to capture eternity with the instruments of his own opinions, demanding that Truth be what he expects it to be. Unconsciously he sets himself up as a judge over the unknown, while in his ignorance he takes the attitude that could be reasonable only if he were all-knowing."[7]

Truth is, of course, far more vast than the sum of all practices, let alone one practice. Yet many practitioners are certain they know what Truth looks like and that their path is the one and only path to that Truth. The result of this is the creation of yet another identity—a spiritual identity—which is a step in the wrong direction. Eliphas

Lévi referred to spiritual identity when he wrote *Transcendental Magic* in the mid-1800s. "The man who loves his own opinions and fears to part with them, who suspects new truths, who is unprepared to doubt everything rather than admit anything on chance, should close this book: for him it is useless and dangerous."[8]

Raymund Andrea tried to avoid the pitfalls of practice by employing a "technique" rather than a "practice." "A technique for Cosmic attainment is a sum total of numerous actual experiences in reaching the goal. A technique is not a result of a process of reasoning, nor a personal belief, faith or theory. It is the accumulation of knowledge of ways and means appropriate to obtain the end with the least loss of effort, both physical and mental. The technique is the aftermath of an eventual venture of blazing a trail through obstacles of ridicule, criticism and false illusions."[9] What Andrea calls a technique is essentially a toolkit of different ideas, methods and practices which are collected by the aspirant during his spiritual journey. A spiritual jack-of-all-trades is less likely to be attached to any one particular practice as the road to Truth.

Whether we utilize a rigid "practice" or a flexible "technique," preparation is an important part of the journey. As Robert Wang explains, "The whole experience is one of preparation of the Personality, and the body in which it is operating, to deal with an influx of Light which would be devastating to a system unready to handle such energy. Most important here is the monitoring of progress, the continual testing from above. It is the angel here which is at once the Higher Self and the initiatory forces of nature, which pours the elixir from vase to vase. This is an ongoing process of testing, measuring to see how much the physical vehicle can bear. When it can handle the stress of the energy interchange here symbolized, the arrow is released. On the other hand, the angel makes certain that no individual is allowed more than it can handle. The result of taking on too much at once is an admonishing jolt, from this angel, not soon to be forgotten. The angels, described as sentinels at each inner gate, are there for our own protection." [10]

Unfortunately, there are many people who pursue the spiritual path unprepared for these "initiatory forces," whether because their practice was inadequate or because they employed no practice at all. They are often badly hurt by an onrush of spiritual energy for which their system was ill-equipped. This problem will be explored in more detail in **The Tower.**

Western Mystery Tradition Correspondences

Roman numeral: XIV

Path number: 25

Hebrew letter: *Samech*

Hebrew number: 60

Astrological or planetary correspondence: Sagittarius

Color: Blue

Deities: Diana, Apollo and Artemis

Gem: Jacinth

Perfume: Lignaloes

Plant: Rush

Creature: Horse and dog

Sefer Yetzirah Path Name: Testing Consciousness

Sefer Yetzirah Hebrew Letter Description: "He made the letter Samekh king over sleep, bound a crown to it, permuted them one with another, and with them He formed Sagittarius in the Universe, Kislev in the Year, and the right hand in the Soul, male and female." [11] *Kislev* is the ninth month of the Jewish calendar.

Meditations

Michael Meditation: Withdraw from your personal concerns and sit quietly. Take a deep, slow breath and discover that the archangel

Michael stands before you. He invites you to ask him a question about an out-of-balance situation in your life. You describe it in some detail to him. When you finish he extends his cup of water, indicating that by holding it you may be able to correct this imbalance. You accept the cup, but in your hand it changes into something entirely different. What does it become? What do you hold that can help you re-balance? When you are ready, return the object to the archangel, thank him, and return to normal consciousness.

Spiritual Practices Meditation: Withdraw from your personal concerns and sit quietly. Take a deep, slow breath and consider the spiritual practices you are currently engaged in. In what ways do these practices highlight your strengths? In what ways do they tap into or avoid your weaknesses? Does your practice address both strengths and weaknesses equally? Consider what a more balanced practice would look like. When you are ready, return to normal consciousness.

Card XV. The Devil

"From the mixture of light and darkness
Do all things proceed,
And I am Prince of Darkness
As well as King of Light.
Shall there be anything
Wherein I, the Lord of all, have no
dominion?"[12]

THE DEVIL.

*The **Devil** is a large bat-winged, goat-faced, horned creature crouching on a black platform. His right hand is raised with fingers parted between the middle and ring finger, the open palm reveals the symbol of Saturn. In his left hand, he holds a downward-facing torch. An upside-down (two points up) pentagram rests on **The Devil**'s forehead. Chained to the platform upon which he sits are two naked figures, male and female. Both are horned, hoofed and tailed.*

This arrangement of a man and a woman standing on either side of a large supernatural figure is also seen in **The Lovers** and **Judgement**. These three cards represent aspects of the Mystical Marriage, forming a path that leads from *Binah* to *Tifaret*, *Tifaret* to *Hod*, and *Hod* to *Malkuth*. **The Lovers** depicts the apparent separation of Divine and human, male and female; **The Devil** asks us to look more closely at that separation.

The Hebrew letter *Ayin*, meaning "eye," is assigned to this path. **The Devil** is **The Lovers** seen through the eyes of misunderstanding.

121

The Devil is actually Auriel, Archangel of Earth. To see the archangel behind the disguise of **The Devil**, we must learn to not be deceived by appearances. The card shows a man and a woman chained to **The Devil**'s platform. The chains imply that when we are bound to the belief that we and the world are not divine, the physical world appears to be evil. Once we are released from this belief, **The Devil** is revealed to be an archangel, the physical world is seen as holy, and what appeared to be evil is discovered to be the action of the One Will.

Seeing through **The Devil**'s deception is accomplished by understanding the true nature of man and the universe. Paul Foster Case explains that "...the Pentagram is the symbol of man, and an inverted Pentagram suggests the reversal of true understanding of man's place in the cosmos. In point of fact, the mistaken estimate of man's power and possibilities is all that keeps any one in bondage."[13] The assignment of this card to the path from *Tifaret* to *Hod* suggests that the revelation of the true nature of **The Devil** necessitates changing the way we think.

If **The Devil** is actually an archangel, does this mean there is no evil? Certainly there are many things in the world that appear to be evil. Consider, however, that we don't view Nature as evil. If a tsunami kills a thousand people, we may be heart-broken at the loss of life, but we do not regard the tsunami as evil. If male lions instinctively kill the cubs of their rivals, we do not think of lions as evil. If a baby is playing with matches and burns the house down, we don't see the baby as evil.

In fact, it seems we only consider an act evil when it is performed by a person who understood what he was doing and had the opportunity to choose otherwise. Thus, the concept of evil is dependent upon the concept of free will. But if we are all conduits for the One Will (hanging on the branch beside **The Hanged Man**), then it may be that there is the appearance of free will but not genuine free will. If there is no free will, there is no choice; if there is no choice, there is no evil. Everything that happens is then the action of the Divine. Paul Foster Case confirms, "Every aspect of evil presenting itself to the human mind is the raw material for transmutation into a beautiful result. Behind all appearances, whatever they may be, is the operation of a perfect law having beauty for its foundation. Apparent evils are temporary and necessary phases of the Cosmic process." [14]

This apparently blithe disregard for the existence of evil and free will obviously doesn't work for everyone, and doesn't always ring true. Some teachers say that our Higher Self has free will, but that our everyday self has about the same free will as a character in a book. We may have the freedom to be our character, to evolve and change in accordance with our character, but we do not have the freedom to do something our character wouldn't do, or to turn into a different character entirely. The question of free will is a difficult paradox that must be resolved by each aspirant if he is to move forward.

Another aspect of **The Devil**'s deception is our belief that certain aspects of our selves—greed, jealousy, hatred—are evil. We often bury these "shadow" aspects beneath rationalizations that will show us in a better light. However, giving into the temptation to hide our darker aspects encumbers us on our journey. It is imperative that we learn to see through the illusion of these shadow aspects and find the wounds that lie beneath. To become a fully functioning Initiate, all aspects of our being must be brought into the light. Acknowledging, embracing and healing our shadow aspects will ground our feet more surely on the path to Initiation.

It is no accident that **The Devil** card looks blatantly sexual; despite the apparent openness of twenty-first-century society, many people remain uncomfortable with their sexuality and regard it as evil. As we will discuss in **Two of Pentacles**, sexuality is a divine gift that has an important place on the spiritual path.

Western Mystery Tradition Correspondences

Roman numeral: XV

Path number: 26

Hebrew letter: *Ayin*

Hebrew number: 70

Astrological or planetary correspondence: Capricorn

Color: Indigo or black

Deities: Khem, Priapus, Pan, Bacchus, Hades and Baphomet

Gem: Black diamond

Perfume: Musk

Plant: Hemp

Creature: Goat and ass

Magical Equipment: Lamp

Sefer Yetzirah Path Name: Renewing Consciousness

Sefer Yetzirah Hebrew Letter Description: "He made the letter Eyin king over anger, bound a crown to it, permuted them one with another, and with them He formed Capricorn in the Universe, Tevet in the Year, and the left hand in the Soul, male and female."[15] *Tevet* is the tenth month of the Jewish calendar.

Meditations

Meditation on Chains: Withdraw from your personal concerns and sit quietly. Take a deep, slow breath and discover that you are chained to a stone pedestal. Standing above you on the platform, clutching the other end of the chain, is a figure that represents a deeply held belief that holds you enslaved. Sit with this cherished belief and the chain by which it binds you. Acknowledge the attractive power of the belief, the security of the chain, and what it means to you to be chained. Can you escape this bondage? What would it feel like to be free? If you are ready, remove the chain that holds you; then return to normal consciousness.

Meditation on Evil: This meditation is suitable for more advanced aspirants. Withdraw from your personal concerns and sit quietly. Take a deep, slow breath and discover that **The Devil** sits opposite you. He represents an event in your life that feels evil to you. While in no way denying the pain and suffering this event caused you, move your awareness to a place where it is clear that this was the action of the One Will—not evil, vindictive, or intending to punish. As you do so, watch **The Devil**'s face turn into that of a beautiful archangel. After a few minutes, bring your awareness back to the recognition of your very real pain and suffering. The ability to shift levels in this manner is part of the adept's training. Practice moving back and forth. When you are ready, return to normal consciousness.

Card XVI. The Tower

THE TOWER.

"Verily destruction is the foundation
of existence,
And the tearing-down thou seest
Is but the assembling of material
For a grander structure." [16]

The Tower *stands on a rocky peak. A flash of lightning strikes* **The Tower,** *knocking a large golden crown from the top of the structure. Flames burst from the top and three windows of* **The Tower** *and a man and a woman fall head-first and screaming. The woman wears a crown and is dressed in blue; the man wears red. Twenty-two* Yods *fall from the sky.*

The crown on top of **The Tower** represents the first *sephirah*, *Keter*, meaning "crown;" this teaches that the forces that wreak this havoc come from a very high level. The position of the three flaming windows, one window centered above two others, represents the Supernal Triangle. The twenty-two *Yod*s symbolize the twenty-two Hebrew letters and the paths of the Tree of Life. The lightning flash on the card is shaped like the Lightning Flash used by Kabbalists to describe the process of creation.

The man is consciousness, the woman is subconsciousness. She is crowned because the destruction of **The Tower** is a subconscious decision; consciousness becomes aware of it only after the event begins. The card is assigned to the Hebrew letter *Peh*, meaning "mouth." The mouth of *Peh* swallows structure and turns it into energy; from this we learn that when the structure of **The Tower** is destroyed, additional energy becomes available for the journey.

The Tower represents our ideas of who we are—our beliefs, ideas, and personality, as well as all the nouns and adjectives we normally use to describe ourselves. If asked "Who are you?" our responses would range from our occupation to our marital status, our voting preference to our diet. We also have unspoken descriptions, things we think about ourselves but would never say aloud; these are our innermost fears and hopes, what we long for, what terrifies us, etc. These stories are the structure of our lives. They are so very fascinating that we spend a good deal of time building them, tall and strong. These are our towers.

Unfortunately, these towers prevent us from discovering who we are beneath the structure of our stories; for us to progress, our towers must be destroyed. Sometimes this destruction is the work of a lifetime; other times, it occurs from just a single glimpse of truth. Paul Foster Case observes, "In terms of consciousness, the lightning-flash symbolizes a sudden, momentary glimpse of truth, a flash of inspiration which breaks down structures of ignorance and false reasoning." [17]

Necessary though this process is, few of us would deliberately choose this destruction. The screaming faces of the falling figures give a pretty accurate idea of what this stage of spiritual progress feels like for the aspirant. If the picture of **The Tower** doesn't put fear into the heart, consider Robert Wang's description of the process. "There is absolutely nothing benign about the perception of personality being washed away. There are no words to describe the terror, the intense inner pain, and the total isolation of this condition for the unprepared Westerner." [18]

W. E. Butler (1898–1978), British occultist and author, penned an excellent description of the experience of **The Tower**. "…remember that the personality is built up during earth life by the experience it meets, and its reactions thereto. Since these experiences are many and varied, and since the personality reactions are exceedingly complex, we usually arrive at middle age with a personality which has been built up without any definite plan. Here we have fought circumstances, there we have given in to them. Here we have faced adverse conditions and learnt the lesson they had to teach, their power being thus obtained for ourselves, there we have attempted to escape from such conditions and from the necessity of having to make a decision concerning them. And so it goes on, so that it will be seen that the temple of our personality is usually a very curious structure, built with ill-assorted materials, and showing very little trace of any coherent plan. Into this structure we draw down the forces and powers of the universe, and it is small wonder if it happens that this house of the personality is overthrown by the lightning-flash of the forces invoked. In simple language, the presence of the power invoked acts upon all parts of our 'psyche', and the repressed 'complexes' as well as the integrated consciousness feel that pressure. So it sometimes happens that a student of magic begins to show signs of mental instability. Under the supervision of a wise teacher, such a condition may become what is known in psychology as a mental 'catharsis' or purification, and the repressed material, having been driven up into the conscious levels, becomes integrated with the normal consciousness. The symptoms of unbalance disappear, and the student has definitely gained by the experience. But sometimes such a happening as this cannot take place. The buried complexes are charged with power, but cannot emerge into, and be integrated with consciousness. The result is a more or less complete disruption of the mind." [19]

Despite the dangers, the destruction shown in this card is the inevitable result of the spiritual practice of **Temperance** and the successful decoding of **The Devil**'s deception.

Getting through the process of **The Tower** without permanent damage requires adequate preparation through spiritual practice, as well as a strong and stable psyche. Individuals without that stability are often drawn to this work, but don't fare well. As Robert Wang observes, "It is a sad fact that many disturbed people are attracted to all forms of occult work. These are people who look for an escape, but do not find it. An unbalanced personality, unable to cope with its own earthly environment, will find little solace in the Tarot or in any other facet of the Mysteries. Instead, such persons may find esoteric research very disconcerting, as they discover themselves required to face aspects of their personalities with which they cannot cope, or increasingly immersed in their own fantasies and losing touch with reality. The dawning awareness of the truth of the universal order is difficult for the most balanced personality, because it involves concepts that totally refute what most people believe themselves to be. There is a cause and effect here, which is the reason that so many esoteric works include a warning. Anyone can learn to manipulate the Kundalini forces of their own body, and open the channels by which Light descends. The methods are basically very simple, and are openly described in works such as Regardie's *Middle Pillar* and in his *Foundations of Practical Magic*. Yet if the basic preparatory work has been ignored, or done casually, the result may be a systemic imbalance, rather than balance and increased vitality and awareness. These dangers are one reason that the Mysteries maintained strict secrecy for so many centuries."[20]

Whether through inadequate preparation or because of inherent instability, some individuals experience psychological difficulties as a result of their spiritual efforts that make it impossible for them to function in everyday life. They may require medical or psychiatric care, which represses, rather than integrates, the experience. This is what Stanislav and Christina Grof refer to as "spiritual emergency." The Grofs are among the founders of the field of transpersonal psychology as well as pioneers in the use of altered states of consciousness. According to the Grofs, spiritual emergencies come in a variety of forms, such as shamanic crisis, awakening of kundalini, episodes of unitive consciousness, psychic opening, past-life experiences, communications with spirit guides, channeling, near-death experiences, etc. [21]

To reduce the likelihood of spiritual emergency, the Western Mystery Tradition advocates a slow, safe rate of spiritual progress. Manly P. Hall says, "True occult growth is so slow that it is almost imperceptible, the faculties unfolding from within outward like the petal of a flower. To hasten these natural processes beyond a certain point is to endanger the sanity and health of the candidate." [22]

During these difficult times, some aspirants like to think that God is testing them. Others prefer the psychological view—we've changed the way we think, so previously undisturbed subconscious material is rising to the surface. Regardless of how we frame the experience, it is helpful to view the process as having purpose, to trust that the roller coaster ride won't go on forever and that reaching this point truly is a milestone on the path and a sign of progress. When we have this trust, **The Tower** ceases to become a symbol of terror and instead becomes the means by which we achieve a new and higher balance. This card's assignment to the path from *Netzach* to *Hod* shows it to be one of the three horizontal and stabilizing paths on the Tree of Life.

There is a common belief that the experience of **The Tower** is a one-shot deal. This is not the case. It is the nature of the personality to build structure. Since the personality is not completely destroyed by Initiation, it gets started on a remodeling project in short order. In fact, most New Age spirituality is simply a newly renovated tower for its adherents. It may look like an improvement over the old tower, but if the aspirant is to progress, this new tower will also have to come crashing down. This process goes on more or less indefinitely, but over time the process becomes easier—the structures built by the personality become progressively weaker and the tools the aspirant possesses to deal with the destruction become more powerful.

Western Mystery Tradition Correspondences

Roman numeral: XVI

Path number: 27

Hebrew letter: *Peh*

Hebrew number: 80

Astrological or planetary correspondence: Venus

Color: Red

Deities: Horus, Mentu, Ares, Mars, Krishna and Odin

Gem: Ruby

Perfume: Pepper

Plant: Rue, pepper and absinthe

Creature: Bear and wolf

Sefer Yetzirah Path Name: Palpable Consciousness

Sefer Yetzirah Hebrew Letter Description: "He made the letter Peh king over dominance, bound a crown to it, permuted one with another, and with them He formed the Sun in the Universe, Tuesday in the Year, and the right nostril in the Soul, male and female."[23] The Tarot tradition assigns Venus to **The Empress** and Mars to **The Tower.**

Meditations

The Tower Meditation: Withdraw from your personal concerns and sit quietly. Take a deep, slow breath and discover that you are sitting inside **The Tower.** There are only three small windows in the tower; though you can see through them, the view is limited. As a result, you are prevented from seeing a good part of the world. Walk around **The Tower** and notice that one brick is loose. If you can wiggle the brick free and push it out, you will have the opportunity to see something new, a part of the world you've never seen before. What does this brick represent? Why is it loose? Push it out of the wall, hear it crash to the ground on the other side, and peer through this new opening. What do you see? When you are ready, return to normal consciousness.

Destruction Meditation: Withdraw from your personal concerns and sit quietly. Think about a time in your life when you felt that your life had been dramatically and catastrophically altered. It might have come about as the result of a death, an illness, a divorce, or anything that ripped up your life. Spend some time thinking about the person you were before that event. What qualities did you have? How might you have described yourself? Now consider the person you are today. What qualities do you have today that came about as a result of that catastrophe? When you are ready, return to normal consciousness.

No Tower Meditation: This meditation is suitable for more advanced aspirants. Withdraw from your personal concerns and sit quietly. Take a deep, slow breath and discover that that you are sitting on the top floor of **The Tower**. Get up and walk down the circular stairs until you are at **The Tower**'s front door. Take a deep breath and deliberately walk out of **The Tower**. You have just left behind your personality, beliefs, culture, etc. You stand outside, unprotected and alone. What does it feel like to stand outside **The Tower**? When you are ready, return to normal consciousness.

Card XVII. The Star

"THINKEST thou, O seeker for wisdom,
That thou bringest thyself into the Light
By thine own search?
Not so.
I am the HOOK,
Cast into the waters of darkness,
To bring men from their depths." [24]

THE STAR.

The card shows a woman kneeling; her left knee is on land and her right foot rests on the surface of a pool. She holds two jugs of water; she pours one into the pool and the other onto the earth. The immediate background shows a tree with an ibis perched in it; the far background shows a mountain. One large star and seven smaller stars dominate the sky.

The Star is assigned to the path between *Netzach* and *Yesod*, and to the Hebrew letter *Tzaddi*, meaning "fishhook." As a fishhook connects the worlds of land and water, the path of **The Star** connects the world of nature (*Netzach*) to the world of imagination (*Yesod*).

This card is reminiscent of **Temperance**, which showed the archangel Michael standing with one foot on land and one on water, pouring water from a jug. But the figure in this card is a mortal being, not an archangel. The lesson of **The Star** is that we must learn to live our earthly lives on several different levels of being simultaneously. Just as the woman pictured on the card has one foot on the

133

ground and one on the water, so do we live, move and have our being in the twin worlds of manifestation and spirit.

Maintaining our balance as we move between these worlds takes skill and practice. And one of the difficulties we face is that sometimes one of these worlds feels more solid and "real" than the other.

In the early stages of the spiritual quest, most people are certain that the world of manifestation is real, but they're not so sure about the spiritual world. At some point on the spiritual path, however, this reverses; we become completely certain that the spiritual world is real, but are no longer so sure about the world of manifestation. Many aspirants, both before and after Initiation, report that their experience of physical reality changes. Where the physical world once felt solid and significant, it now seems thin and insubstantial. As the material realm fades out, it begins to seem like a dream from which we are about to awaken, and some aspirants begin to lose interest in the events of their physical lives. At this point, the question of which world is more "real" becomes acute.

Scottish historian Andrew Webb argues that the question of reality is a fairly recent one that occurred only when we began to put our faith in definitions of reality supplied by science. "Among practical people there is a certain amount of agreement on what constitutes the 'real.' 'Real' objects are those which possess some physical characteristics by which they can be identified—they can be felt, seen, heard, tasted, or smelled. The category of the real can then be extended to emotions, thoughts, and practical concerns which are registered on the consciousness—they are remembered or perceived, and are therefore 'real.' This is the Aristotelian approach: observation and conclusion.

"By the turn of the century there were present, and in competition with one another, two differing versions of reality which have since become confused, although in essence they remain diametrically opposed: the material and the 'spiritual.'"[25]

However, while experiencing the physical plane as "unreal" is common to more advanced aspirants, it may also arise from an aspirant's inability or unwillingness to confront the difficulties inherent on the physical plane. These aspirants view the spiritual world as a kinder, gentler reality. In transpersonal psychology, this is called "spiritual bypass." Spiritual bypass occurs when we choose to avoid dealing with our unhealed wounds because they "aren't real." While those of us in spiritual bypass may have very high-sounding beliefs, the truth is that we are frozen in place, using spiritual jargon to avoid confronting our pain.

The two realities, physical and spiritual, must be understood and reconciled. Most teachers of the Western Mystery Tradition recognize that both are real. *The Kybalion* summarizes: "... if Man, owing to half-wisdom, acts and lives and thinks of the Universe as merely a dream (akin to his own finite dreams) then indeed does it become so for him, and like a sleepwalker he stumbles ever around and around in a circle, making no progress, and being forced into an awakening at last by his falling bruised and bleeding over the Natural Laws which he ignored. Keep your mind ever on the Star, but let your eyes watch over your footsteps, lest you fall into the mire by reason of your upward gaze. Remember the Divine Paradox, that while the Universe IS NOT, still IT IS. Remember ever the Two Poles of Truth—the Absolute and the Relative. Beware of Half-Truths."[26]

Indeed, the physical plane may sometimes feel like a dream. But it is not a dream; we treat it as such at our peril. Even after the most profound Initiation imaginable, the world of manifestation will not vanish. This world will be understood differently and so our relationship to it will change; but manifestation itself will not change. It will be what it has always been.

While the aspirant may come to understand that both the material and spiritual worlds are "real," he may still need to learn that each is governed by its own set of rules, and that the rules of one must not be confused with the rules of another. This seems obvious in theory, but can be difficult in practice; particularly, as Dion Fortune points out, since each plane functions on its own but is nonetheless affected by the others. "Each plane of manifestation has its own laws and conditions; the spiritual plane is governed by spiritual law; the mental plane by the laws of the functioning of mind; the astral plane has its own laws, and so have the etheric sub-planes of matter; dense matter itself is also a kingdom which has a constitutional government.

"This does not mean, however, that each plane is autonomous. Each level is ruled and ensouled by the next subtlest level, the physical by the etheric, the etheric by the astral, the astral by the mental, and the mental by the spiritual. But although the subtler levels rule and ensoul each its denser neighbour, they rule as constitutional monarchs according to the laws of the country, and not as arbitrary autocrats. Mind can influence matter profoundly, and yet it cannot do just as it pleases with matter. It must always rule by availing itself of the inexorable laws of the physical plane."[27]

The modern version of this wisdom comes from transpersonal psychologist Ken Wilber. "Let us simply assume that all men and women possess an eye of flesh, an eye of reason, and an eye of contemplation; that each eye has its own objects of knowledge (sensory, mental, and transcendental); that a higher eye cannot be reduced to nor explained in terms of a lower eye; that each eye is valid and useful in its own field but commits a fallacy when it attempts, by itself, to fully grasp higher or lower realms.

"The only point I wish here to emphasize is that when one eye tries to usurp the role of any of the other eyes, a category mistake occurs. And it can occur in any direction: the eye of contemplation is as ill-equipped to disclose the facts of the eye of flesh as the eye of flesh is incapable of grasping the truths of the eye of contemplation. Sensation, reason, and contemplation disclose their own truths in their own realities, and any time one eye tries to see for another eye, blurred vision results."[28]

Nowhere do category mistakes occur more frequently—and heatedly—than in the healing arts. Many aspirants feel quite strongly that every ailment can be cured by spiritual means. It's this category mistake or confusion of levels that encourages so many New Age groupies to expect all their problems to be solved by spiritual means. Toothache? They're off to a shaman to exorcise the monster in the molar. Head cold? Mercury must be in retrograde—again.

Denying the obvious link between the physical and the spiritual is pointless. We all recognize that spiritual disharmony can produce physical effects and alternative medicine certainly has an important place in the healing arts. Nonetheless, denying the physical in favor of the spiritual can be a costly mistake. As Hugh Roscoe explains in *Occultism and Christianity: A Restatement of Faith*, "To the true occultist a belief in the reality of spiritual healing does not involve the absurdity of denying that pain and illness exist in matter, nor a refusal to make use of proper medical care of the physical body as an accompaniment of spiritual healing."[29]

Recognizing and affirming the existence of different levels should help the aspirant understand that his life in the world of manifestation will not, and should not, be replaced by a completely new life in the spiritual world. Instead, our lives in manifestation will be supplemented by the spiritual. After Initiation and a full experience of the Self, the Initiate becomes aware that, from the standpoint of the immortal Self, there is no pain, suffering or death. However, from the standpoint of that person's life in manifestation, all these things most certainly do exist. Life still goes on and we still get our share of suffering. We still pay taxes, our bodies continue to play out their genetic destinies, and our karma, whatever that means to us, persists. As Manly P. Hall summarizes, "Even after many initiations all the laws of human limitation hold good. Initiates are subject to birth, growth, and old age. Sickness and sorrow still confront them at every turn. They must return to this life again like other normal beings until their development carries them to a state of consciousness much higher than that which the average individual can hope to reach in one lifetime."[30]

Western Mystery Tradition Correspondences

Roman numeral: XVII
Path number: 28
Hebrew letter: *Tzaddi*
Hebrew number: 90
Astrological or planetary correspondence: Aquarius
Color: Sky blue
Deities: Venus, Juno, Athena, Ganymede, Ahepi and Aroueris
Gem: Chalcedony
Perfume: Galbanum
Plant: Olive
Creature: Eagle and peacock
Magical Equipment: Censer
Sefer Yetzirah Path Name: Natural Consciousness

Sefer Yetzirah Hebrew Letter Description: "He made the letter Tzadi king over taste, bound a crown to it, permuted them one with another, and with them He formed Aquarius in the Universe, Shevat in the Year, and the right foot in the Soul, male and female."[31] *Shevat* is the eleventh month of the Jewish calendar.

Meditations

Meditation on Water and Earth: Withdraw from your personal concerns and sit quietly. Take a deep, slow breath and discover that you are standing with one foot on land and one in water. The foot on land represents your normal, everyday life; the foot in water is in the world of spirit. The foot in water feels wonderfully warm and comfortable; you want to get more of your body into the water. However, try as you might, you can't lift your other foot off the land. To what extent is this a true picture of your life? Consider what it is in the spiritual world that attracts you and what it is in the physical world you'd like to leave behind. When you are ready, return to normal consciousness.

Meditation on Stars: This meditation is suitable for more advanced aspirants. Withdraw from your personal concerns and sit quietly. Take a deep, slow breath and discover that you are gazing upon the surface of a still pool of water. Reflected on the surface of the pool are the stars in the sky above you. These stars are truths about your self that you have not yet brought to full awareness. You are holding a *Tzaddi*, a fishhook, on a long nylon line. This fishhook will catch whatever truth you most desire from the pool of stars, but to make its magic work you must articulate very clearly what you are looking for. When you know what truth you want to learn, tell the fishhook what it's looking for. Then lower it slowly into the pool. When you feel something tugging at the line, pull the fishhook up to see what you've hooked. The star on your hook is alive, glowing, breathing. Spend some time with it; address it if you wish. When you are finished, drop it back into the pool of stars and return to normal consciousness.

Card XVIII. The Moon

THE MOON.

"This is my hidden being
Behind the face of the Vast Countenance;
Therefore am I called
The BACK of the Head which is not a
Head."[32]

A large moon with a somber face gazes down upon a desolate scene. A wolf and a dog howl at the moon; a lobster-like crustacean crawls up out of a pond. A long path leads from the water's edge to two towers before disappearing into the distant mountains. Fifteen Yods fall from the sky.

This strange card evokes thoughts of dreams and fantasies. Such things are very common on the spiritual quest—we all know people who have fallen victim to an alluring combination of imagination and wishful thinking. Examples include the belief that the aspirant was someone special in a past life; is marked for an extraordinary destiny; is frequently approached by fairies, sprites, elves or angels; etc. As Dion Fortune says, "When, however, I listen to the talk of some of those who are interested in occultism, I feel as if I had returned to the Dark Ages, so much of it is sheer credulity and superstition. Such romantic previous incarnations, such wonderful auras, such authoritative teachings received from the Masters; everything accepted without any counterchecking or attempt at verification."[33]

The Moon gives us clues as to why these illusions persist. Our spiritual quest, symbolized by the path, moves ever onward and upward to the mountains in the distance. However, our ego (the dog and wolf) howls and strange creatures (the lobster) crawl up from our subconscious. It is the conscious ego and subconscious ideas that create psychic visions, memories of past lives, and notions of grand destinies. Overseeing all of it is our waxing and waning personality (the moon).

This card connects *Netzach*, the world of instincts, sensuality and emotions, with *Malkuth,* the physical world. As the moon exerts its unseen but powerful influence on the seas, much of what happens in *Malkuth* comes about as a result of the hidden action of *Netzach.* Similarly, what appear to be spiritual experiences are actually the work of the unseen influences of the ego and the subconscious. The card is also assigned to the Hebrew letter *Kuf* or *Qoph*. Robert Wang explains, "The meaning of Qoph is the back of the head. It is behind the head itself, which is Resh (*The Sun*). Thus, what is symbolized by *The Moon* is anterior to the bright intellectual awareness of *The Sun*."[34] The home of fantasy is, in a sense, in the "back of the head," behind the intellectual awareness of the mind.

It's all too easy to fall under **The Moon**'s spell. Experiences such as dreams of angels, psychic events, stigmata and so on convey a feeling of great significance and immense personal achievement. These often become a red carpet invitation to Fantasyland. There are many, many aspirants and teachers who have allowed their spiritual experiences to turn their heads. The masters of the Western Mystery Tradition have all recognized the tendency toward excessive imagination among those who seek Initiation. As Manly P. Hall explains, "It is important to understand that the imaginative faculty is closely associated with and may be the direct cause of a kind of pseudo mysticism. A confusion of imagination and wishful thinking will result in what appears to be genuine spiritual development. Unless a student is protected during the first years of his development he is quite likely to become involved in the illusions of the astral light, the imaginative sphere." [35]

Fantasy may also serve to help us escape pain. Many of us who are attracted to spirituality aren't actually interested in spiritual growth. Instead, we're seeking a bandage, a balm, a distraction or an analgesic for a desperately wounded ego. Life involves a great deal of suffering, and spirituality is probably as good an escape from that suffering as drugs, alcohol, or daytime soaps. In ancient times, there were certain "virtues" required for admission to a Mystery School. These virtues had nothing to do with morality and everything to do with selecting candidates who were emotionally healthy, well-balanced individuals. Today, because so many Mystery Schools operate online or by mail, it is virtually impossible to exclude candidates who are not well-suited to this discipline.

Once we get caught up in fantasy, we've left the narrow spiritual path of Initiation for the well-paved highway of delusion. This change of roadway often happens imperceptibly; only the most scrupulous self-honesty will keep us on track. Armed with this self-honesty, the well-balanced and mature spiritual aspirant will be able to identify and restrict his tendency toward fantasy. If he experiences such phenomena as past life memories or psychic abilities, he will attach no importance to them.

Western Mystery Tradition Correspondences

Roman numeral: XVIII
Path number: 29
Hebrew letter: *Kuf* or *Qoph*
Hebrew number: 100
Astrological or planetary correspondence: Pisces
Color: Buff
Deities: Vishnu, Neptune, Poseidon and Khephra
Gem: Pearl
Perfume: Ambergris
Plant: Poppy, hibiscus and nettle
Creature: Dolphin
Magical equipment: Magic mirror
Sefer Yetzirah Path Name: Physical Consciousness
Sefer Yetzirah Hebrew Letter Description: "He made the letter Kuf king over laughter, bound a crown to it, permuted them one with another, and with them He formed Pisces in the Universe, Adar in the Year, and the left foot in the Soul, male and female."[36] *Adar* is the twelfth month of the Jewish calendar.

Meditations

Howling Meditation: Withdraw from your personal concerns and sit quietly. Take a deep, slow breath and discover that you are sitting beside a still, dark pool of water. Beside you is a wolf. It sits on its haunches, stares up at the moon and begins to howl. This wolf symbolizes some part of you that is howling for attention. What does it want? How can you give it what it needs? You may speak to the animal if you wish. When you are ready, thank the wolf and return to normal consciousness.

Moonlight Meditation: Withdraw from your personal concerns and sit quietly. Take a deep, slow breath and discover that you are standing in the moonlight beside a still, dark pool of water. Hiding beneath the surface of the water are odd, dark creatures; they are ideas about yourself you've been harboring, notions you don't want to look at in the light of day. As you peer into the water, something slowly crawls out and sits beside you on the sand. What is this creature? What does it represent to you? You may speak to it if you wish. When you have learned enough, thank it and return to normal consciousness.

Card XIX. The Sun

"Yea, in that day
Shalt thou sing unto the Lord a new song,
A song of rejoicing in His
beautiful countenance,
The FACE of thine own true Self." [37]

THE SUN.

A child with open arms, legs and face rides a gray horse. In his left hand, the child holds a large red banner. The blue sky is dominated by an enormous yellow sun with an impassive human face. Behind the child is a wall, above which peek four sunflowers, three on one side of the card and one on the other.

The Sun represents that unforgettable moment when the sun comes out from behind the clouds and shines full upon human awareness—Initiation. It is significant that this is the only card featuring a child as the sole human figure; the child symbolizes the sense of rebirth that accompanies Initiation. Just as the child rides the horse with neither bridle nor saddle, the Initiate maintains effortless balance and control of his animal self. The red banner is proof of his victory.

The Hebrew letter *Resh*, meaning "head," is assigned to this card. As the head is the guiding power of the individual, **The Sun** represents the guiding power of the spirit. **The Sun** is assigned to the path from *Hod* to *Yesod*, indicating that the illumination pictured

145

here has occurred in the mind. It has not yet changed our lives, but it has altered our minds' perceptions.

Spiritually inclined writers from every tradition and generation have made an effort to describe Initiation/Enlightenment/Illumination/Samadhi. And though it is generally acknowledged that the experience is ineffable and can never be rendered in words, masters of the Western Mystery Tradition have contributed to the literature on this subject.

Paul Foster Case describes it as, "...the extinction of the illusion that there are two in the sphere of being. It is the extinction of the candlelight in the blaze of the sun. Samadhi is not of long duration, usually not more than half an hour. For the space of a half hour, there was silence in heaven, we are told in Revelation. But the man who returns from Samadhi is changed forever. He has become what Will Levington Comfort called 'one of those who know and cannot tell.'"[38]

Israel Regardie explains, "Not until man does recognize that he is himself a microcosm of the macrocosm, a reflection of the universe, a world within himself, ruled and governed by his own divinity, can he escape from the wheel. It is the achievement of this one realization which all schools of mysticism, magic, and various forms of occult teaching refer to as the Great Work."[39]

Dion Fortune attempts more detail. "The word Initiate, as used in these pages, means one in whom the Higher Self, the Individuality, has coalesced with the personality and actually entered into incarnation in the physical body. An Initiate, therefore, is one whose Higher Self it is that looks out at us through his eyes. The personality is reduced to a set of habit-complexes of living, leaving the Higher Self free to carry on its work with the minimum demands upon its attention from the physical plane."[40]

Manly P. Hall gives us what may be the most accurate description of Initiation provided by a Mystery Tradition author. "Many are the popular misconceptions about the metaphysical significance attached to the word illumination. Illumination is not to be interpreted as some kind of an external experience; it is an entirely natural consequence of living an enlightened life. Illumination does not confer perfection, nor does it bestow a sudden extension of spiritual powers. Rather, it is a kind of dawning within the Self, the beginning of a greater light, the Aurora of Jakob Boehme.

"Illumination should never be interpreted as an acceptance into some elite body of initiated adepts, nor as an introduction into some arcane storehouse of secret lore. It has no association with fantastic pageantries, robed figures, priests and altars, soul flights, or similar absurdities so often suspected by the uninformed. Illumination is simply a process of awakening...of opening one's eyes, lifting another veil, opening another door...and looking toward the face of Truth. It is the consciousness having penetrated a little farther into the wonders of living.

"There is no cause for pride in illumination—if anything, the illumined student becomes more gentle and more humble. But there is no groveling humility. The disciple approaches Truth because it is his birthright. He neither demands nor supplicates. He obeys the Law, fits himself to receive light, and the light comes.

"Illumination is not a single experience marked by an abrupt transition from a state of ignorance to a state of wisdom. It is a series of related experiences, a series of spiritual discoveries. There will be moments that seem more radiant than others, but the whole experience will extend over a period of many lives. Growth is a sequence of unfoldment, an orderly procedure marked by the gradual increase of internal light."[41]

Surprisingly, Initiation may not be as rare as we have been led to believe. As Bernadette Roberts says, "In kind and number we underestimate those who have made the journey thus far, or those who have made the existential leap—transcended the ego, have been through the ordeal of transformation, and realized true being as the condition of mature human existence." [42] In spiritual life today, there are many people who have experienced at least some degree of awakening and are struggling through the confusion and uncertainty that often results.

But despite these increasing numbers of awakened aspirants, this level of consciousness is not a common state of being; at least, not at this point in humanity's history. To attain Initiation through any form of spiritual practice requires as much devotion, determination and discipline as, say, becoming a world-class tennis player. Natural ability is essential, but it's not enough. It is a lifetime effort that carries no certainty of success, no awards or medals, and no advertising contracts. We do it in addition to raising a family, working a job, paying bills and dealing with a deteriorating physical body. We do it only because we are driven to do it and will be satisfied with nothing else.

Western Mystery Tradition Correspondences

Roman numeral: XIX
Path number: 30
Hebrew letter: *Resh*
Hebrew number: 200
Astrological or planetary correspondence: Mercury
Color: Yellow
Deities: Ra, Helios, Apollo, the child Horus and Surya
Gem: Chrysoleth
Perfume: Cinnamon and olibanum
Plant: Sunflower, heliotrope and laurel
Creature: Lion and the sparrowhawk
Magical Equipment: Bow and arrow
Sefer Yetzirah Path Name: General Consciousness

Sefer Yetzirah Hebrew Letter Description: "He made the letter Resh king over peace, bound a crown to it, permuted one with another, and with them He formed Mercury in the Universe, Thursday in the Year, and the right ear in the Soul, male and female." [43] The Tarot tradition assigns this card to the Sun, rather than to Mercury.

Meditations

Child's Play Meditation: Withdraw from your personal concerns and sit quietly. Take a deep, slow breath and discover that you are riding a horse with no saddle, stirrups or bridle. What is your experience of this ride? Is the horse moving quickly or slowly? Are you able to remain on its back? Do you feel safe? Deliberately smooth out the horse's gait and cultivate a feeling of effortless ease as the horse moves along. When you are ready, return to normal consciousness.

Gate Meditation: This meditation is suitable for more advanced aspirants. Withdraw from your personal concerns and sit quietly. Take a deep, slow breath and discover that you are separated from Initiation by a wall. Four sunflowers grow behind the wall; as you approach, they speak to you. The first one says, "Find the gate." The second one says, "There is no gate." The third says, "There never was a gate." The fourth says, "And there is no wall." Sink deeply into yourself to experience the meaning of the sunflowers' messages. When you are ready, return to normal consciousness.

Card XX. Judgement

JUDGEMENT.

"This living Flame is the power of
the Anointed One,
The Power of the mighty thunders
of the swift flash
Which divideth the One into the Two,
And in its return
Absorbeth the Two into the perfect Unity."[44]

An archangel dressed in blue appears from the clouds, blowing a gold trumpet. A flag with a red cross on a white background hangs from the trumpet. Below the archangel is the sea, upon which float many coffins. In the immediate foreground are three coffins in which stand a woman, a man, and a child. Their eyes are closed and their arms upraised. Beyond them are shown three similar figures.

This is the final card in the Mystical Marriage trilogy; the other two cards are **The Lovers** and **The Devil**. All three cards show a man and a woman in the presence of a supernatural being. The supernatural being in **Judgement** is the Archangel of Water, Gabriel, identified by the blue robe. However, this time there is an additional figure—the child, representing a new level of spiritual awareness. This awareness is the child of the Mystical Marriage, the union between consciousness (male) and subconsciousness (female).

Judgement shows the rebirth that occurs as a result of Initiation. The person we thought we were has died; we are now reborn. The unusual color of the skin on the figures shown on the card teaches that this is not a physical rebirth, but a spiritual one.

The assigned Hebrew letter is *Shin*, meaning tooth. Paul Foster Case explains, "We may understand this letter as being a symbol of the power which tears down the limitation of form, as teeth break up food. As the serpent's fang, it represents the power which 'kills' the false personality and its sense of separateness." [45] Equally relevant, the *Sefer Yetzirah* assigns the element of fire to *Shin*; fire symbolizes the awareness that leads to the end of separateness.

This rebirth means that we will live our lives differently now; this is true even of our spiritual practices. An old teaching says that once the river has been crossed, the boat must be abandoned. The boat alluded to here is the aspirant's spiritual practice. The people standing from their coffins in this card are preparing to leave their boats behind in order to experience a new life.

At this point, the inward, seeking movement that characterized the spiritual path ends. What is required now is exactly the opposite of that which was required before. This is counter-intuitive and very difficult. It is a strange paradox that the moment we discover that our practice worked is the moment we must abandon it. However, a key insight that occurs after Initiation is that none of our practices were actually necessary. In fact, we may feel a little embarrassed when we think back over what we thought we had to do to get here, and even more embarrassed when we remember how we sneered at the practices of others. We realize now that pouring our morning coffee is as much an act of worship as any ritual ever devised and saying "Good night" to the kids is as much a prayer as twelve hours on our knees.

If we elect to carry the boat on our shoulders, rather than abandon it at the shore, we encumber ourselves unnecessarily. The most common example is meditation. Almost every spiritual practice includes some form of meditation. Many aspirants meditate for hours every day. After Initiation, they often report that the experience of entering an altered state has ceased and meditation no longer "works." This is because they are already in that altered state.

The tools that aided us on the Western Mystery Tradition path were analogy, symbol and law. During the unfolding of awakening, these things actually get in the way. This is because these tools are mental constructs; when we begin to awaken, we rely on our minds less and less. Consciousness increases, mentation decreases. Words lose their value as more appropriate methods of understanding become available. This card's assignment to the path from *Hod* to *Malkuth* indicates that the mental Initiation that occurred in **The Sun** has now become manifest on another level.

Dion Fortune is one of the few classic occultists to understand that practices must eventually be abandoned. "It must again be emphasized that the study of occultism is only a means to an end, and that end is the Way of Divine Union. Some there are who can take that journey direct, but others have to proceed by stages through the planes of form of which the mental plane is not the least, and for them the mind has to be trained and raised and taught to function under new forms that shall more nearly approximate to the spiritual actuality, But let it never be forgotten that all forms but obscure the light, and we only know them by the shadows they throw upon a lower plane. The aspirant should use the symbols of occultism to train consciousness, not to furnish it, and it should be his aim to cast them aside at the earliest possible moment that pure consciousness can dawn upon him."[46]

The archangel blowing the trumpet shows another activity that may occur during this phase—helping others on their spiritual paths. The potential danger, of course, is that we may get involved in others' processes before being quite done with our own. To the extent that none of us are ever done, and the process of realization and unfolding continues throughout our lifetimes, this is unavoidable. But only strict self-honesty will tell us if we are ready to sound that trumpet.

Western Mystery Tradition Correspondences

Roman numeral: XX
Path number: 31
Hebrew letter: *Shin*
Hebrew number: 300
Astrological or planetary correspondence: Pluto
Color: Red
Deities: Agni, Hades, Vulcan, Horus and Pluto
Gem: Fire opal
Plant: Poppy and hibiscus
Perfume: Olibanum
Creature: Lion
Magical equipment: Wand and lamp
Sefer Yetzirah Path Name: Continuous Consciousness

Sefer Yetzirah Hebrew Letter Description: "He made the letter Shin king over fire, bound a crown to it, permuted one with another, and with them formed the heavens in the Universe, the hot in the Year, and the head in the Soul, male and female."[47] Today Pluto (despite its current non-planet status), rather than the heavens, is assigned to this card.

Meditations

Meditation on Outgrown Belief: Withdraw from your personal concerns and sit quietly. Take a deep, slow breath and discover that you are standing in a coffin that floats upon an open sea. This coffin represents a particular belief or spiritual practice that is no longer serving you. What belief might this be? How has this belief helped you in the past? In what way might it be hard to leave this behind? Now notice that the coffin is sinking beneath the waves, but you are actually floating on the water unaided. Experience the freedom of knowing that you no longer need this belief or practice to hold you up. Return to normal consciousness.

Helping Hand Meditation: Withdraw from your personal concerns and sit quietly. Take a deep, slow breath and discover that in your lap you are holding a large, golden trumpet. Raise it to your lips tentatively and blow. Your breath activates some magic inside the instrument; the sound that comes out is huge, magnificent, awe-inspiring. Take a closer look and realize this trumpet is actually your own life. The part of you that is blowing it is your Higher Self and the sound issuing from the trumpet is a particular truth that can only be expressed through your life. Spend some time appreciating the uniqueness of the life you are living and how it contributes to the Divine Symphony that is going on all around us, all the time. When you are ready, return to normal consciousness.

Card XXI. The World

"Therefore is the end of all wisdom
Hid within the one word A Th H, THOU,
What thou seekest,
Truly that thou art.
The treasure thou journeyest afar to find
Is the Jewel of Eternity
In thy heart of hearts." [48]

THE WORLD.

The card shows a female figure partially covered by a long scarf, holding a baton in each hand. She appears to be dancing in air. Each corner of the card displays the head of a creature representing one of the four elements: eagle (water), man (air), bull (earth) and lion (fire).

The World is assigned to the final path that brings us into conscious physical manifestation, *Yesod* to *Malkuth.* On this path, we take all that we've learned on the previous paths and incorporate these lessons into our lives. The Hebrew letter *Tav*, meaning "signature," is assigned to this letter. As the signature on the canvas is the artist's final step in his task, so **The World** represents the last step in the creation of fully awakened person. The title of the card and the presence of the four elements indicate that this fully awakened person is in, not above or beyond, the world.

Whereas **Judgement** represents the relinquishing of spiritual practices, **The World** symbolizes the Initiate's re-entry into the world. This aspect of Initiation is often depicted in glowing terms. In describing this card, A. E. Waite says, "It represents also the perfection and end of the Cosmos, the secret which is within it, the rapture of the universe when it understands itself in God. It is further the state of the soul in the consciousness of Divine Vision, reflected from the self-knowing spirit."[49]

Paul Foster Case was also enthusiastic in his description. "The Dancer is the All-Father and the All-Mother. She is the Bride, but she is also the Bridegroom. She is the Kingdom and the King, even as *Malkuth,* the Kingdom, is by Qabalists called the 'Bride,' but has also the Divine Name ADNI MLK, Adonai Melek, Lord King."[50]

Despite the blissful prose, however, Initiates often find that post-Initiation life doesn't go quite the way they pictured it. Bernadette Roberts maintains that this is because there has been a fundamental change in the Initiate. "For most authors, the contemplative life ends on the downbeat of the soul's plunging into the world of social welfare and reform, of missionary or charitable work. It is said that after his years in the sheltered cocoon, the individual now rejoins society to roll up his sleeves, get to work, and finally do something for God and man. What these authors do not realize is that the butterfly can never rejoin the caterpillars as long as he lives. The butterfly is not an extraordinary caterpillar; rather, he is a different type altogether.

"When the butterfly returns, the caterpillars do not recognize him anymore; he is an outsider. Nobody wants what he has to give; nobody is interested in his new knowledge. If the butterfly tries to give them some perspective on their creeping lives they are outraged, call him a fraud, and bring him down. They may even put him to death. Because the butterfly has returned full and over-flowing, being dismissed, ignored, and misunderstood is a bewildering predicament. Like Santa Claus returning with good things for all men, he discovers he cannot give anything away. What we have here is no success story; there will be no glory in this unitive life. It will not be easy—indeed, Christ lasted only three years among the caterpillars. Yet to be put down, put out, and put away is the way it is supposed to go. To be rejected is the way forward now; it is the essence of the new movement, and what will demand the exercise of the full unitive life."[51]

However, it's not entirely true that the caterpillars do not recognize their old companion in this new butterfly. The truth is that most people don't notice a difference at all. God does not put up a sign over the Initiate's front door saying "Enlightened Person: Inquire Within." This apparent blindness on the part of friends and family can be hard, particularly for Initiates who have been the family weirdo since birth and still entertain a secret fantasy that involves their families suddenly "getting it," apologizing, and humbly asking the Initiate for spiritual guidance. It's best for the Initiate to surrender such fantasies, which reflect nothing more than a persistent attempt on the part of the ego to participate in this new phase of life.

Once Initiates adjust to this new life—which may take considerable time—they soon come to realize that they are not "more" now than they were before. They see that they were just as much a part of the One Will before Initiation as afterward; the only difference is that now they know what they are. The fact that they are not recognized as special is no longer surprising—they know they are nothing more (or less) than a manifestation of the One Will, with no separate existence. They eventually learn to delight in their ordinariness.

The Initiate also comes to realize that there is nothing wrong in the universe, nothing waiting to be fixed. There are indeed Initiates driven to extraordinary deeds; but this comes either from the personality or from karmic impulses that are not yet spent, not from the higher awareness brought by Initiation.

The true prize of awakening is not power, fame or fortune but freedom. This freedom is not sought after or prized because most people don't realize that they lack it. Everywhere the Initiate looks, he sees people enchained, barely able to move, yet completely unaware of it. These chains are forged by the fear of other people's opinions; the belief that certain things are right and certain things are wrong; the fear of death; the fear of God; and myriad other fears and constraints that incarcerate the lower self. Initiation dissolves these chains and life changes completely. This is what it means to be the dancer on the card of **The World**.

This new freedom doesn't necessarily translate into flight from the Initiate's existing life. Many Initiates remain in place, fulfilling whatever tasks fall to their lot. However, we are, each of us, unique expressions of the One Will. So life after Initiation will look different for different people. For one person, fulfilling his tasks might look like working in a 9-to-5 job. For another person, fulfilling his tasks might look like quitting his 9-to-5 job. No one can judge the true course of the Initiated life for another. As Manly P. Hall explains, "Truth brings to the wise man exactly what the wise man brings to Truth. Therefore Truth is a sort of living legend, which he interprets according to himself. Each finds in Truth what he himself is; according to his own knowledge he understands." [52]

Western Mystery Tradition Correspondences

Roman numeral: XXI
Path number: 32
Hebrew letter: *Tav*
Hebrew number: 400
Astrological or planetary correspondence: Saturn
Color: Black
Deities: Brahma, Pan, Saturn, Vidar and Gaea
Gem: Onyx
Perfume: Frankincense
Plant: Ash and cypress
Creature: Crocodile
Sefer Yetzirah Path Name: Worshipped Consciousness
Sefer Yetzirah Hebrew Letter Description: "He made the letter Tav king over grace, bound a crown to it, permuted one with another, and with them He formed the Moon in the Universe, Friday in the Year, and the left eye in the Soul, male and female. The Tarot tradition assigns Saturn to this card and the moon to **The High Priestess.**"[53]

Meditations

Meditation on Freedom: Withdraw from your personal concerns and sit quietly. Take a deep, slow breath and think about what freedom would feel like to you. What personal, social, cultural or psychological chains constrain you from living your life according to the boundless wisdom of your Higher Self? What keeps you from removing these chains? When you are ready, return to normal consciousness.

Dancer Meditation: Withdraw from your personal concerns and sit quietly. Take a deep, slow breath and realize that you are floating in the air. While you may feel a little frightened at first, you soon feel comfortable and safe up here. You find that you can move through the air with ease and grace, just by intending to do so. You begin to dance and spin, never feeling dizzy or tired; you feel intoxicated by the effortless freedom of dancing in air. Dance for as long as you wish; then return to normal consciousness.

Chapter Four Bibliography

1   Case, Paul Foster. *Book of Tokens: Tarot Meditations.* Los Angeles, CA: Builders of the Adytum, 1968, p. 131.

2   Jung, Carl. *Memories, Dreams, Reflections.* New York, NY: Random House, 1965, pp. 314-315.

3   Case, Paul Foster. *Tarot: A Key to the Wisdom of the Ages.* Richmond, VA: Macoy Publishing Company, 1947, p. 144.

4   Wang, Robert. *The Qabalistic Tarot: A Textbook of Mystical Philosophy.* Canada: Marcus Aurelius Press, 2004, p. 181.

5   Kaplan, Aryeh (Trans.). *Sefer Yetzirah.* York Beach, Maine: Samuel Weiser, Inc., 1997, p. 278.

6   Case, Paul Foster. *Book of Tokens: Tarot Meditations.* Los Angeles, CA: Builders of the Adytum, 1968, p. 140.

7   Hall, Manly P. *Self-Unfoldment by Disciplines of Realization.* Los Angeles, CA: Philosophical Research Society, 1995, pp. 145-146.

8   Levi, Éliphas. *Transcendental Magic.* (Waite, A.E. Trans.) York Beach, ME: Weiser Books, 2001, p. 27.

9   Andrea, Raymund. *The Technique of the Master.* Kingsport, TN: Kingsport Press, 1979, p. 11.

10 Wang, Robert. *The Qabalistic Tarot: A Textbook of Mystical Philosophy.* Canada: Marcus Aurelius Press, 2004, pp. 177-178.

11 Kaplan, Aryeh (Trans.). *Sefer Yetzirah.* York Beach, Maine: Samuel Weiser, Inc., 1997, p. 299.

12 Case, Paul Foster. *Book of Tokens: Tarot Meditations.* Los Angeles, CA: Builders of the Adytum, 1968, p. 148.

13 Case, Paul Foster. *Tarot: A Key to the Wisdom of the Ages.* Richmond, VA: Macoy Publishing Company, 1947, p. 158.

14 Case, Paul Foster. *The True and Invisible Rosicrucian Order.* York Beach, ME: Samuel Weiser, Inc., 1985, p. 232.

15 Kaplan, Aryeh (Trans.). *Sefer Yetzirah.* York Beach, Maine: Samuel Weiser, Inc., 1997, p. 278.

16 Case, Paul Foster. *Book of Tokens: Tarot Meditations.* Los Angeles, CA: Builders of the Adytum, 1968, p. 156.

17 Case, Paul Foster. *Tarot: A Key to the Wisdom of the Ages.* Richmond, VA: Macoy Publishing Company, 1947, p. 162.

18 Wang, Robert. *The Jungian Tarot and Its Archetypal Imagery.* Canada: Marcus Aurelius Press, 2001, p. 33.

19 Butler, W. E. *The Magician: His Training and Work.* No. Hollywood, CA: Wilshire Book Company, 1969, pp 20-21.

20 Wang, Robert. *The Qabalistic Tarot: A Textbook of Mystical Philosophy.* Canada: Marcus Aurelius Press, 2004, pp. 7-8.

21 Grof, Stanislav and Christina Grof. "Spiritual Emergency: Understanding Evolutionary Crisis" in Grof, S. and Grof, C. (Eds.), *Spiritual Emergency: When Personal Transformation Becomes a Crisis.* New York, NY: Penguin Putnam Inc., 1989, pp. 13-14.

22 Hall, Manly P. *Spiritual Centers in Man.* Los Angeles, CA: Philosophical Research Society, 1999, p. 14.

23 Kaplan, Aryeh (Trans.). *Sefer Yetzirah.* York Beach, Maine: Samuel Weiser, Inc., 1997, p. 275.

24 Case, Paul Foster. *Book of Tokens: Tarot Meditations.* Los Angeles, CA: Builders of the Adytum, 1968, p. 161.

25 Webb, Andrew. *The Occult Underground.* La Salle, IL: Open Court, 1974, p. 360.

26 Three Initiates. *The Kybalion.* Chicago, Illinois: Yogi Publication Society, 1940, p. 78.

27 Fortune, Dion. *Aspects of Occultism.* York Beach, ME: Samuel Weiser, Inc., 2000, p. 55.

28 Wilber, Ken. "Eye to Eye: Science and Transpersonal Psychology" in Walsh, R. and Vaughan, F. (Eds.), *Paths Beyond Ego.* New York, New York: Penguin Putnam, Inc., 1993, pp. 185-186.

29 Roscoe, Hugh. *Occultism and Christianity: A Restatement of Faith.* London, UK: Rider & Co., 2004, p. 72.

30 Hall, Manly P. *What the Ancient Wisdom Expects of Its Disciples.* Los Angeles, CA: Philosophical Research Society, 1982, p. 51.

31 Kaplan, Aryeh (Trans.). *Sefer Yetzirah.* York Beach, Maine: Samuel Weiser, Inc., 1997, p. 278.

32 Case, Paul Foster. *Book of Tokens: Tarot Meditations.* Los Angeles, CA: Builders of the Adytum, 1968, p. 169.

33   Fortune, Dion. *Sane Occultism and Practical Occultism in Daily Life.* Wellingborough, Northhamptonshire, UK: The Aquarian Press, 1987, p. 37.

34   Wang, Robert. *The Qabalistic Tarot: A Textbook of Mystical Philosophy.* Canada: Marcus Aurelius Press, 2004, p. 157.

35   Hall, Manly P. *Self-Unfoldment by Disciplines of Realization.* Los Angeles, CA: Philosophical Research Society, 1995, p. 169.

36   Kaplan, Aryeh (Trans.). *Sefer Yetzirah.* York Beach, Maine: Samuel Weiser, Inc., 1997, p. 279.

37   Case, Paul Foster. *Book of Tokens: Tarot Meditations.* Los Angeles, CA: Builders of the Adytum, 1968, p. 176.

38   Case, Paul Foster. *The True and Invisible Rosicrucian Order.* York Beach, ME: Samuel Weiser, Inc., 1985, p. 240.

39   Regardie, Israel. *The Middle Pillar: The Balance Between Mind and Magic.* Woodbury, Minnesota: Llewellyn Publications, 2006, pp. xxv–xxvi.

40   Fortune, Dion. *Training and Work of an Initiate.* York Beach, Maine: Samuel Weiser, Inc., 2000, p. 34.

41   Hall, Manly P. *Self-Unfoldment by Disciplines of Realization.* Los Angeles, CA: Philosophical Research Society, 1995, pp. 185-186.

42   Roberts, Bernadette. *What Is Self? A Study of the Spiritual Journey in Terms of Consciousness.* Boulder, CO: Sentient Publications, 2005, p. 29.

43   Kaplan, Aryeh (Trans.). *Sefer Yetzirah.* York Beach, Maine: Samuel Weiser, Inc., 1997, p. 276.

44   Case, Paul Foster. *Book of Tokens: Tarot Meditations.* Los Angeles, CA: Builders of the Adytum, 1968, p. 182.

45   Case, Paul Foster. *Tarot: A Key to the Wisdom of the Ages.* Richmond, VA: Macoy Publishing Company, 1947, p. 189.

46   Fortune, Dion. *Esoteric Orders and Their Work.* York Beach, ME: Samuel Weiser, Inc., 2000, p. 88.

47   Kaplan, Aryeh (Trans.). *Sefer Yetzirah.* York Beach, Maine: Samuel Weiser, Inc., 1997, p. 274.

48   Case, Paul Foster. *Book of Tokens: Tarot Meditations.* Los Angeles, CA: Builders of the Adytum, 1968, p. 188.

49   Waite, Arthur Edward. *The Pictorial Key to the Tarot.* Mineola, New York: Dover Publications, 2005, p. 78.

50   Case, Paul Foster. *Tarot: A Key to the Wisdom of the Ages.* Richmond, VA: Macoy Publishing Company, 1947, p. 198.

51   Roberts, Bernadette. *Path to No-Self*. Albany, NY: State University of New York Press, 1991, pp. 121-122.

52   Hall, Manly P. *Self-Unfoldment by Disciplines of Realization*. Los Angeles, CA: Philosophical Research Society, 1995, p. 101.

53   Kaplan, Aryeh (Trans.). *Sefer Yetzirah*. York Beach, Maine: Samuel Weiser, Inc., 1997, p. 276.

Chapter Five

INTRODUCTION TO
THE MINOR ARCANA

The paths to Initiation embrace the four primary aspects of the human being—physical, emotional, intellectual and spiritual. The path that focuses on the physical is known as the Path of Service; the path that utilizes the emotions is the Path of Devotion; the path of the intellect is the Path of Knowledge; and the path of awareness is the Mystic Path. In eastern traditions, these paths are called, respectively, Karma Yoga, Bhakti Yoga, Jnana Yoga and Raga Yoga.

The four suits of Tarot's Minor Arcana may be interpreted as symbolizing these four paths. The Suit of Pentacles symbolizes the physical Path of Service, corresponding to the Kabbalistic world of *Assiah*, the final *Heh* in the Divine Name *Yod Heh Vav Heh*, and the element of earth. The Suit of Cups symbolizes the emotional Path of Devotion and corresponds to the world of *Yetzirah*, the letter *Vav* in the Divine Name, and the element of water. The Suit of Swords symbolizes the intellectual Path of Knowledge, and corresponds to the world of *Briah*, the first *Heh* in the Divine Name, and the element of air. The Suit of Wands symbolizes the Mystic Path of awareness, and corresponds to the world of *Atziluth*, the letter *Yod* in the Divine Name, and the element of fire.

Some Tarot teachers reverse the order of Cups and Swords, assigning Cups and the emotions to *Briah*, and Swords and the intellect to *Yetzirah*. The reason for this difference is that some teachers consider emotions to be closer to awareness than intellect, while others maintain the opposite to be true. The order used in this book is based on the Kabbalistic system and correlates with the progression of elements associated with the four worlds. *Atziluth* is associated with the least dense element, fire, which corresponds to the spirit. *Briah* is associated with the next densest element, air, which corresponds to the intellect. *Yetzirah* is associated with the third densest element, water, corresponding to the emotions. *Assiah* is associated with the densest element, earth, corresponding to the body.

We usually choose our spiritual path based on what we believe to be our greatest strength and most reliable tool. For example, those who pride themselves on the power of their minds, believing that emotions are false but the mind knows the truth, tend to be drawn to the Path of Knowledge. Those who connect to the world primarily through the emotions, feeling that the mind is treacherous but the heart never lies, usually find themselves on the Path of Devotion.

We often entertain the hope that we can reach our destination by walking the path of our choice and ignoring the others. This hope is often based on distaste (conscious or subconscious) for certain aspects of our being. For example, those on the Path of Knowledge, whose strong preference for their intellect may make them suspicious of their emotions, usually avoid utilizing their emotions on their journey. Similarly, those on the Mystic Path often would like to avoid the experience of being embodied. However, since we each possess a body, emotions, intellect and awareness, our journey actually encompasses all aspects of our being and thus all spiritual paths. Eventually, in order to reach full Initiation, body, heart, mind and awareness must all be awakened.

The Suit of Pentacles

The Suit of Pentacles symbolizes the Path of Service. On this physical, earth-based path, we are led toward God by working in His
service, which usually takes the form of helping other people, animals, the environment, etc. The Path of Service is a wide, well-paved
avenue walked by many people, many of whom are not spiritual
aspirants. A great many people are engaged in service because they
believe it's the right thing to do, or because they are emotionally
moved to do so. The spiritual aspirant walks the Path of Service for
the sole purpose of achieving Initiation.

This path is often embedded in other paths. Those embarked on a
magical path, for example, are expected to "desire to know in order
to serve." As W. E. Butler says, "In the early stages of our magical
training, our motives are usually mixed, but from the beginning our
motive must be present in our minds if we wish safely to tread the
magical path. This motive we have already referred to. It is the
desire to know in order to serve, and it must be the primary motive
of our interest in magic. Other motives, such as intellectual curiosity, emotional appeal or aesthetic appreciation, may co-exist with
this primary desire, and may each in their own way be catered for.
But this motive of service must always come first." [1]

The eastern counterpart of the Path of Service is Karma Yoga.
In describing this path, religious scholar Huston Smith advises,
"Throw yourself into your work with everything you have; only do
so wisely, in a way that will bring the highest rewards, not just triv-
ia. Learn the secret of work by which every movement can carry
you Godward even while other things are being accomplished, like
a wristwatch that winds itself as other duties are performed." [2]

To be carried "Godward," the aspirant must continually focus
his attention within, rather than without. Raymund Andrea explains
this as the need to focus on the soul, rather than the personal self.

"The neophyte...will regard himself as a volunteer to a life of dis-cipline, the object of which is to give him skill in service. As a pre-liminary in this discipline he is to cultivate a responsiveness of the personal self to the soul which is to ultimately dominate all his activities. He will seek to transfer the emphasis he has placed so completely upon the objective self, to that informing entity within which will gradually assert its control and initiate him into new areas of consciousness through a growing responsiveness to subtle vibrational measures hitherto unrecognized."[3]

The concept of service to the world is also fundamental to the Kabbalistic tradition upon which the Rider-Waite Tarot is based; in particular, Rabbi Isaac Luria (1534–1572) stressed the idea of *tikkun olam*, meaning "repair of the world," as the primary responsibility of humankind.

The Path of Service is based on the perception that the world is in trouble and needs to be fixed. But this belief, which, seemingly, lies at the very heart of the Path of Service, is held only by the egoic, indi-vidual self. After Initiation, we realize that there is nothing wrong on Planet Earth. Thus, the Path of Service begins with our earnest de-sire to save the world (or some portion of it) and ends with our reali-zation that everything is really fine. Our personality had a belief that the world needed help; eventually we discover that our Higher Self sees the world as a paradise. This change comes about not because we succeeded in making the world better, but because our aware-ness shifted from the level of the personality to that of the Higher Self. After Initiation, we may very well continue to lead a life of service, but we will do so with a very different sense of what we are doing and why.

The Suit of Cups

The Suit of Cups symbolizes the Path of Devotion to God. This path is experienced as a close, personal, One-on-one relationship between Divine and devotee. All the emotion and attachment most people have for their spouse, children, or automobile is funneled into this relationship with God. It's been said that this is the easiest path to walk because love is such a powerful part of the human experience. But while this path may be easy in the early stages, walking this path to its conclusion requires a level of all-consuming devotion that is far beyond the average person's capability. Most people actually have very little interest in loving God; they want to bargain with God, seeking favors in exchange for prayer or sacrifice. But the aspirant on the Path of Devotion asks only the privilege of loving God.

Swami Vivekananda (1863–1902), chief disciple of the nineteenth-century mystic Ramakrishna, describes the eastern version of this path. "Bhakti Yoga is a real, genuine search after the Lord, a search beginning, continuing, and ending in love. One single moment of the madness of extreme love to God brings us eternal freedom."[4]

There are many practices on this path—purity, non-injury to other beings, sacrifices of various kinds, creation of spiritual art, chanting, devotion to images and churches, etc. These practices help us maintain our focus on loving God in the face of life's many distractions.

While those on other paths may experience God as impersonal, the aspirant on the Path of Devotion experiences God in a very personal way. The devotee understands that it is impossible to engage in a relationship with an impersonal God, so he chooses a personal representation of the One Will and establishes his relationship with that representation. Far from being inappropriate or childish, this is a perfect and beautiful understanding of the human need to relate to the un-relatable.

The aspirant's experience of God is a reflection of his own level of development. In essence, we make God in our own image. A loving aspirant creates a loving God. A fearful person creates a God who must be feared. As an aspirant becomes deeper and wiser, his God becomes deeper and wiser; as the aspirant's capacity for love increases, his God's capacity for love likewise increases.

Since the Path of Devotion is based on a relationship with the Divine, this path requires the existence of two separate beings, an "I" and a "Thou." If the path is walked to the end, the final sacrifice required of the aspirant is that of the relationship itself. When the aspirant realizes that lover and Beloved have been one and the same all along, the relationship ceases to exist.

The Suit of Swords

The Suit of Swords symbolizes the Path of Knowledge, also called the Path of the Mind. This path seeks God through study, analysis and theosophy. It is not held in particularly high regard in today's popular spiritual culture. We often believe that if it weren't for the restless mind, we'd be at peace; if it weren't for the mind's illusions, we'd be aware of our Self. But such preferences go in cycles—a century ago, it was the physical body which was considered the bane of spiritual life and had to be shunned, disregarded, punished and tortured into acquiescence.

Despite our modern distaste for the mind, a fair number of aspirants still walk the Path of Knowledge. They read, study, analyze and meditate on ancient and modern manuscripts, symbols and glyphs in search of new insights, which are then examined thoroughly. Emotional content and physical experience are considered unimportant on this path; students do not typically consider their feelings to be an authentic test of truth, nor do they ask their bodies for an opinion.

Huston Smith describes the eastern version of this Path, Jnana Yoga. "The yoga of knowledge is said to be the shortest path to divine realization. It is also the steepest. Requiring as it does a rare combination of rationality and spirituality, it is for a select few." [5]

On the Path of the Mind, aspirants begin with a deep curiosity about the workings of the Universe and the belief that the mind is the best tool to discover these secrets. The path leads deeply into many mysteries and aspirants often have a sense of being on the verge of great discovery. Old "truths" are revealed as falsehoods, new realities are exposed; then, in an instant, the mind sees the ultimate truth—its own non-existence. The power of the mind vanishes and the soul wakes up.

The Suit of Wands

The Suit of Wands symbolizes the Mystic Path. The mystic gift—the ability to find divine awareness directly through human awareness, rather than through the intermediaries of body, mind and heart—is a rare one. Few aspirants walk this path.

The mystic searches for God directly, turning the high beams of his trained awareness upward. Kabbalistic scholar Gershom Scholem (1897–1982) points out, however, that the mystic experience isn't always the result of effort. "A mystic is a man who has been favored with an immediate, and to him real, experience of the divine, of ultimate reality, or who at least strives to attain such experience. His experience may come to him through sudden illumination, or it may be the result of long and often elaborate preparations." [6]

The eastern version of this path is Raja Yoga, described here by Huston Smith. "…a determined refusal to allow the pitter-patter of daily existence to distract from the unknown demands of some waiting urgency within: a kind of total strike against the terms of routine, prosaic existence. The successful yogi succeeds in carrying life's problems to this plane of new magnitude and there resolving it. The insights of such people will pertain not so much to passing personal and social predicaments as to the unquenchable source by which all peoples and societies are renewed, for their inspiration will be drawn from direct contact with this primary spring. In body they will remain individuals. In spirit each will have become unspecific, universal, perfected."[7]

Evelyn Underhill (1875–1941), whose book *Mysticism: The Nature and Development of Spiritual Consciousness*, originally published in 1911, remains a seminal text on the subject, explores the nature of the mystic gift. "The true mystic is the person in whom such powers [spiritual awareness] transcend the merely artistic and visionary stage, and are exalted to the point of genius: in whom the transcendental consciousness can dominate the normal consciousness, and who has definitely surrendered himself to the embrace of Reality... As other men are immersed in and react to natural or intellectual life, so the mystic is immersed in and reacts to spiritual life. He moves towards that utter identification with its interests which he calls 'Union with God.' He has been called a lonely soul. He might more properly be described as a lonely body: for his soul, peculiarly responsive, sends out and receives communications upon every side."[8]

Underhill's description of the mystic as a "lonely body" is an accurate one. The mystic generally regards body, mind and emotions as impediments to the full flowering of his gift. The body gets sick and becomes useless, the mind weakens and becomes forgetful, the emotions are a veritable roller-coaster—none of these are fit instruments for the mystic on his journey. The mystic's goal is to do away with form entirely and focus on will and awareness. He employs his will to block out distraction, while his awareness searches the heavens for Grace.

It's worth noting that another, less well-known version of this path is the Path of the Magician. While exoteric magic seeks change in the practitioner's external world, magicians on a spiritual path, like mystics, concentrate the trained will and awareness on internal change, believing this path to be the shortest and most direct route to God. As Israel Regardie asserts, "Herein lies the value of magic. Under ordinary conditions, months may be required for the flowering of a plant, but the use of a hot-house will produce identical results within a few weeks. An understanding and application of magic can telescope the time required for man to acquire the realization of his own divinity." [9]

Magic attempts to actually "reprogram" the human mind to encompass the spiritual realm. Bill Whitcomb, contemporary author and student of the magical arts, argues that, "From a neuropsychological standpoint, traditional magic is a collection of rule-of-thumb techniques for altering the focus and content of consciousness. Magic could be described…as a larval technology for programming and metaprogramming the human biocomputer. Some of the techniques used to alter the focus of consciousness include breath control, celibacy, dance, drugs, exhaustion, fasting, flagellation, music (drumming, singing, etc.), sensory deprivation, sexual activity, sleeplessness, and visualization. Techniques used to alter the content of consciousness include the use of hypnotic language structures, the visualization of colors and archetypes, manipulation of symbolic alphabets, and sensory saturation (through chanting, incantations, mantras, and visualization of symbols.)" [10]

The techniques described by Whitcomb have been used in spiritual systems throughout history; the difference is that magicians regard these techniques as part of a scientific endeavor, with predictable and repeatable results. Most of our discussion of the Mystic Path and the problems encountered as we move through the Suit of Wands may also be applied to the Path of the Magician.

Chapter Five Bibliography

1   Butler, W. E. *The Magician: His Training and Work*. North Hollywood, CA: Wilshire Book Company, 1969, p. 151.

2   Smith, Huston. *The World's Religions*. New York, NY: Harper Collins, 1991, p. 37.

3   Andrea, Raymund. *The Technique of the Disciple*. San Jose, CA: Grand Lodge of the English Language Jurisdiction, 1999, pp. 19-20.

4   Vivekananda, Swami. *What Religion Is*. New York, NY: Julia Press, 1962, p. 165.

5   Smith, Huston. *The World's Religions*. New York, NY: Harper Collins, 1991, p. 32.

6   Scholem, Gershom. *On the Kabbalah and Its Symbolism*. New York, NY: Schocken Books, 1996, p. 3.

7   Smith, Huston. *The World's Religions*. New York, NY: Harper Collins, 1991, p. 43.

8   Underhill, Evelyn. *Mysticism: The Nature and Development of Spiritual Consciousness*. Oxford, UK: Oneworld Publications, 1999, pp. 75–76.

9   Regardie, Israel. *The Middle Pillar: The Balance Between Mind and Magic*. Woodbury, Minnesota: Llewellyn Publications, 2006, p. xxvi.

10   Whitcomb, Bill. *The Magician's Companion: A Practical & Encyclopedic Guide to Magical & Religious Symbolism*. Woodbury, MN: Llewellyn Publications, 2007, pp. 5–6.

Chapter Six

THE SUIT OF PENTACLES

Ace of Pentacles

A Hand holding a Pentacle emerges from a cloud. Below the Hand is a garden; mountains are beautifully framed through the arched, fruited entrance. A path leads across the garden and directly to the mountains.

ACE of PENTACLES.

This card is assigned to *Keter*, the first *sephirah*, and is the beginning of the Path of Service. The Hebrew word for "hand" is *Yod*, which is also the first letter of the four-letter Name of God. The Hand in this and the other Ace cards is a Divine Hand, as is indicated by the halo (hard to see in black and white) surrounding it. The Pentacle in the Hand teaches us that physical manifestation comes from God: the everyday is sacred and the ordinary is holy. This is the creed of the aspirant on the Path of Service.

The arch reminds us of *Daleth*, the letter assigned to **The Empress** and the Hebrew word for "door." The natural doorway in the **Ace of Pentacles** represents the womb through which we enter the world; the mountains symbolize a distant goal. We reach the goal by following the path out of the womb and into the world.

Pentacles represent our lives in physical manifestation. By existing on this planet, we walk the Path of Pentacles. When we attain a deep realization of the inherent holiness of the physical, we find a new way of being in the world. We respect the earth, the physical world, and our bodies as divine gifts, releasing our old beliefs that there are aspects of the world and of our bodies that are flawed and imperfect. Remembering that each one of us has walked through the rose-entwined gateway of the **Ace of Pentacles** in order to live on this earth, in this particular body, may help us see the physical experience as entirely divine.

The Path of Service requires us to live in paradox, seeing the world as undamaged and needing no help while simultaneously serving and helping it. It demands that we remain unattached to how our work helps or hinders the world. Our service must be offered freely to God without expectations or demands.

Two of Pentacles

A juggler holds an odd contraption that consists of two Pentacles with what appears to be a rubber band around them. The band is twisted in the center to look like an infinity sign. Behind the figure is a rolling sea; ships ride the waves. The juggler wears red clothing and an odd hat.

From *Keter*, the Path of Service moves downward into *Chokmah* on the Pillar of Force. *Chokmah* is the seed that fertilizes the womb of *Binah*, further suggested by the juggler's phallus-shaped hat.

The **Two of Pentacles** teaches us about sexuality. Sexuality is an important issue on the spiritual path. This may seem puzzling or even disturbing to those who come from a traditional religious background, but the Western Mystery Tradition, like the Kabbalistic Tradition on which it is based, is frank about the role of sexuality in creation and does not support any notion of sexuality as impure or evil. All that lives and breathes on the earth owes its existence to sexuality.

Further, spiritual energy and sexual energy are believed to be linked. Dion Fortune writes, "Those who have entered into the deeper aspects of occultism know that Kundalini, the Serpent Force which lies curled up at the base of the spine, is really the sex force..."[1] And Gershom Scholem observes, "It is well known that those deepest regions of human existence which are bound up with the sexual life play an important part in the history of mysticism. With few exceptions mystical literature abounds in erotic images."[2]

The Western Mystery Tradition utilizes the link between spiritual and sexual energies, creating certain practices that employ sexual energy for spiritual purposes. For example, the aspirant may be taught to direct sexual energy toward God or up the spine in order to energize kundalini. Modern Kabbalist Aryeh Kaplan gives a brief description of this use of sexual energy. "By meditating on the fact that the ten toes represent the ten *Sefirot*, one is able to concentrate spiritual energy into the sexual organ. Through such methods, one can gain complete control over one's sexual activities, even in the midst of intercourse. By sanctifying oneself in this manner during sexual intercourse, one is able to determine the qualities of the child that will be conceived...The sexual drive is one of the most powerful psychological forces in man, and when it is channeled along spiritual lines, it can help bring one to the highest mystical states."[3]

There are, of course, dangers implicit in such practices. For example, if there is even a remnant of doubt as to the "suitability" of sexual energy used for spiritual purposes, this underlying belief can damage the psyche. Further, if the individual has not had adequate preparation, he may be physically, emotionally and psychically unable to withstand the release of kundalini. The Western Mystery Tradition encourages aspirants to both recognize the divinity implicit in sexuality and understand that it is a potent force to be handled with care.

Three of Pentacles

Three men—a builder, an architect and a monk—stand together inside a church. The builder is up on a bench, elevated above the other figures. Three Pentacles and a mystic rose are engraved on a stone arch.

The elevation of the builder above the other two symbolizes the elevation of work. The placement of the scene inside a church teaches that work is inherently spiritual.

A deeper reading of the **Three of Pentacles** tells us that the architect holding the plans represents our mind; the monk who wants the church to be built represents our heart or desire; and the person actually doing the work represents our body. In terms of the human psyche, these three figures comprise a heart/mind/body interaction.

In the **Three of Pentacles**, the Path of Service moves into *Binah*. *Binah* takes the desire of *Keter* and the force of *Chokmah* and sets patterns that will eventually become physical reality. This card may be viewed as a picture of the Supernal Triangle—shown as the three Pentacles in the arch—in action.

We often believe that certain kinds of work are "more spiritual" than others. However, Manly Hall insists that whatever work stands before us—whether manual labor, household chores or office work—is the work that will serve us best on the spiritual path. "If in his zeal to unfold his spiritual nature he neglects those daily labors which have been assigned to him in the material world, he can never hope to attain true spirituality. Each individual born into the physical world has obligations which if not assumed by him must be carried by others."[4]

Domestic work is no exception. Dion Fortune used the term "Path of the Hearth-Fire" to describe the Path of Service in a domestic context. "If we rule our homes in a spirit of selfless love and serenity of heart, asking no return, but doing our duty for the sake of the need of those to whom we minister, our house will be a true Temple of the Hearth-Fire in which we can receive our initiation. But let it be remembered that the serenity of heart must be there as well as the faithful performance of duty. It is this serenity which is the proof of karma overcome. As long as we are kicking against the pricks we still have something to learn from our circumstances."[5]

There is undoubtedly great wisdom in the acceptance of whatever work is placed before us, and certainly all work is equally divine. However, history teaches us that acceptance of the responsibilities before us, as defined by conventional wisdom, isn't necessarily the right approach. Moses' real responsibility was not to the Pharaoh and his daughter, but to the tribe of Israel; Buddha's real responsibility was not to his wife and child, but to the untold millions who would find enlightenment by following in his footsteps. Determining our real responsibilities, separating what can and should be changed from what cannot and should not be changed, is in itself a difficult spiritual task. There is no virtue in sticking with boring, awful work if there are other ways in which we are called to serve; there is no virtue in running out on boring, awful work if it must be done and there is no one else to do it.

Four of Pentacles

A crowned man sits on a stone bench with one Pentacle in his arms, another Pentacle above his head and two more beneath his feet. He appears to be hunched over, as if guarding himself. A large city is seen in the background.

From *Binah*, the Path of Service drops down across the Abyss into *Chesed*, the *sephirah* of expansion and growth. But there is danger in growth, and that is the lesson of this card. In *Chesed*, the Path of Service encounters material wealth.

At first glance, we might suppose that this man is in control of his Pentacles. Notice, however, that in actuality the Pentacles are in control of the man, literally from head to toe. Similarly, we are often imprisoned by what we own. If we have a large home, we must clean and maintain it. A beautiful yard must be planted, trimmed, raked and mowed. Nice possessions generally require care, perhaps even an alarm system to keep them safe. Maintaining our possessions is practically a full-time job, making us the servants, not the masters, of our wealth.

The things we own also create a prison by constructing identities for us. The objects we covet define us as rich, poor, trendy, dowdy, an antique collector, a book lover, a car buff, and so on. Another person can look at our stuff and know "who we are." If we are attached

181

to our possessions, we are inevitably attached to the identities they create for us as well.

In this same way, identities can be created by our attachment to the roles we play in life. On the Path of Service we often find ourselves attached to our identities as helpers, servers and givers. We might readily surrender our possessions, time, effort and money—especially for what we perceive to be a good cause—but still remain attached to the identities such acts of surrender create. This is often rooted in our belief that being perceived (by ourselves and others) as selfless and saintly is proof of our spiritual progress. This is an egoic desire masquerading as spirituality.

Just as the figure in the card is clutching and being clutched by the Pentacles, so too are we often clutching and clutched by our possessions, by the identities we derive from these possessions, and by our egoic desires. Progress on the Path of Service requires us to loosen our attachments to these possessions, identities and desires. The concept of becoming unattached is often misunderstood. P. D. Ouspensky (1878–1947), philosopher, author and student of George Gurdjieff, reminds us, "Non-attachment does not mean indifference. It is a kind of separation of self from what happens or from what a man is doing. It is not coldness, nor is it the desire to shut oneself off from life."[6] Similarly, non-attachment on the Path of Service does not mean that we should have no possessions or roles in life; it means that we must separate our essential self from these possessions and roles. A person may live in a hovel with few possessions and be quite attached to them; a person may live in a palace full of beautiful things and be non-attached.

Some people believe the concept of non-attachment derives from eastern cultures and spiritual system and so is out of place in the Western Mystery Tradition. However, the idea of non-attachment has a place in both eastern and western spiritual systems. For example, in discussing the view of Kabbalist Rabbi Isaac of Acco

(1250–1340), Aryeh Kaplan notes, "One of Rabbi Isaac of Acco's important teachings involves *Hishtavut*, a term derived from the root *Shava*, meaning 'equal.' The term denotes making all things equal for oneself, and can be translated as equanimity, or more accurately, as stoicism…The Talmud clearly states that those who attain this level of stoicism are able to radiate spirituality." [7]

Five of Pentacles

Two poor, ragged people struggle through the snow. The figure with crutches has a bandage on his head. Author Isabel Radow Kliegman points out that the bell around his neck indicates he is a leper.[8] *The other figure is barefoot and clutches a thin shawl. Both figures pass under a church window illuminated by five Pentacles.*

The Path of Service now veers into *Gevurah*, a *sephirah* of restrictive energy on the Pillar of Severity. This phase of the Path of Service can manifest as the sudden eruption of a great many problems in our lives —hardship, financial loss, poverty, neglect, illness, despair and exhaustion. Some of us view this as intense spiritual practice or even a test; others view it as a quick "finishing-up" of karma which will then allow us to move on to bigger and better things.

In Dion Fortune's opinion, "When people have arrived at a certain degree of development, they are more sensitive and have more spiritual force, and so their problems are more acute. The soul may have decided to go rapidly on, and brings down in a concentrated form all the Karma due. Trouble seems always to come down on this soul, and through an incarnation of trouble the soul is purified, and then the next incarnation opens up free of these conditions."[9]

Some of us bring trouble into our lives deliberately, thinking it will enhance our spirituality or perceiving it as a type of personal sacrifice. Sacrifice has an important place in spirituality. It is interesting to note that the Hebrew word for sacrifices, *qorbanot*, comes from a Hebrew root word spelled *Kuf Resh Bet*, which means "to draw near." A sacrifice is one way of drawing near to the Divine.

Sacrifice often manifests as certain forms of spiritual practice. It's important to distinguish ascetic and ritual practices, which can indeed be helpful to us, from mortification practices, which are not helpful. Ascetic practices are intended to simplify, to pare away the unessential in order to find the essential. Mortification practices, on the other hand, are forms of self-punishment. A number of religious and spiritual groups encourage mortification with hair shirts, whips, beating, piercing, cutting, starvation, etc. While these practices are ostensibly based on the belief that estrangement of flesh will draw us closer to spirit, they actually reflect a denial of the physical aspects of our lives. It is impossible for such practices to draw us closer to God; instead, they draw us into an unbalanced egoic identity.

A subtle mortification practice on the Path of Service takes the form of working harder and harder, faster and faster, obsessed with trying to fill a need that cannot be filled. We may ultimately give everything we've got—money, time, health—in the service of this need; but what looks like sainthood is really a mortification practice.

Six of Pentacles

A man holds scales with one hand while dispensing coins with the other. Two kneeling figures open their hands to receive the coins. Six Pentacles float in the air.

In the **Six of Pentacles**, the Path of Service comes into balance in *Tifaret*, on the Middle Pillar. It is here that we encounter the bliss of experiencing God.

The **Six of Pentacles** is actually a pictorial representation of the Divine Name. The hand, with its five fingers, is often symbolized by the Hebrew letter *Heh*, which is also the number five. The Hebrew letter *Vav* means "and," so it joins two things together. The *Yod*, as the smallest Hebrew letter, often represents something small but valuable. Thus, the *Yod* in the Divine Name represents a coin; the first *Heh* represents the Hand of God; the second *Heh* represents the hand of man; and the *Vav* between the two *Heh*s represents Hand and hand touching one another.

The coins in this card symbolize the "coin" of *Tifaret*—spiritual experiences of bliss, connection and joy. These spiritual experiences, in which we actually feel God's presence within our being, are the early fruits of spiritual practice. The experience of *Tifaret* may last a minute, an hour, a day, or even a week, but rarely longer. Though such experiences are necessarily temporary, the inspiration and strength they provide help us continue on our paths, even when these paths get narrow and steep.

As the picture indicates, the bliss experienced in *Tifaret* is not something we have earned; it is given only by the grace of God. However, most of us believe that spiritual practice increases the likelihood that we'll receive this gift. One teacher says that spiritual practice is like sitting in the front row of the classroom waving your hand madly, hoping to be called on; but the teacher may decide instead to call on the quiet kid at the back of the room.

This card reminds us that everything we receive every moment of our lives and everything we give to others actually comes from the Hand of God. Those of us on the Path of Service serve merely as the *Vav*, the joining, that passes the coin from the Hand of God to the hand of its recipient.

Seven of Pentacles

A man who appears to be tending or harvesting a crop leans on a farm implement and looks down on a bush fruited with six Pentacles. A seventh Pentacle stands on the ground before him.

In the **Seven of Pentacles**, the Path of Service comes out of *Tifaret* and moves down to *Netzach*, the *sephirah* of emotion on the Pillar of Mercy.

The man in the card looks puzzled, as if he had planted an apple tree and found pineapples growing instead. Life has a way of rewarding our efforts in unanticipated ways; at this point on the Path of Service we begin to suspect that the fruits of our labor—the benefits of our practice—aren't going to be quite what we expected.

For example, we may begin to feel disconnected from the service that has occupied us for so long. We may even begin to feel impatient with those we're supposed to be helping. Some of us regard these unanticipated fruits as evidence of our wrong-doing, wrong-thinking or wrong-feeling. To compensate, we may chastise ourselves and work harder than ever to cast out these apparent demons.

But oddly enough, these thoughts and feelings may well be the proper fruit of our labor, and represent progression, not regression, on the Path. This is often the beginning of the necessary detachment from the belief that our service is needed. In our discussion of the **Four of Pentacles**, just above the **Seven of Pentacles** on the Pillar of

Mercy, we explored the need for this detachment; here in *Netzach* and the **Seven of Pentacles**, our practice has borne its fruit.

To determine whether our new feelings and attitudes mean that we've lost focus and gone astray or that we're actually making progress, we must clearly analyze our practice and what has come from it, refraining from both self-punishment and self-aggrandizement. Those of us who are lucky enough to have a trusted spiritual guide or fellow aspirant will find that person to be of tremendous help at such times; those of us who walk a solitary path must rely on our own strict self-honesty.

Eight of Pentacles

A man sits on a bench engraving a Pent-acle. Another Pentacle sits on the ground near his feet and six more hang on the right hand side of the card.

In the **Eight of Pentacles**, the Path of Service moves into *Hod*, the *sephirah* of ritual. The engraver in the card performs his work as a ritual, completely focused on his task. There is no audience and no fanfare; the town, symbolizing other people, is far away.

This focus and devotion is difficult to achieve in modern life. As Manly P. Hall remarks, "One of the great problems of Western living is interruption. The Truth seeker is constantly beset by interruptions that tend to divert him from his spiritual ideals. These unexpected happenings are a testing of his one-pointedness. They are external interruptions and will continue as long as man's internal life is negative to his external environment. However, when discipline makes the inner life positive and renders the environment negative, such interruptions cannot occur." [10]

When Hall refers to a positive inner life and negative environment, he means that when we focus our attention on our inner life, it becomes more important than the events of our outer life. As a result of this continuous training, our attention becomes impervious to interruption from the outer world. Our physical work may be interrupted; but our attention, focused always within, is not.

This focusing of attention is particularly difficult on the Path of Service, where our work appears to lie in the external world. One way to maintain this inner focus while serving the world is to regard our work on the Path of Service as ritual, rather than as activity designed to accomplish earthly goals in the outer world. Robert A. Johnson, author and psychoanalyst, provides an excellent description of how ritual works and why it is important. "...the highest form of ritual has this characteristic: Those who participate sense that they are doing an act that has symbolic meaning, and they consciously seek to transform that act into an active, dynamic symbol. Their every movement becomes a symbol-in-motion that carries the power of the inner world into visible and physical form.

"Whether we are aware of it or not, much of our behavior is symbolic. But what transforms physical acts into high ritual is the expression of symbolism within a conscious act. At its best, ritual is a series of physical acts that expresses in condensed form one's relationship to the inner world of the unconscious." [11]

Work performed by the aspirant on the Path of Service is, as Johnson says, a physical act that expresses our relationship to both our inner world and to the Divine. By performing work in this way, we become God's hands and feet. The more consciousness we bring to our work and to this relationship, the more transformative our ritual becomes.

Nine of Pentacles

A woman stands in a grape arbor. She wears a long, flowing robe decorated with flowers. On one hand she wears a glove, on which perches a hooded falcon. Nine Pentacles stand behind her; she rests her hand on one of them. A tiny snail crawls in front of her.

In the **Nine of Pentacles**, the Path of Service moves into *Yesod* on the Middle Pillar. *Yesod* is the *sephirah* of dreams, and that's what this lovely picture of a woman standing in a garden is—a dream of paradise.

Many of us on the Path of Service believe the world really could be paradise, if we all worked on it. But in order to move ahead on this path, we must recognize that the idea of paradise as a goal to be attained is a dream of the lower self, not the Higher Self. The Higher Self knows that it is in paradise right now, at this moment, no matter what the external circumstances of life may be.

On another, related level, this card illustrates how man alters Nature to suit his purposes. The grapes have been trained to grow up the trellises in the arbor. The falcon is hooded, indicating that it, too, has been pressed into man's service. The old alchemical maxim, "Nature unaided fails," seems everywhere demonstrated on this card—effort and training are necessary to bring out nature's potential. The esoteric understanding of this maxim is that it is ourselves we must train, in order to bring out the best of our spiritual potential. The presence of the snail teaches that this is a long, slow process.

Yesod also corresponds to the genitals; it is worth noting that the covenant of circumcision, a deliberate alteration of nature, comes from the belief that men are born imperfect, but may become perfect through certain actions. A deeper understanding of this belief is that effort is required for us to see the perfection around us.

The idea that something must be changed or trained in order to be bettered lies at the very heart of the Path of Service and of all human life. We seem unable to be content with life as it is or with ourselves as we are. It is human nature to want to change and "improve" our situation. As we train nature in order to make it serve us better, so we believe we must train ourselves in order to serve God better. We cling to this belief stubbornly, right up until the moment of Initiation.

Ten of Pentacles

Beneath an arch in the middle of town a man and woman engage in conversation. A child peeks out from behind the woman's red dress and pets a dog. The dog stands before an old man sitting with his back to us; the old man pets another dog. A third dog, disguised as a fold of the old man's cloak, sits beside the second. Behind the old man is what appears to be a lyre; below the lyre are grapes. Upon the wall of the arch, three tapestries depict a fortress, a mountain surrounded by a castle, and a pair of scales. Ten Pentacles arranged in the pattern of the Tree of Life float in the immediate foreground.

It is interesting to note that this card contains hints of the other Pentacle cards on the Middle Pillar. The **Ace of Pentacles** is represented by the mountain, the **Six of Pentacles** by the scales and the **Nine of Pentacles** by the grapes. The **Ten of Pentacles** is thus portrayed as the sum total of all the *sephirot* on the Middle Pillar.

This card has many layers of imagery and symbols, leading to many different interpretations of this card. Some Tarot students focus on the man and woman as the central figures and conclude that they are having relationship problems; others focus on the old man and decide that he represents neglected old age. Still others look at the child and believe he is unprotected and afraid. However, the Initiate sees this entire scene—childhood, adulthood, old age, animals, plants, cities, mountains, trees—as nothing more or less than God in His dazzling, dizzying array of forms. There are no judgments, no concerns and nothing wrong.

This card represents the conclusion of the Path of Service in *Malkuth*. We realize now that the idea of God needing our help in any way is absurd. As Swami Vivekananda says, "He allows you to work. He allows you to exercise your muscles in this great gymnasium, not in order to help him but that you may help yourself. Do you think even an ant will die for want of your help? Most arrant blasphemy! The world does not need you at all. The world goes on; you are like a drop in this ocean. A leaf does not move, the wind does not blow, without him." [12]

Astonishingly, however, the realization of this truth rarely results in our spending the rest of our lives in a hammock, sipping lemonade. Work still happens, activity still occurs; but we no longer have the perception that we are working. Our activity seems to result from the motion of the universe rather than from personal volition; we remain non-attached to the results of our efforts, content to leave the responsibility where it has truly rested all along—in the hands of the One Will.

Chapter Six Bibliography

1   Fortune, Dion. *What Is Occultism?* York Beach, ME: Samuel Weiser, Inc., 2001, p. 125.

2   Scholem, Gershom. *Major Trends in Jewish Mysticism.* New York, NY: Schocken Books, 1995, p. 225.

3   Kaplan, Aryeh (Trans.). *Sefer Yetzirah.* York Beach, Maine: Samuel Weiser, Inc., 1997, p. 37.

4   Hall, Manly P. *Spiritual Centers in Man.* Los Angeles, CA: Philosophical Research Society, 1999, p. 9.

5   Fortune, Dion. *Training and Work of an Initiate.* York Beach, Maine: Samuel Weiser, Inc., 2000, pp. 47-48.

6   Ouspensky, P. D. *A New Model of the Universe.* Mineola, NY: Dover Publications, 1997, p. 260.

7   Kaplan, Aryeh. *Meditation and Kabbalah.* Northvale, NJ: Jason Aronson, Inc., 1995, p. 140.

8   Kliegman, Isabel Radow. *Tarot and the Tree of Life: Finding Everyday Wisdom in the Minor Arcana.* Wheaton, IL: Quest Books, 1997, p. 54.

9   Fortune, Dion. *Applied Magic.* York Beach, ME: Samuel Weiser, Inc., 2000, p.8.

10   Hall, Manly P. *Self-Unfoldment by Disciplines of Realization.* Los Angeles, CA: Philosophical Research Society, 1995, pp. 33-34.

11   Johnson, Robert A. *Inner Work: Using Dreams & Active Imagination for Personal Growth.* San Francisco, CA: Harper & Row, 1986, pp. 102-103.

12   Vivekananda, Swami. *What Religion Is.* New York, NY: Julia Press, 1962, p. 124.

Chapter Seven

THE SUIT OF CUPS

Ace of Cups

A Hand holds a Cup in its open palm; the halo around the Hand indicates that this is the Hand of God. The Cup, inscribed with a "W" or an upside-down "M," overflows like a fountain into the sea below. Above the Cup, a bird holds what appears to be a communion wafer in its beak.

ACE of CUPS.

This first card on the Path of Devotion is assigned to *Keter*, the first *sephirah*. Cups symbolize our emotional lives. As white light is split into a spectrum of many colors, emotions are split into love, hate, fear, sympathy, etc. The emotional spectrum is symbolized by the five different streams falling out of the Cup. The **Ace of Cups** is the sum of all the different emotions.

    Like water, emotions are fluid and lack clear definition. Emotions often combine with other emotions in ways that make it difficult for us to tease them apart. Fear may masquerade as anger; resentment may distract us from the underlying envy. If we find our emotions confusing and painful, we tend to suppress them. But when we force our emotions underground, we eventually become dry and parched. Part of our work on the spiritual path is to learn to set our emotions free. The goal is not to allow our emotions to flood our lives, but to allow them to become as clear and clean as the streams of water on the **Ace of Cups**.

The creed of the aspirant on the Path of Devotion is "God is love," but of course the One Will actually contains all emotions. In fact, Kabbalists suggest that God has more emotions than we do. In Genesis 1:6–7, "God said, 'Let there be an expanse in the midst of the water, that it may separate water from water.' God made the expanse, and it separated the water which was below the expanse from the water which was above the expanse. And it was so." Water is separated into water above and water below, teaching us that God has emotions that we do not. Assuming that we know what the One Will is feeling is always a mistake. God does not feel as we do, and we cannot imagine how He feels.

The Cup shown on this card recalls the legend of Joseph of Arimathea, who was said to have been sustained for 35 years by a wafer placed into the Holy Grail every day by a dove. In the same way that Joseph was kept alive by that wafer, so are those of us on the Path of Devotion kept alive by the love we feel for and from God.

No one knows for certain what the letter on the Cup means. The "W" may stand for water or for Waite; it might also stand for the three founders of the Golden Dawn, of which Waite was a member—Woodman, Westcott and Mathers.

Two of Cups

A man and a woman stand facing one another. Each holds a Cup and he is reaching for her Cup. A red winged lion is perched on a caduceus above the Cups. The background is a pastoral scene.

When the Suit of Cups moves into *Chokmah*, the element of water meets primal force. This card concerns the enormous power of emotion, particularly the longing of male and female for one another.

Almost everyone experiences a feeling of incompleteness. We are usually taught that this feeling is the result of our longing for a mate. On that level, this card is a picture of a man and a woman uniting in love or marriage. On a spiritual path, however, the feeling of being incomplete is usually interpreted as the longing for God.

Kabbalists symbolize God as male and humankind as female; this often feels like a slight to womankind. However, in the Kabbalistic view, the woman represents the *Shekhinah*, a Hebrew word meaning "the Indwelling Presence of God," which is that part of God that exists in manifestation. Though God and the *Shekhinah* are ultimately one Being, Kabbalists speak metaphorically of the *Shekhinah* and God as being involved in a romantic relationship and refer to the *Shekhinah* as the "Bride" of God.

The longing experienced by male and female, Divine and human, is an immensely powerful force. It provides the energy that fuels us on our quest to find a mate, an endeavor that consumes an enormous amount of our time and attention; it is also the energy that fuels us on our spiritual paths. All paths are based on the power of longing; the focus of that longing may differ, but the emotion at the root of all our efforts is the same.

The red lion shown in the card is a Western Mystery Tradition symbol for transformation; the caduceus symbolizes healing through the resolution of opposites. "According to Greek myth, the god Hermes (Roman, Mercury) was given a rod by his fellow god, Apollo. Traveling to Arcadia, Hermes came upon two snakes engaged in deadly combat. He cast his rod down between them and the snakes peacefully entwined themselves about the rod. The rod, the serpent-girt caduceus, thus became a symbol of peace—of balance and equilibrium between two warring energies." [1] The caduceus may also be seen as another symbol of the Tree of Life, with the rod serving as the Middle Pillar and the Pillars of Force and Form twining about it.

The relationship of male and female can lead to healing and transformation. Since this card is assigned to *Chokmah*, meaning "wisdom," we learn that wisdom is an essential part of the transformation that can result from human relationships. Our relationship with God is no different; if we do not enter into this relationship wisely, our love for God may result instead in fanaticism and fantasy.

Three of Cups

Three women dance in a circle, their Cups raised high. Their mood seems to be one of joy and celebration. Vines, leaves and fruit surround them.

The Path of Devotion moves now into the womb of *Binah*, where force is tamed, often painfully, into form. *Binah* also creates time, which leads inevitably to death. The **Three of Cups** represent the three things brought into existence by *Binah*—birth, life and death.

When we experience fear, we tend to enter into a supplicative, rather than loving, relationship with God. We beg God for health, wealth and a variety of other favors. To move away from supplication and fear and towards gratitude and love, we must recognize that all three aspects of *Binah* are necessary steps in the dance of creation.

Mythologically, these dancing women may be seen as Clotho, Lachesis and Atropos, the three Fates. Clotho spins the thread of each person's life and represents the aspect of birth. Lachesis measures the thread and represents the aspect of life. Atropos cuts the thread and represents death.

We can begin to enter willingly into this dance of creation by becoming aware of the rhythms of birth-life-death that are all around us every day. For example, when sitting down to dinner, we can remember that death was required—animal, vegetable or both—

201

to bring our meal to us. As we eat, we can be aware that life is being renewed within us as a direct result of those deaths. Recognizing the universality of life and death is not morbid or unhealthy. Learning to celebrate, rather than fear and ignore, the essential rhythms of life allows us to become conscious participants in the dance.

Four of Cups

A youth sits on the grass beneath a tree with his arms and legs crossed. Three Cups sit on the grass before him. A hand holding a fourth Cup appears from a cloud, but the youth does not look at it.

The Path of Devotion crosses the Abyss and enters *Chesed*, the *sephirah* of expansion, growth and devotion. Here we feel that we love and understand God, and He loves and understands us.

This sounds like a wonderful place to be, but too much of a good thing can blind us to other possibilities. The **Four of Cups** shows a man whose devotion to what he loves keeps him from experiencing further growth. This man is certain that his current level of understanding and spiritual experience is enough. His eyes remain fixed upon what he already possesses, and he has no interest whatsoever in the fourth Cup. He sits like Buddha under this tree, awaiting enlightenment; but he won't take it when it is offered.

It's common for people to feel that they have all the answers. Their book-of-choice tells them everything they need to know, their religious leader assures them that they're on the right path, and further questions are not encouraged. As long as they are comfortable —seated on a grassy hill in the shade, for example—they cannot be tempted from their stronghold. If allowed to remain in this comfortable place long enough, their stubborn hold on their beliefs can turn into fanaticism. And while we often believe that fanaticism exists only within organized religion, the reality is that it is a common malady in all walks of spiritual life.

Few of us move away from a nice, shady spot of our own volition; life pushes us away. The next card, **Five of Cups**, shows us that it is usually grief, pain and loss that get us back onto the spiritual path; however, those who are not ready to make that move may retreat defensively even further into their belief systems. It takes great courage to give up comfortable beliefs to continue on the journey.

Five of Cups

A cloaked figure, shoulders hunched with grief, stares down at three Cups lying on their sides, contents spilled upon the earth. The figure's back is turned upon two Cups that remain standing behind him.

The Path of Devotion swings away from *Chesed*, a *sephirah* of openness and expansion, into *Gevurah*, a *sephirah* of restriction. This is a painful, but necessary, correction.

The **Five of Cups** is a card of perceived loss. The three Cups that had been right in front of us in the **Four of Cups** have tipped over and have spilled their contents onto the ground. This situation manifests in our lives as our sudden inability to experience the love we believed the Divine had for us. An emotional state that we had come to depend upon is now unavailable to us. We may wonder what we did wrong and how we lost what we had. We may try to go back to that happier time, but it's impossible; there is no way open for us now but forward.

Every path must move through *Gevurah*, but it is a particularly difficult experience on the Path of Devotion because it feels personal. On this path, the relationship we have with God, whether that of servant-Master, friend-Friend, or lover-Beloved, is the most important relationship in our lives. The apparent disappearance of that relationship in *Gevurah* feels like the worst possible loss.

205

Difficult as it is, however, this is a crucial stage of the journey. It is here that we have the opportunity to experience God as more than sweetness and light. Just as we have difficulty accepting our negative and destructive emotions, we often have trouble accepting the negative and destructive facets of God. It's easy for us to love God when things go well for us; we may find it less easy to love God when poverty and bad health come our way. This card challenges us to love the aspects of God that appear negative to our human eyes as much as we love those that appear positive. The Path of Devotion requires us to keep our faith and trust in God no matter what the circumstances of our lives might be.

Six of Cups

Two figures stand before a village. Though one figure is quite a bit larger than the other, it is difficult to know whether they are children or adults. The larger figure, whose gender is unclear, offers a Cup of flowers to the smaller (and clearly female) figure. A Cup of flowers rests on a stand, and four more Cups of flowers occupy the immediate foreground.

From the difficulties of *Gevurah*, the Path of Devotion now moves into *Tifaret*, the *sephirah* of spiritual experience at the heart of the Tree. The fact that all the Cups are filled with flowers is important; what is shown in the **Six of Cups** is the Divine giving a person something beautiful, and ephemeral. This is a picture of the spiritual experience of *Tifaret*. The flowers represent the bliss that grew from the water of devotion; they are beautiful and to be received with a glad heart, as well as with the certain knowledge that they will soon fade. The village in the background teaches us that this experience is available in everyday life.

The **Six of Cups** symbolizes our reunion with God. *Gevurah* was a long, difficult experience; in *Tifaret* our faith and trust are finally rewarded. Our experiences in *Chesed* and *Gevurah* have made us larger, more mature and stronger than before. We have become more suitable containers, larger Cups, to hold God's love. The bliss we experience here is heart-bursting, overwhelming, and possibly even physically painful in its intensity. Many people mistake *Chesed* for *Tifaret*; it is only after we've experienced *Tifaret* for ourselves that we know the difference. *Chesed* is smiling happiness; *Tifaret* is trembling ecstasy.

The **Six of Cups** may come upon us whether we expect it or not, and whether we deserve it or not. It's as if an inner window opens, for no reason at all, and lets in all the sunlight. This experience is so wonderful, so life-altering, so astounding that we want nothing more than to live in this place forever. We would gladly give up all our ambitions, our strivings, our ideas, everything—if we could just stay here.

But we can't. And trying to hold onto the experience is not only impossible, but sets us up for failure and defeat. The nature of the Universe is to move and change; human awareness is no exception. We focus on something with all our might, but in a matter of moments our focus changes. We are pulled down, inexorably, out of *Tifaret* and down toward *Malkuth*. *Tifaret* is a vacation in Hawaii; *Malkuth* is home base. *Tifaret* is a brief experience; *Malkuth* is where we live.

Seven of Cups

Seven Cups float on dark clouds before a silhouetted figure. The Cups are filled with fantastic images—a human head, a snake, a cloaked and glowing figure, a castle, a mound of jewels, a victory wreath and a dragon.

The images shown in the Cups are the ego's fantasies—riches, self-importance, dangers, etc. In the **Seven of Cups**, the Path of Devotion comes out of balance in *Tifaret* and veers into *Netzach*, the *sephirah* of emotion on the Pillar of Mercy.

When this emotionally extreme spiritual path encounters the emotional *sephirah* of *Netzach*, the result is uncontrollable emotional content and egoic fantasy. Rather than quenching our thirst and nourishing our being, these emotions are destructive. The fantasies that burgeon forth often have their roots in the repressed childhood emotions and trauma we neglected to resolve during our period of preparation. Carl Jung reminds us, "A man who has not passed through the inferno of his passions has never overcome them. They then dwell in the house next door and at any moment a flame may dart out and set fire to his own house. Whenever we give up, leave behind, and forget too much, there is always the danger that the things we have neglected will return with added force."[2] There may be people who have emerged from their childhoods without emotional wounds; the rest

209

of us must contend with issues that, if left unresolved, will eventually erupt and cause great damage in our lives.

These issues result in a faulty view of the world; there are very few spiritual practices that help us unmask the emotional injuries that lie at the root of this faulty view. We can be told by a spiritual teacher, adept, guru or priest that we should neutralize dark energies and rise to a higher plane, or subsume our pain in our love of God, but these well-meaning exhortations rarely succeed; emotional healing more often comes from some form of therapy. Therapy operates by bringing unconscious beliefs into consciousness. It is, in essence, a way of contacting our High Priestess with the help of someone who knows her language.

Many aspirants feel that getting therapy is an admittance of spiritual failure. There's nothing un-spiritual about going to a therapist; however, there may be something un-spiritual about needing therapy and not going. Israel Regardie felt very strongly about the need for therapy. "Today I will not so much as consider even discussion of the Great Work with a student until he has experienced some form of psychotherapy, I care not which." [3] He adds, "For until one understands himself according to that peculiarly penetrating light which psychology has thrown upon our motives, he cannot hope to bring effectively into operation the dormant side of his nature. And lest anyone casually dismiss this desirable self-knowledge as a goal easily attained to or, it may be, already obtained, one can only utter a solemn warning that this is not so simple as at first sight seems." [4]

The spiritual world is full of people who should take off their robes, beads, crosses and pentagrams and lie down on a therapist's couch every week for a few years. For spiritual aspirants, the goal of therapy is not to rehearse the miseries of our lives at $150 an hour but to learn which aspects of our experience are real and which are not. One word of warning—traditional therapy is designed to make us into better-adjusted, happier people, while spiritual practice is designed to make us into no one at all. Happily, there are many therapists today who also walk a spiritual path and are able to apply therapeutic techniques to further the goals of spirituality. These techniques help us distinguish the real from the unreal, allowing us to release, rather than reinforce, our identification with old ideas and roles.

Eight of Cups

Eight Cups are neatly stacked in the foreground. A figure walks away from the Cups; he wears boots and carries a staff, as if embarking on a long journey. Mountains loom in the background and the moon eclipses the sun overhead.

The moon is often used as a symbol for the personality. Like the moon, the personality is always changing; like the moon, the personality has no light of its own and can only reflect light from the sun, which is a symbol of our higher awareness and the Divine. But the moon may eclipse the sun, as seen here; so too our personalities may block our awareness of our higher Selves and Divine love.

In the **Eight of Cups**, the Path of Devotion moves into *Hod* to recover from the unbalanced emotional overload of *Netzach*. As we begin to heal our damaged psyches, we realize just how thoroughly our personalities have been blocking our higher awareness and our love of the Divine.

Our "moon" may also seem to comprise not just our present personality, but personalities from past lives, or incarnations, as well. It's not uncommon for spiritual aspirants to actually remember events from the past and even experience snippets of feelings that apparently belong to another time or place. While memories of facts and ideas are seldom problematic on the spiritual path, emotional memories from another life can be difficult to manage.

Raymund Andrea felt that while past life memories are a sign of progress on the path, they may also be the source of some difficulty. "In the case of the man who is graduating in the technique, whose vibration is raised and stabilized and the force of the soul recognized, I believe that the accumulated faculty of the past will be working very strongly in consciousness... It is to be welcomed, because it signifies advancement, and it is inevitable at some time... There are several personalities playing into the man by virtue of the storied past which is sounding forth from higher planes; and while he plays his humble part within the present circumstances of time and space, and in so doing appears no doubt to his fellow man recollected and able and intent upon the one aim of dedication and service—nor are they mistaken in this—he feels that insistent past striving for expression, too, in an environment which does not provide a medium for it. There is an orator in that man who has stirred men to action; there is a priest who has ministered with the multitude in the temple; there is a musician whose transcripts of harmony come back with haunting emphasis for reiteration. These hidden personalities are with him; they possess his hands, brain and heart, and would live in their fullness again. They must not be slain. They give him keys to the soul of the world and for the interpretation of the hearts of men... It is a phase of the double vision; and I conceive it to be one of the hardest stages in the initiate's progress." [5]

Some of us have the unpleasant experience of what appear to be past life personalities actually fighting to take over our lives, evidently intent on completing some mission from an earlier time and place. William Gray (1913–1992), British occultist and author, explains, "Persistence of personality from one incarnation to another eventually builds up a kind of artificial ego or Pseudoself which can cause very serious spiritual trouble if it tries to 'set up in business for itself' ... This is something on the principle of a theatrical role specially created by an actor persisting after the play has ended and making difficulties for its designer. Just as such temporary constructions of consciousness have to be equated out of existence for the sake of mental health, so do our incarnationary personalities have to be dealt with likewise if spiritual health is to be safeguarded."[6]

Unfortunately, many of us become enamored of past life personalities, forgetting that past life personalities are a favorite hiding place for the ego. Further, we must remember that there can be no guarantee that these are "our" past lives. As Buddhist writer Alexandria David-Neel (1868–1969) notes, "When the student becomes aware of this crowd in himself, he should avoid imagining, as some do, that it represents memories of his preceding lives. There is no lack of those who state and are convinced that such and such a personage, who lived in the past, is reincarnated in them. Stories depicting reincarnations are innumerable in Asia where they keep alive the childish thirst for the marvellous [sic] among the masses."[7]

The hard fact is we can never be absolutely certain of the truth of these past-life phantoms; allowing ourselves to become emotionally invested in them is always counter-productive. The most useful thing to do with what appear to be past life personalities is put on our boots and walk onward, as does the figure in this card, regarding these personalities merely as aspects of self that are waiting to be healed. This allows us to deal with the emotional issues they present without becoming attached to yet another identity.

Nine of Cups

A happy, satisfied man sits on a chair be-
fore nine Cups that sit high above him.

In the **Nine of Cups**, the Path of Devotion
comes into a place of balance in *Yesod*.
Yesod is the home of the astral template,
that which is about to become manifestation. On the Path of Devotion, this means
that our union with God has not yet occurred, or that it occurs erratically. The
result is that we still experience ourselves as
separate from God.

Just as this man has placed his nine
Cups high up on a pedestal, so we have
placed God on a pedestal high above us.
We needed the perception of separation in
order to sustain the Divine-devotee relationship, but both perception
and relationship now stand in the way of our completion of the path.

As we see from the expression on the face of this figure, *Yesod*
can be a nice place; as a result, many of us will move no further than
the **Nine of Cups**. We enjoy the feeling of loving God and we want
the experience of separation that brings us these joyful, happy feelings. Huston Smith explains this viewpoint, saying that the practitioner "…will reject all suggestions that the God one loves is oneself, even one's deepest Self, and insist on God's otherness. As a
Hindu devotional classic puts the point, 'I want to taste sugar; I
don't want to be sugar.'" [8]

Smith explains this idea further with a poem, translated by John S. Hoyland in *An Indian Peasant Mystic*, which describes the feelings of the practitioner who chooses to stop at this point.

> "Can water quaff itself?
> Can trees taste of the fruit they bear?
> He who worships God must stand distinct from Him,
> So only shall he know the joyful love of God;
> For if he say that God and he are one,
> That joy, that love, shall instantly vanish away.
> Pray no more for utter oneness with God;
> Where were the beauty if the jewel and setting were one?
> The heat and the shade are two,
> If not, where were the comfort of shade?
> Mother and child are two,
> If not, where were the love?
> When after being sundered, they meet,
> What joy do they feel, the mother and child!
> What were joy, if the two were one?
> Pray, then, for no more oneness with God."[9]

Most people aren't trying to wake up from their dream of separation—they're just trying to make the dream more pleasant. Here at the **Nine of Cups,** the dream has become pleasant indeed; the only aspirants who will move away from this happy place are those whose commitment to truth is greater than their desire for personal happiness.

Ten of Cups

*A husband and wife stand together with their arms upraised; two children frolic beside them. A rainbow of ten Cups dominates the heavens; a house, trees and a stream are seen in the background. The smug man from the **Nine of Cups** has become an entire family; the Cups that sat on his altar now soar in the air, alive with color.*

The Path of Devotion is based on the belief that Someone or Something needs, wants, or deserves our devotion. But this same belief that forced us onward also kept us from our ultimate goal.

When the Path of Devotion comes to rest in *Malkuth,* we experience the Initiation of the emotions. We discover that God is the earth, the sky, our spouse and our own selves. The Path of Devotion, based on the belief of separation, dissolves; the powerful longing that sent us out on this long journey is satisfied. This does not mean we stop loving God; it means that this love now exists, in and of itself, with neither subject nor object. There is no sense of self-sacrifice, no sense of "doing what's right" and no effort expended; love emanates from us in this way not as the result of a conscious decision but because we cannot do otherwise.

The rainbow is an ancient symbol of God's promise to us. Genesis 9:12–13: "God further said, 'This is the sign that I set for the covenant between Me and you, and every living creature with you, for all ages to come. I have set My bow in the clouds, and it shall serve as a sign of the covenant between Me and the earth." The rainbow is also a symbol of a bridge built between human and Divine awareness. Everyday life, beautifully and idyllically pictured here, has become paradise. This occurs not because our lives have physically changed, but because our perception of our lives has changed.

Chapter Seven Bibliography

1 Goddard, David. *The Tower of Alchemy: An Advanced Guide to the Great Work*. York Beach, ME: Samuel Weiser, Inc., 1999, p. 68.

2 Jung, Carl. *Memories, Dreams, Reflections*. New York, NY: Random House, 1965, p. 277.

3 Regardie, Israel. *The Middle Pillar: The Balance Between Mind and Magic*. Woodbury, Minnesota: Llewellyn Publications, 2006, p. xxx.

4 Regardie, Israel. *The Middle Pillar: The Balance Between Mind and Magic*. Woodbury, Minnesota: Llewellyn Publications, 2006, p. 6.

5 Andrea, Raymund. *The Technique of the Master*. Kingsport, TN: Kingsport Press, 1979, pp 93-95.

6 Gray, William. "Patterns of Western Magic: A Psychological Appreciation" in Tart, C. (ed.) *Transpersonal Psychologies*. New York, NY: Harper San Francisco, 1992, p. 425.

7 David-Neel, Alexandra and Lama Youngdon. *The Secret Oral Teachings in Tibetan Buddhist Sects*. San Francisco, CA: City Lights Books, 1967, pp 101-102.

8 Smith, Huston. *The World's Religions*. New York, NY: Harper Collins, 1991, p. 33.

9 Smith, Huston. *The World's Religions*. New York, NY: Harper Collins, 1991, p. 33.

THE SUIT OF SWORDS

Ace of Swords

A Hand holding an upright Sword appears from a cloud. The halo around the Hand indicates that this is a Divine Hand. The tip of the Sword is crowned with a gold circlet, from which hang a palm branch and an olive branch. Six Yods float above the hilt of the Sword.

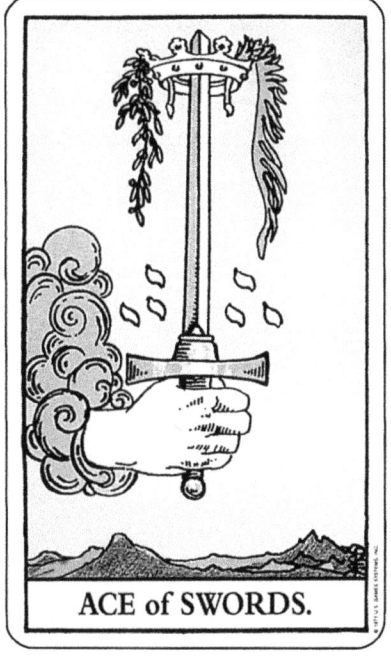

ACE of SWORDS.

The **Ace of Swords** is the beginning of the Path of the Mind. Since this is the Hand of God, this card reminds us to honor our intellect as a gift from God.

Both the Sword and the mind are powerful weapons. The Sword shown here is double-edged, meaning that the mind brings both joy and suffering. It is the mind that creates all of human society —philosophy, science, opera, French cooking and Superman comics. But the mind also creates interpretations of events that lock us into false and painful beliefs. It is thus simultaneously our best friend and worst enemy. This dual nature is further symbolized by the palm and olive branches, representing suffering and peace.

We tend to forget that the mind creates the interpretations that we believe are real. We accept the stories that make us feel sad as well as those that make us feel happy: once we believe the stories, we believe all the stories. But the dual nature of the mind is ultimately a good thing; if its interpretations brought only joy, we would never seek to go beyond what the mind can experience. We would never learn that the mind invents stories more often than it discerns truth.

The Path of the Mind covers a great deal of terrain; however, if we are to make progress, the mind must eventually turn its attention to its own nature, using its powers of discernment to discover its own nature.

The crown in the picture symbolizes *Keter* and the six *Yod*s symbolize *Tifaret*; the Sword symbolizes the path from *Keter* to *Tifaret*. As we know from our journey through the Major Arcana, this is the path of **The High Priestess**. This suggests that the Path of the Mind benefits from the subconscious mind, which offers insights and hunches that allow us to reach levels of understanding unattainable by the conscious mind alone.

Two of Swords

A blindfolded woman seated on a bench holds two Swords in her crossed arms. Behind her is the sea and two small islands; a tiny crescent moon hangs in the sky.

In the **Two of Swords**, the Path of the Mind has left *Keter* and moved into *Chokmah*, the beginning of perceived duality. This card shows the mind's essential dilemma —it refuses to acknowledge that it cannot see reality. The thin crescent moon overhead suggests that the mind provides little illumination.

The card suggests isolation, immobility, and powerlessness; yet this appears to be by choice. If the figure would put the Swords down, she could remove the blindfold. Her refusal to relinquish the Swords keeps her in this position.

Despite the somber aspect of this and most of the Sword cards, the mind in and of itself is not a bad thing. Walking the Path of the Mind leads us to Initiation as surely as any other path. It is also a valid means of worship. Those of us who walk the Path of the Mind worship by studying symbols and models of the Divine, thus refining our understanding. As worship through the heart and body have created churches and art, so worship through the mind has created vast libraries of books dedicated to the understanding of the Divine.

While walking this path, we must remember that despite the mind's belief in its own knowledge, we cannot actually know God or even know God's way of knowing. In fact, we know very little at all. Those of us who identify with our minds are often drawn to walk this path; but, because of that identification, we have a difficult time acknowledging the mind's limitations.

Three of Swords

A red heart is pierced through by three Swords. Rain pours from dark clouds above the heart.

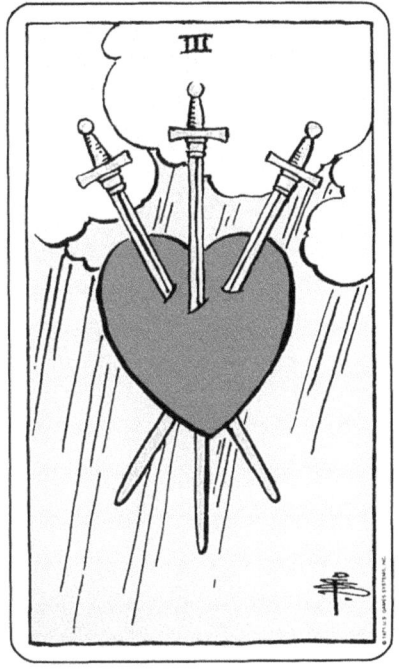

In the **Three of Swords**, the Path of the Mind crosses from *Chokmah* to *Binah*. As we know, the experience of *Binah* is a difficult one, encompassing birth, life and death. These are the three Swords that pierce this heart.

The **Three of Swords** is a difficult card to look at; similarly, the mind has a hard time looking at its own mortality. We may indulge in fancies about physical immortality, take vitamins and supplements until we choke on them, and pray until our knees bleed—but it doesn't matter. All that we love and all that we believe ourselves to be will perish from this earth in the near future. These Swords can never be drawn from the heart.

How do we live with that? How do we keep from being pierced to the heart by this knowledge? The answer is—we don't. The message of this card, difficult as it is to accept, is that we must recognize the truth of our own mortality and bring this understanding even deeper, allowing it to cut through and break us open. We must become large enough to understand and accept what *Binah* means to each of us, and live in full awareness of those Swords in our hearts.

Doing so is not easy; it may take a lifetime to fully acknowledge and accept our mortality.

The pain we experience in this process is not pointless, nor is it without benefit. Becoming aware of the Swords in our heart helps us honor the pain experienced by every self-aware creature. This pain comes not just from contemplating the end of our own existence, but also from the many kinds of suffering we encounter throughout our lives. Each of us is fighting a battle of some kind—often many battles—in more or less silent agony.

Finally, accepting the fact of our mortality frees up the energy we spend denying it, allowing us to focus our efforts instead on discovering that within us which truly is immortal.

Four of Swords

The stone effigy of a knight rests atop a coffin. One Sword adorns the side of his coffin; three more Swords hang on the wall of the church.

In the **Four of Swords**, the Path of the Mind moves into *Chesed*. Here there is peace, a state not easily achieved on the Path of the Mind. In fact, there is a strong belief in spiritual circles that the restlessness of the mind prevents us from experiencing the Divine. In eastern traditions, the term "monkey mind" is widely used to describe the endless jumping about and chattering of the untrained, unsettled mind. Learning to quiet the mind is an important part of our training on this path.

Meditation is the generic name for the many practices employed to quiet the mind. There are an enormous variety of meditation techniques, many of which seem downright contradictory. Some practitioners advocate mental images; others insist that using mental images is disastrous. Some practitioners use sensory aids, such as mandalas and chanting; others are certain that closed eyes and absolute silence are required. Some meditators move, dance, and assume postures; others insist on stillness. A wide variety of paraphernalia is available to help us—candles, cushions, garments, magical tools, etc. When we become more advanced, we are able to quiet our minds without such aids.

Meditation does more than just quiet the mind. Raymund Andrea explains that meditation builds a bridge between two different states of consciousness. "....mind consciousness and soul consciousness are two distinct organisms, with vastly different values and possibilities. One functions within and is circumscribed by its self-imposed form. The other is formless and the source of divine love and of all inspiration. It is the bridging form between the two which he [the aspirant] is to build in meditation, until the form of the personal self is surmounted and free access to the soul sphere is made." [1]

Continued meditative practice over many years builds a bridge of awareness between what Andrea calls "mind consciousness and soul consciousness," or everyday awareness and Divine awareness. Eventually, this bridge becomes strong enough to allow us to be aware of and live from both levels of consciousness—mind and soul, everyday and divine—simultaneously.

Five of Swords

A young man with a smile of triumph on his face holds three Swords. Two men walk away, defeated, their Swords left behind upon the ground. The sky looks dark and troubled.

In the **Five of Swords**, the Path of the Mind moves into *Gevurah*. At this point on the journey, our intellectual understanding that our minds play us false becomes an experiential realization.

Though convinced that our bodies and emotions could not be trusted, those of us on the Path of the Mind believed we could rely on the sharp, incisive powers of our minds. To finally realize that our minds too cannot be trusted is often terrifying; at this stage of the path, it feels like a defeat.

Manly P. Hall writes, "To perceive that the mind is the interposer of doubt, the very source of the impulse of negation, the root of fear, the origin of unbelief and disbelief; to discover through realization that weakness is not in the Self, but in the mind, is to emerge victorious from life's greatest battle. Armageddon is the war against the shadows that have been set up by thought." He adds, "The struggle between the Self and its lower selves, between realization and opinion, between illumination and thought—this is the last great war. Each must fight this battle within his own nature. Before he can proceed he must emerge victorious from his battle with his own thoughts."[2]

How can we do battle with our own thoughts? It seems impossible. However, as Hall explains, what achieves victory over thought is awareness or knowing. "His victory must be in the simple fact of knowing, which scatters the ghosts opposing him. There is no struggle or warfare between light and darkness. When light comes, darkness fades away. Man wins by the steadfastness of his light. His victory is a gentle attainment of truth. His enemy cannot strike back. Shadows and unrealities have no power except that which is bestowed upon them by one of the numerous attributes of ignorance. As ignorance ceases, the adversary is left powerless; but the ghosts do not return to their caverns and their grottoes. All vanish together in the presence of the Knower."[3]

Those of us on the Path of the Mind tend to put all our eggs in the basket of our intellect; we may have a difficult time understanding the difference between the knowing that is achieved by the intellect and the knowing of awareness. The knowing of the mind can answer questions, but it cannot realize God. Experiencing and understanding the differences between these two kinds of knowing is an important step on this path.

Six of Swords

A ferryman poles a boat carrying a wo-man, a child and six upright Swords to the opposite shore.

The **Six of Swords** represents the Path of the Mind in *Tifaret*. On this path, we give everyday awareness (the ferry-man) responsibility for guiding us (the boat) on our journey. The boat includes both our subconscious (the cloaked wo-man) and our awakened awareness (the child).

This card represents the particular spiritual experience that occurs when the mind stops its activities. The Swords are upright in the boat, showing that the mind is present; however, the fact that the Swords have not pierced the boat indicates that the mind is not active during the *Tifaret* experience.

This often occurs as the result of our meditative practice from the **Four of Swords**, coupled with the lesson of the **Five of Swords**, which teaches us the difference between the knowing of awareness and the knowing of the mind. It also may happen as a result of study. When the mind makes a particular connection or reaches a certain understanding, it is momentarily satisfied and quiescent; realization often slips into this stillness. It's a wonderful moment. Everything suddenly falls into place. We have arrived at a new shore.

It's important to recognize that during this brief time the mind is aware but quiet. The mind must remain in abeyance for the duration of the *Tifaret* experience. It acts only as a witness, observing and remembering, but not using its blade to pierce the boat.

This is the lesson of all the paths. The various instruments we use to define ourselves and to apprehend the One Will—mind, heart, body, will—must wait quietly outside the door while Grace shines upon us.

Like all the gifts of *Tifaret*, this spiritual experience does not last long. The mind may cease for a moment, a minute, or even ten minutes, but it soon rushes in to define what it thinks was experienced, to find language and create stories that will put this realization into a context—and we are back on the path again. The realization fades as the mind strives to capture, record, explain and analyze.

Seven of Swords

A man tiptoes furtively away from a village, holding five Swords in his arms. Two more Swords stand upright behind him.

In the **Seven of Swords**, the Path of the Mind moves reluctantly out of *Tifaret* and into *Netzach*, the *sephirah* of the emotions. Those of us on the Path of the Mind typically have considerable difficulty dealing with our emotions; but none of us can escape this aspect of our journey.

As we discussed in the **Seven of Cups**, the emotional content we choose to repress will eventually work toward our destruction later. On the Path of the Mind, we usually try to avoid not just our own emotions; we hope to avoid those of other people, too. Just as the figure on this card is hoping to slip away unseen, those of us on the Path of the Mind would generally prefer not to get involved in the messiness of other people's lives. We often disappear with our thoughts and ideas gathered in our arms.

The most commonly cited reason for this departure is the aspirant's desire to remain fixed in higher awareness and not be distracted by others. As Raymund Andrea says, "We read much of the mastering of the opposites, of standing upon a point of balance, poised and aloof above all the oscillations of life; and so ambitiously and conscientiously has this coveted altitude been striven for, that it is small wonder if a sympathetic and emotional participation in the lives of others should indicate retrogression and a condition of ignoble bondage."[4]

But it may be that our discomfort with others is the result of our own unresolved emotional content, which is triggered by that of other people. Once our issues are resolved, our poise will no longer be disturbed by other people.

Occasionally, reluctance to be involved with others stems from an overly sensitive nature, which can make us the unwitting and unwilling psychic recipient of the strong emotions of other people. Until we are strong enough to remain unaffected by the emotional influence and unconscious persuasion of other people, we may indeed be better off keeping ourselves in relative isolation.

Only strict self-honesty can tell us if we're avoiding other people because of our "psychic sensitivity" to their emotions or because we are disturbed by answering or matching emotions within ourselves.

Eight of Swords

A bound and blindfolded woman stands surrounded by eight Swords stuck into the earth. The landscape is desolate.

In the **Eight of Swords**, the Path of the Mind moves into the intellectual sphere of *Hod*. This card teaches us that studying and learning can trap the mind in its own fears. Each of the books, ideas and philosophies we study are certain that they are right and offer convincing evidence; nonetheless, they contradict one another. The mind begins to suspect that none of them are true; worse, it soon suspects it might never know the truth.

At this point, a million fears pour in. These fears may be little, insignificant things, but more often they are the "great fears" that have always plagued humankind—the unlikelihood of an afterlife, the inevitability of death, the extinction of our individual selves, and so on. Those of us who walk the Path of the Mind may find it difficult to lean upon faith or God's love; our mind has taught us to both fear the dark and be skeptical of the light. This can result in materialism, scientism, atheism—and despair.

Without the leavening of tender emotions or faith, our minds easily fall prey to these damaging anxieties. We may listen to rational counter-arguments for each anxiety, but our minds aren't convinced by them for long and won't be talked out of its fears. Notice, however, that the woman in the card isn't completely trapped; her feet are unbound and she can walk away, with small steps, carefully, gingerly, to find someone who will help her. This teaches us that we need to rely on other aspects of our being—heart, body and soul— to break the hold these fears have on the mind.

Nine of Swords

A figure sits up in bed, hands over eyes, in an attitude of despair. Hanging on the wall—or perhaps in space—are nine Swords. This person has just awoken from a nightmare.

In the **Nine of Swords**, the intellect encounters the dream world of *Yesod*. What happens in *Yesod* often presages that which will occur in *Malkuth*, and that's exactly what's happening here. Turning the page to the **Ten of Swords** shows us what the nightmare was about—death.

In the **Nine of Swords**, we suddenly have the nightmarish realization that our spiritual journey is going to kill us; or, at least, our mind's belief about who we really are. At this point, we see no happy resolution. If we move forward, the self we believe ourselves to be will die. If we go backward into the **Eight of Swords**, we descend again into the blindness of our fears. If we choose not to move at all, we are stuck in *Yesod* with our nightmares. It's not a happy choice.

All the paths involve giving up an identity; the process is always painful. On the Path of the Mind, we become quite attached to the identity we've created through learning and study. Surrendering the idea that our mind is what matters means surrendering the importance of all the knowledge we have gained; this is an intolerable position for the ego.

To move past *Yesod*, we must go beyond knowledge by forcing the mind to recognize, through its own logic, that it is a phantasm, that it cannot know God, and that the Higher Self lies elsewhere. There are no guarantees that this will happen. The spiritual path is choked with people who have decided to sit it out at *Yesod* and move no further. They cannot imagine who they would be without the identity they have so painstakingly patched together. They are afraid they would be nobody—and they are right.

People move in the direction of least pain; if moving ahead appears more painful than staying in place, that's what they will do. One teacher says that the only reason anyone takes this process to the very end is that they are driven to do so; there is no other reason. If we have this drive, we will be satisfied with nothing less than the Truth; in that case, the direction of least pain will always be forward.

Ten of Swords

A body lies face down, pierced by ten Swords. Dawn breaks over the mountains in the distance.

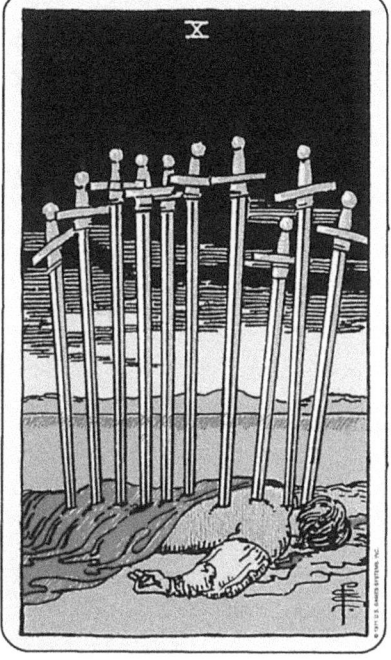

In the **Ten of Swords**, the Path of the Mind comes to rest in *Malkuth*. The dawn shown here is the dawn of the knowing of awareness and Initiation.

Throughout most of our lives, this knowing is obscured by the noise and clatter of our thoughts; so it is generally believed that stopping our thoughts allows the knowing to arise. As Dion Fortune says, "The training…is designed to teach the mind to rise to the abstract and transcend thought, for it is only when thought ceases that apprehension begins."[5] Fortune uses the word "apprehension" to mean "understanding" or "knowing."

However, it is almost impossible to stop thought for more than a few moments at a time. The key here is not to stop thinking, but to stop identifying with thought and knowledge. Thought continues, but we no longer believe that these thoughts are who we are.

At the **Ten of Swords**, we have reached this Initiation of the Mind. We understand now that it is impossible to know either ourselves or the One Will through the mind. We may massage and manipulate ideas, rearrange the letters of the name of God, and find new correspondences for the paths on the Tree of Life—but none of that can bring us to an awareness of God. After initiation, there are no more arguments, no positions left to hold, no points to argue. While the mind may still race away and get tangled in all sorts of logical knots, the sense of meaning these gymnastics once had vanishes. We now realize that this is just our mind doing what the mind does and that it is of no particular importance.

Chapter Eight Bibliography

1   Andrea, Raymund. *The Mystic Path*. San Jose, CA: Grand Lodge of the English Language Jurisdiction, 1999, p. 23.

2   Hall, Manly P. *Self-Unfoldment by Disciplines of Realization*. Los Angeles, CA: Philosophical Research Society, 1995, pp. 209–210.

3   Hall, Manly P. *Self-Unfoldment by Disciplines of Realization*. Los Angeles, CA: Philosophical Research Society, 1995, p. 210.

4   Andrea, Raymund. *The Mystic Path*. San Jose, CA: Grand Lodge of the English Language Jurisdiction, 1999, p. 75.

5   Fortune, Dion. *Sane Occultism and Practical Occultism in Daily Life*. Wellingborough, Northhamptonshire, UK: The Aquarian Press, 1987, p. 19.

THE SUIT OF WANDS

Ace of Wands

A Hand holding a Wand issues from a cloud. The halo surrounding the hand indicates that this is the Hand of God. Trees, a river, rolling hills, a castle and mountains are seen in the background.

ACE of WANDS.

Wands represent the element of fire. In human beings, fire symbolizes spirit. Spirit manifests as awareness and will, particularly the will to live. When a person dies, there is still water in their bodies, air in their lungs, clay on their bones—what is missing is fire. And in fire's absence, the other elements soon vanish and the body decomposes.

In exploring the correlation between fire and life, Paul Foster Case notes, "To define the primal mode of the Life-power—the first aspect of the cosmic vital principle—is impossible. Yet wise men have ever agreed that it is like fire, and the most recent discoveries of modern physics demonstrate the fact that the 'something' whereof all things are made is a radiant, fiery energy. Occultism adds the thought that this energy is the working power of pure consciousness, which plays upon that energy, is inseparable from it, and directs all its manifestations from within."[1]

Just as we each have a body, heart and mind, we each have this mysterious fire within us. For some of us, the fire appears as a very strong will or desire. This may be the will to live or the will to succeed in a particular endeavor. The will is not always fully appreciated. While our powerful brain and opposable thumb distinguish us from the other beasts, a developed will separates a more advanced human being from his neighbor. We all know people who are very determined. They set their minds to something and they achieve it, come what may. Other people seem to have a very low fire; they reach a decision only to countermand it the next day or give up as soon as the first real obstacle appears. A person may have enough intelligence to study hard, save money, exercise, and so on—but it is the will that brings such plans to fruition.

Fire also symbolizes awareness of the spiritual world, or God. Some people seem to have been born with an innate awareness of this world, experiencing visions and altered states while still in childhood. Those not so gifted must rely on special practices, techniques or even drugs to achieve this awareness.

The Path of Wands, known also as the Mystic Path, relies on both will and awareness to find the Divine. Because will and awareness are silent, invisible and not well understood, the Mystic Path is a particularly difficult path to comprehend and walk. Of course, will and awareness are utilized on other spiritual paths as well. It is the strength of our will that keeps us moving through difficult times; those with an underdeveloped will get stuck early on. As we progress, our awareness helps us recognize that we are growing, changing and coming closer to God. At the end of each path, it is awareness that will bring us into conscious awakening. Each of us, regardless of our chosen path, must develop will and awareness if we are to succeed.

Two of Wands

A man looks out over a wide vista of moun-
tains, forests, buildings and the sea. He
holds a globe in his right hand and a Wand
in his left. A second Wand stands on its
own to his right. The stone parapet upon
which he stands is decorated with red roses
and white lilies, the traditional Tarot floral
motif.

In the **Two of Wands**, the Mystic Path
takes its first step out of *Keter* and into *Chok-*
mah. *Chokmah* represents desire, the force
that fertilizes the womb of *Binah*. The roses
on the parapet symbolize *Chokmah*'s desire, while the globe in the man's hand
suggests that the intent of this path is to
master our experience of manifestation.

Properly understood and focused,
desire is an aspect of the will. In fact, Creation was willed into existence by the desire of the Divine. The Western Mystery Tradition
employs the will to control and focus desire. The phrase "burning
desire" reflects the Path of Wands perfectly, both in reference to the
element of fire and to the emphasis on desire controlled by will. The
mystic's burning desire to find God is the foundation of this path.

Kabbalah teaches that it is mutual desire that forms the connection between God and humankind. The *Zohar* explains, "Rabbi
El'azar said, 'I see that arousal above transpires only with arousal
below, for arousal above depends on desire below.'"[2] This statement from the *Zohar* is deliberately sexual; God above is viewed as

male while physical manifestation below is viewed as female. Arousal and desire, symbolized by fire and Wands, create a channel of communication between God and humankind, the spiritual and physical.

Three of Wands

A man looks out over a sea, where three ships sail in the distance. He holds a Wand; two more Wands stand behind him.

In this card, the Mystic Path moves out of *Chokmah* and into *Binah* on the Pillar of Severity. The **Three of Wands** is structured much like the **Two of Wands**, though in this card the man looks out only over the sea. This is appropriate, for this card is assigned to *Binah*, often referred to as the Great Sea from which life sprang.

The goal of the mystic is to become aware of the Self that lies behind the mind, body and heart. This is accomplished via an ongoing process of seeing through that which isn't real. Raymund Andrea explains, "The aspirant's ascent on the mystic way is a twofold process of the destruction of form and the building of form, until he enters the life of the soul which is formless. He is imprisoned within the mental and emotional form which his life experience has created; his object is to transcend that form."[3]

The form to which Andrea refers is our body, mind and heart. Of course, we cannot completely destroy this "form" as long as we are embodied in physical manifestation. What we can do, however, is to create different forms; we do this by working out the mental and emotional knots that encumber us, healing old wounds, seeing through false ideas, and so on. As we grow, learn and heal, our "form" changes. Andrea concludes, "The finer form is building. The soul responds; the vibration of the personality is heightened; repolarization of consciousness is gradually taking place. The personality feels the energizing and life-giving force of the soul."[4]

No sooner is one form transcended than another one is built; the moment the aspirant gets comfortable in the new form, he is required to destroy that form, too. Life on the spiritual path is a continuous experience of **The Tower**. Over time, we learn to let our Towers crumble easily and not get hit by falling bricks; we even learn to welcome this destruction as a sign of progress.

Four of Wands

Two figures stand side by side, one garbed in blue and the other in red. Both wear crowns of flowers and hold bouquets high in the air. The mood is one of celebration. Four Wands in the immediate foreground are tied together with vines, garlands and fruit. A stone castle or walled city is shown in the background.

When awareness moves into *Chesed*, we experience joy and delight. The marriage pictured here is the marriage of our human awareness with Divine awareness. As anyone who has been married knows, the marriage ceremony represents an early stage in the relationship as well as a high point in the relationship.

Evelyn Underhill describes five phases of the mystic journey— Awakening, Purgation, Illumination, Dark Night of the Soul and Union. The **Four of Wands** symbolizes the first phase, Awakening. "The awakening of the Self to consciousness of Divine Reality... usually abrupt and well-marked, is accompanied by intense feelings of joy and exaltation."[5]

This joyful experience is often so powerful that those of us on the Mystic Path tend to believe absolutely and literally that this awakening represents unquestionable truth. This often reinforces the mystic's belief that he is worshipping the one and only deity in the one and only correct manner. Few mystics are able to recognize that their particular experience of the Divine is nothing more than a reflection of their personality and culture.

Gershom Scholem asks, "Why does a Christian mystic always see Christian visions and not those of a Buddhist? Why does a Buddhist see the figures of his own pantheon and not, for example, Jesus or the Madonna? Why does a Kabbalist on his way of enlightenment meet the prophet Elijah and not some figure from an alien world? The answer, of course, is that the expression of their experience is immediately transposed into symbols from their own world."[6]

This means that any individual's experience is right and true for him, but not necessarily right and true for someone else; the face we see beside us under the marriage canopy is always a product of the subconscious material from our own minds or the group mind of our culture. Getting overly attached to one particular expression of the Divine keeps us from moving forward on our path.

Five of Wands

Five figures battle with Wands. It's impossible to tell who is on which side or if there even are sides. There is no apparent cause for the fracas—no treasure to be won or helpless maiden to rescue.

In the **Five of Wands**, the Mystic Path moves into the *sephirah* of *Gevurah* and the phase that Underhill calls Purgation. "The Self, aware for the first time of Divine Beauty, realizes by contrast its own finiteness and imperfection, the manifold illusions in which it is immersed, the immense distance which separates it from the One. Its attempts to eliminate by discipline and mortification all that stands in the way of its progress towards union with God constitute Purgation: a state of pain and effort."[7]

Purgation is the phase in which we first recognize just how many as yet unconquered aspects of body, mind and heart live within us. This will be the first of many battles. Since success on this path involves bringing thoughts and emotions under control, it is inevitable that these aspects of self will stage a revolution, not just once but many times on the path. This is a battle in which there is no strategy and no plan—there's just the battle. These conflicts require a lot of energy, making Purgation an exhausting and difficult phase.

We may feel quite overwhelmed at this point. We feel so far from our goal, so mired in materiality and lost in emotional turmoil, that it seems impossible for us to ever succeed. This can apply to our spiritual practices as well as life in general. It can feel like an uphill battle just to say a prayer or light a candle. We may be tempted to give up entirely. Those of us who cannot muster the will to continue often fall back into memories of the **Four of Wands**, becoming fixated on the particular experience and image we enjoyed in that phase. The tendency to regress to an earlier, happier time is one of the pitfalls of spiritual life; we become overly enamored of the happy feeling we remember so well.

However, as Manly P. Hall reminds us, "A little enlightenment does not bestow immunity from future effort, nor does it promise peace and security in some psychic summerland."[8] In reality, a little enlightenment means a lot more work ahead. It is important for each of us on the spiritual journey to understand very clearly that a "psychic summerland," in which all our endeavors prosper and all our prayers are answered, simply does not exist. If we have embarked upon this journey in order to reach such a place, we have wasted our time.

Six of Wands

A man crowned with a wreath sits on a horse; he holds a Wand upon which hangs another wreath. Surrounding horse and rider are figures carrying five more Wands.

In the **Six of Wands**, the Mystic Path moves into balance in *Tifaret*, the spiritual center of the Tree. Here we achieve a brief victory on the spiritual path, symbolized by the laurel wreath which has been a sign of victory since antiquity. In Roman times, a successful hero was awarded a "triumph" or parade in which he was pulled through the streets of Rome by white horses. In this card, we are the hero sitting on the white horse and wearing the laurel wreath.

The **Six of Wands** represents the third of Underhill's phases, Illumination. Underhill explains that the joy of Illumination is a direct result of the experience of Purgation. "When by Purgation the Self has become detached from the 'things of sense,' and acquired those virtues which are 'ornaments of the spiritual marriage,' its joyful consciousness of the Transcendent Order returns in an enhanced form.... This is Illumination: a state which includes in itself many of the stages of contemplation, 'degrees of orison,' visions and adventures of the soul described by St. Teresa and other mystical writers...illumination is the 'contemplative state' par excellence. It forms, with the two preceding states, the 'first mystic life.' Many mystics never go beyond it; and, on the other hand, many seers and artists, not usually classed amongst them, have shared, to some extent, the experiences of the illuminated state. Illumination brings a certain apprehension of the Absolute, a sense of the Divine Presence: but not true union with it. It is a state of happiness."[9]

After the inner battle in the **Five of Wands**, this re-awakening of Divine Awareness is the sweetest victory imaginable. Just as the horse serves as a vehicle for the man, the man serves as the vehicle of the Divine; just as the horse is clearly aware of its rider, the man is aware of the presence of the Divine. However, they are not yet one Being.

This stage is certainly a sign that we are on the right path and headed in the right direction. Like the victory ride, it is validation of all that has gone before; also, like the victory ride, it's bound to be of short duration. The expression "resting on one's laurels" refers to the reliance on past success. On a spiritual path, resting on our laurels is impossible. The moment we think "I'm done, I've made it!" or "Hey, aren't I something!" or even "Don't think about anything because then this will end," we are cast out from *Tifaret*.

Seven of Wands

A man holding a Wand stands on top of a hill, prepared to do battle with six other Wands. We do not know who wields those six Wands, but we receive the impression of an unequal fight. Despite this, the lone man looks determined but not panicked.

In the **Seven of Wands**, the Mystic Path moves out of balance in *Tifaret* and into *Netzach* on the Pillar of Mercy. *Netzach* is a *sephirah* of emotions. In the beginning of this phase, we may begin to lose our emotional balance. Just as the attacking Wands in this card come from below our line of sight, so it is our subconscious that dredges up the old issues and concerns that threaten our realization and bring on Underhill's fourth phase, the Dark Night of the Soul.

This is an early stage of this phase; the later stage is depicted in the **Nine of Wands**. What we experience here is just the loss of Illumination, described here by Manly P. Hall. "As the growing plant may be destroyed by an unseasonal frost, so the unfolding realization cannot survive any immoderate mental or emotional complex. Imperceptibly, under a false stimulus, the realization is undermined; it shifts back to the status of opinion, affirmation, or emotion. The disciple, often unaware of what has occurred, has thus impeded his own progress. The surest symptom by which he may discover that error is entering into his realization is the diminution of his placidity. When he loses poise, he has lost realization." [10]

In using the term "unseasonal," Hall gives the impression that this is an unnatural occurrence that might have been avoided; however, Evelyn Underhill explains that this is a normal part of the process. "...the typical mystic seems to move toward his goal through a series of strongly marked oscillations between 'states of pleasure' and 'states of pain.' The existence and succession of these states—sometimes broken and confused, sometimes crisply defined—can be traced, to a greater or lesser degree, in almost every case of which we possess anything like a detailed record." [11]

Kabbalah teaches that a relationship with God requires three things from us—*Emunah*, *Bitachon* and *Diveykut*. *Emunah* (pronounced eh-moo'-nah) means maintaining our faith in the existence of God. *Bitachon* (pronounced bih-tah-khon') means feeling trust and confidence that God knows what He's doing. *Diveykut* (pronounced dih-veh-koot') is clinging to God and not letting go. It's easy to experience *Emunah*, *Bitachon* and *Diveykut* when life is good; it's considerably more difficult when our lives become painful. When our realization has been lost, practicing *Emunah*, *Bitachon* and *Diveykut* can help get us through the backlash emotions of disappointment, self-pity and self-blame, and put us back on track.

We may be encouraged by the fact that the figure in the card has the advantage of position, high above the other contestants. His teachers have told him to expect this battle, and he knows he can win.

Eight of Wands

Eight Wands fly through the air. In the background is a grassy hill, a building and a river; there are no human or animal figures.

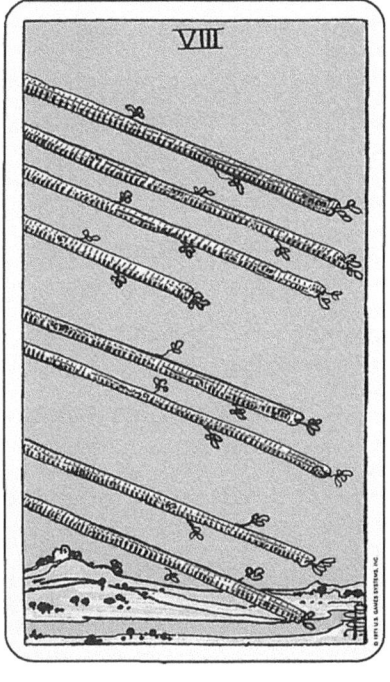

In the **Eight of Wands**, the Mystic Path moves horizontally out of *Netzach*, the emotional *sephirah*, and into *Hod*, the *sephirah* of the mind.

This is the only card in the entire Tarot deck that contains no portion of a human figure. It symbolizes a common complaint lodged against those on the Mystic Path—its lack of value to the rest of the world. The mystic is involved entirely in his own awareness and practices; there's no room for anyone or anything else. This doesn't sit well with many who follow other paths, particularly with those on the Path of Service.

Itzhak Bentov (1923–1979), scientist, inventor, mystic and author, tells an allegorical story about those who have elected to follow the Mystic Path. He and a spirit guide, Naga the snake, have come upon Nirvana, a Sanskrit term for a place of spiritual bliss. Bentov describes Nirvana: "It is really a nice place. What a contrast to the dark void outside! It's difficult to describe the good 'vibes' and the all-pervading light. As you move along, you find high throne-like structures, all luminous, with people sitting cross-legged on them,

253

meditating. Some angels are hanging over them, apparently for decoration. Bliss pervades everything. The people are totally unaware of what is happening around them, for they are immersed in their meditation, experiencing constant and intense bliss."

It sounds appealing; but Naga the snake soon sets us straight. "'Nirvana, as you know,' he says, 'is really a blind alley of evolution. People are interested solely in their own bliss, and they don't care about others. That's why I'm supposed to scare them away from here. But if they decide to come in anyway, in spite of my warnings, it's their right. They worked for it and are entitled to their bliss. However, they will not evolve beyond this.'"

Naga then introduces us to those who have chosen to go beyond bliss. "'Upon closer scrutiny, you find that these people are every bit as developed as the population in Nirvana—even more so. Pure consciousness flows through their bodies, entering through their heads, where again no thought process is visible, and emerging from the bottom of their spines. From there it flows into the Manifest Creation. The difference is that these people tamper a little with the void as it flows through them. They are adding a slight vibration to it, prebiasing the flow of consciousness, in order to produce a certain effect on the evolution of their particular planets.

"'We have here, then, a group of people whose compassion makes them work hard for the evolution of beings on their respective planets. They are, in effect, a planetary lobby, doing a twenty-four-hour-a-day job day in, day out. They have renounced the option of eternal bliss in Nirvana, and instead sit in the dark void, doing thankless jobs. But, as we all know, this kind of selfless work eventually pays off. They will keep evolving, and in time leave the population of Nirvana far behind.'"[12]

This demand that we be of service is such a powerful one that aspirants rarely question its validity. Many people do not realize that this need to be of service was originally imposed on mystics to keep them in line. As Gershom Scholem explains, "Especially in monotheistic religions the religious authorities had still another method of avoiding conflict with the mystics of the community. This was to charge them with social responsibility. They put pressure on the mystics to mingle with the simple folk, to participate in their activities, instead of remaining among themselves in communities of the 'enlightened.' In Christianity, where since the beginnings of monasticism mystics have always been able to band together, this trend has not always been as clear as in Judaism. Since Talmudic times we find a decided disinclination to let mystics organize committees of their own. Time and time again the rabbis insisted that mystical experience, the 'love of God,' must be confirmed by activity in the human community, that it was not enough for an individual to pour out his soul to God...Suffice it to say that it has been highly effective in 'taming' mystics and holding them within the limits imposed by traditional authority." [13]

This requirement to be "useful" has infiltrated all walks of spirituality, but it is actually an attempt at social control. We resist those who want to send us on an all-expenses-paid guilt trip by remembering that God does not need our help to run the world. Those of us who are drawn to serve will do so; those who are not so drawn need feel no remorse.

Nine of Wands

A weary figure leans on a Wand. His head is bandaged; he is grim-faced and determined. Eight more Wands form a fence behind him.

In the **Nine of Wands**, the Mystic Path comes into balance in *Yesod*. The path has been walked almost to its end; but getting through *Yesod* is no easy matter. Here we enter the depths of the Dark Night of the Soul, a phase which began in the **Seven of Wands**. Here our awareness of God's presence completely vanishes. This apparent loss of connection with God is a terrifying experience for anyone who has come to rely upon it.

Though the Wands lined up behind the figure in the card appear formidable, this person has clearly endured many battles and is prepared to do so again. Accustomed to the ups and downs of this path, we call upon the various practices that have aided us in the past—awareness, faith, prayer, therapy, meditation and so on.

But the passage from *Yesod* to *Malkuth* requires something very different from us. As Underhill explains, "In the development of the great and strenuous seeker after God, this is followed—or sometimes intermittently accompanied—by the most terrible of all the experiences of the Mystic Way: the final and complete purification of the Self, which is called by some contemplatives the 'mystic pain' or 'mystic death,' by others the Purification of the Spirit or Dark Night of the Soul. The consciousness which had, in Illumination, sunned itself in the sense of the Divine Presence, now suffers under an equally intense sense of the Divine Absence: learning to dissociate the personal satisfaction of mystical vision from the reality of mystical life. As in Purgation the senses were cleansed and humbled, and the energies and interests of the Self were concentrated upon transcendental things: so now the purifying process is extended to the very centre of I-hood, the will. The human instinct for personal happiness must be killed."[14]

We move forward now not by finding happiness again, but by recognizing the unimportance of happiness. For most of us, this is an incomprehensible idea. We started on the spiritual path because we sought happiness; we believed that happiness waited, like a pot of gold, at the end of the journey. Now we must recognize that the goal of the caterpillar is not the goal of the butterfly; what was important to the person who undertook this journey is not important to the person we are preparing to become.

Ten of Wands

A man grasps ten Wands in both arms, burying his face in them as he walks toward a village.

In the **Ten of Wands** the Mystic Path drops into *Malkuth,* the final *sephirah.* This is a picture of Underhill's final phase —Union. This is the only card that depicts a figure holding all the suit symbols. This teaches us that in the **Ten of Wands**, all aspects are united and the battles are over. The figure walks toward a village, not necessarily to embark upon a Path of Service, but to interact in the world to whatever degree he wishes.

Underhill describes this fifth and final phase. "Union: the true goal of the mystic quest. In this state the Absolute Life is not merely perceived and enjoyed by the Self, as in Illumination: but is one with it. This is the end towards which all the previous oscillations of consciousness have tended. It is a state of equilibrium, of purely spiritual life; characterized by peaceful joy, by enhanced powers, by intense certitude. To call this state, as some authorities do, by the name of Ecstasy, is inaccurate and confusing: since the term Ecstasy has long been used both by psychologists and ascetic writers to define that short and rapturous trance—a state with well-marked physical and psychical accompaniments—in which the contemplative, losing all consciousness of the phenomenal world, is caught up to a brief and immediate enjoyment of the Divine Vision. Ecstasies of this kind are often experienced by the mystic in Illumination, or even on his first conversion." She continues, "Union must be looked upon as the true goal of mystical growth; that permanent establishment of life upon transcendent levels of reality, of which ecstasies give a fore-taste to the soul." [15]

The **Ten of Pentacles, Ten of Cups, Ten of Swords** and **Ten of Wands** represent, together, the complete and total union with God. To the outside world, those who achieve this union may look no dif-ferent than before; but the inner experience is drastically altered. While there is generally at least a vestigial sense of individuality, the main content of this person's awareness is occupied with the experience of being a walking, breathing, manifestation of Grace. His face is completely hidden in the Wands, showing that he has realized that there is really no one there.

Does this awareness bring him long life? It does not. Does he enjoy better health as a result? He does not. Does his personality continue to operate in the world? It does. Is he happy? It doesn't matter.

Chapter Nine Bibliography

1   Case, Paul Foster. *Tarot: A Key to the Wisdom of the Ages.* Richmond, VA: Macoy Publishing Company, 1947, p. 30.

2   Matt, Daniel (Trans.). *The Zohar, Volume Two.* Stanford, CA: Stanford University Press, 2004, p. 53.

3   Andrea, Raymund. *The Mystic Path.* San Jose, CA: Grand Lodge of the English Language Jurisdiction, 1999, p. 21.

4   Andrea, Raymund. *The Mystic Path.* San Jose, CA: Grand Lodge of the English Language Jurisdiction, 1999, p. 28.

5   Underhill, Evelyn. *Mysticism: The Nature and Development of Spiritual Consciousness.* Oxford, UK: Oneworld Publications, 1999, p. 169.

6   Scholem, Gershom. *On the Kabbalah and Its Symbolism.* New York, NY: Schocken Books, 1996, p. 15.

7   Underhill, Evelyn. *Mysticism: The Nature and Development of Spiritual Consciousness.* Oxford, UK: Oneworld Publications, 1999, p. 169.

8   Hall, Manly P. *Self-Unfoldment by Disciplines of Realization.* Los Angeles, CA: Philosophical Research Society, 1995, p. 187.

9   Underhill, Evelyn. *Mysticism: The Nature and Development of Spiritual Consciousness.* Oxford, UK: Oneworld Publications, 1999, p. 169.

10   Hall, Manly P. *Self-Unfoldment by Disciplines of Realization.* Los Angeles, CA: Philosophical Research Society, 1995, pp. 175-176.

11   Underhill, Evelyn. *Mysticism: The Nature and Development of Spiritual Consciousness.* Oxford, UK: Oneworld Publications, 1999, p. 168.

12   Bentov, Itzhak. *A Brief Tour of Higher Consciousness: A Cosmic Book on the Mechanics of Creation.* Rochester, VT: Destiny Books, 2000, pp 69-73.

13   Scholem, Gershom. *On the Kabbalah and Its Symbolism.* New York, NY: Schocken Books, 1996, p. 26.

14   Underhill, Evelyn. *Mysticism: The Nature and Development of Spiritual Consciousness.* Oxford, UK: Oneworld Publications, 1999, p. 169.

15   Underhill, Evelyn. *Mysticism: The Nature and Development of Spiritual Consciousness.* Oxford, UK: Oneworld Publications, 1999, p. 170.

Chapter Ten

COURT CARDS

The Court Cards are also placed on the Tree of Life, though these assignments are not as standardized as the Major and Minor Arcana. Some Tarot students link the Court Cards to particular *sephirah*—Kings to *Chokmah*, Queens to *Binah*, Knights to *Tifaret* and Pages to *Malkuth*. Others assign the Court Cards to so-called "secret" or "invisible" paths. There is nothing particularly secret or invisible about these paths; these are the paths that connect the *sephirot* but are not assigned to Hebrew letters by either the Kabbalistic or Tarot traditions. *The Tarot of Awakening* assigns the Court Cards to the invisible paths. These paths are shown in Figure 6.[1] Using the invisible paths for the Court Cards allows the entire Tree of Life to become a pictorial diagram of the Tarot deck.

Traditionally, the Court Cards are thought to represent people of a particular character or profession who have appeared in the life of the person for whom the reading is being done, referred to as "the Querent." For example, A. E. Waite describes the **King of Cups** as "Fair man, man of business, law, or divinity; responsible, disposed to oblige the Querent; also equity, art and science, including those who profess science, law and art; creative intelligence."[2]

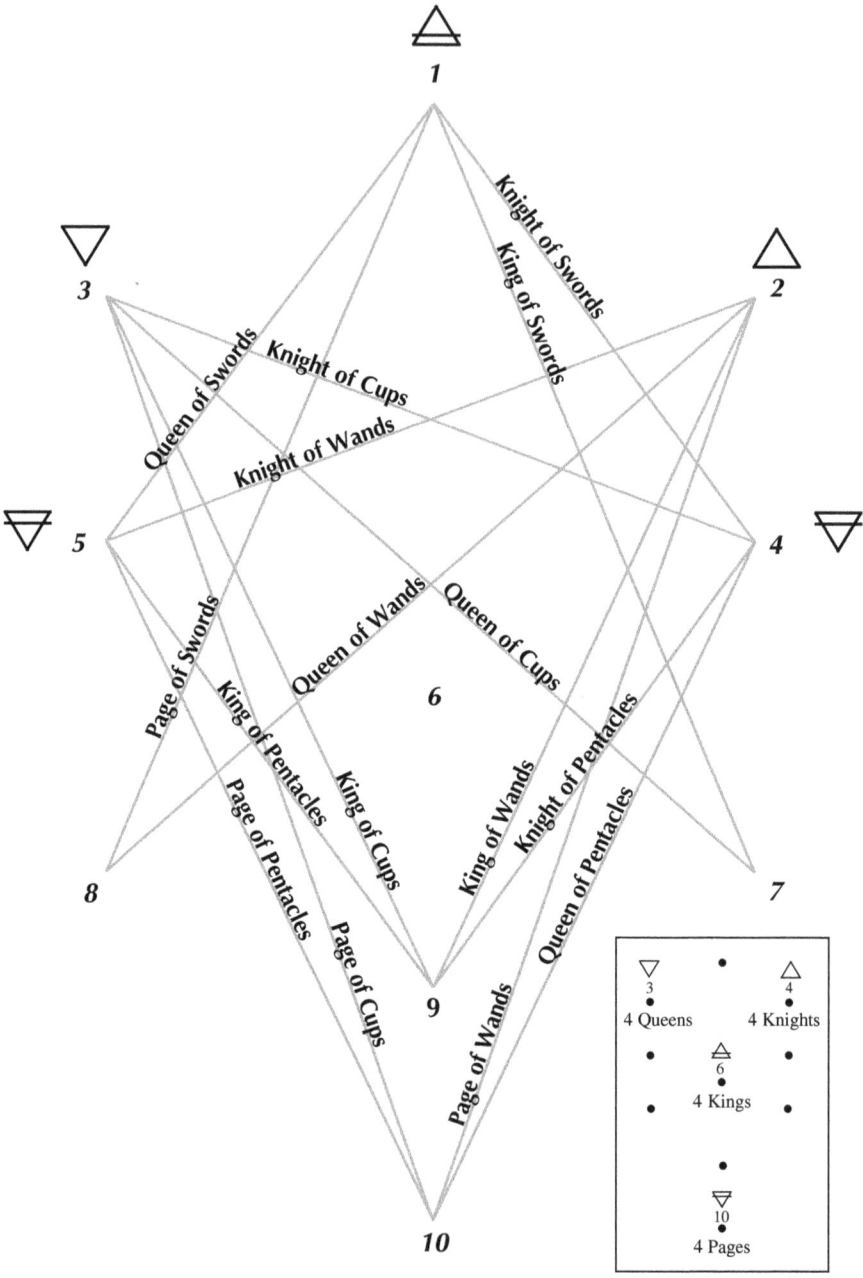

Figure 6. The Court Cards on the Tree of Life as 16 Invisible Paths

The Court Cards are also associated with physical appearances. Again, according to Waite, "The four Court Cards in Wands represent very fair people, with yellow or auburn hair, fair complexion and blue eyes. The Court Cards in Cups signify people with light brown or dull fair hair and grey or blue eyes. Those in Swords stand for people having hazel or grey eyes, dark brown hair and dull complexion. Lastly, the Court Cards in Pentacles are referred to persons with very dark brown or black hair, dark eyes and sallow or swarthy complexions." [3]

More modern interpretations of the Court Cards also revolve around the people in our lives, but tend to focus less on profession or physical characteristics and more on relationships. Kate Warwick-Smith, author, teacher and psychotherapist, gives an example of this in her description of the **King of Cups**. "The Benefactor sits upon the grail throne as the font of goodwill and inexhaustible love. The **King of Cups** is someone in our life who loves us unconditionally. We can rely on the Benefactor to love us no matter what we do or say. He or she may be angry at us and even at times dislike who we are, yet the Benefactor's love for us is unfailing. Grandparents, parents, or offspring can act as Benefactors. Another permutation may be a counselor or therapist who shows unconditional positive regard and accepts us 'as is.'" [4]

In *The Tarot of Awakening*, however, we are concerned not with physical appearance, profession or relationship, but with personality characteristics that help or hinder us on the spiritual path. Since the personality continues to operate even after a high degree of Initiation, these characteristics continue to affect our experience of life and of the Divine.

Most of us have trouble seeing our own personalities clearly. Other people can serve as mirrors for us, reflecting back our own otherwise invisible aspects. Some of our personality aspects are positive, contributing to our progress on our spiritual path; others are negative and pose a liability to our progress. And still others are a combination of positive and negative, which can both help and hinder us.

The Court Cards are affected by three factors. First, the suits retain their customary elemental correspondences—Pentacles are assigned to earth, Cups to water, Swords to air and Wands to fire. Second, there are elemental correspondences assigned to the Court Cards themselves: Kings symbolize fire, Queens symbolize water, Knights symbolize air and Pages symbolize earth. Court Cards thus have elements assigned both from the suit and from the character portrayed. Third, each Court Card is influenced by the path on the Tree of Life to which it is assigned. For example, the **King of Wands** corresponds to fire on two counts, since both the Suit of Wands and the character of the King are associated with the element of fire. Assigned to the path from *Chokmah* to *Yesod*, this King also partakes of the merciful nature of *Chokmah* and the imagination of *Yesod*.

In reading through the descriptions of the Court Cards, it is often helpful to note how these aspects show up within ourselves as well as in the people we tend to attract into our lives. Often we will react to aspects that we see in others because of a matching aspect within ourselves that we are either lacking or that make us uncomfortable.

Certain personality traits are helpful on one specific spiritual path and not helpful on others. It may be instructive to note which aspects of our personalities have steered us in a particular direction. Note that the apparent gender of the Court Cards is irrelevant—both men and women may have King, Queen, Knight and Page aspects;

also note that there is no clear progression of development from Page to Knight, Knight to Queen, etc. The interaction of the various elements and path on the Tree that affect the Court Cards is complex and the results are often surprising.

King of Pentacles

KING of PENTACLES.

The King sits on a throne decorated with bull's heads. He holds a scepter in one hand and a yellow Pentacle in the other. His crown is adorned with roses. He is heavily swathed in a robe embroidered with bunches of grapes; beneath the robe he is encased in armor. A castle is shown in the background.

The **King of Pentacles** is associated with the elements of earth (assigned to Pentacles) and fire (assigned to Kings). The King thus unites the strength of will associated with fire and the physical power associated with earth. This card is also assigned to the path from *Gevurah* to *Yesod*. The armor worn by the **King of Pentacles** suggests the war-like *sephirah* of *Gevurah*, often depicted as a king wearing armor. The astral quality of *Yesod* is countered by the earthiness of Pentacles.

This castle is the only building shown in the Court Cards; it represents the structure of physical manifestation. The bull's heads, and the armor worn beneath the robe, are reminiscent of **The Emperor**, which symbolizes rational awareness. This suggests that the **King of Pentacles** is rational awareness applied to physical manifestation. The grapes on the King's robe represent the element of earth; they also recall the **Nine of Pentacles** and the labor required to domesticate nature. The roses on his crown symbolize desire, a characteristic associated with fire.

The **King of Pentacles** represents an aspect of self that is strong, active, and completely at ease in the physical body and in the world. He is the most strong-willed and self-aware of the Pentacles Court Cards, as well as the earthiest of the Kings. There is no emotional component associated with this card; it may be his own emotions against which the King is armored. He may tend to be overly restrictive, unforgiving, judgmental and insensitive.

When viewed externally, the **King of Pentacles** may look like someone who is powerful in the world and in his body. Discomfort with such people may indicate discomfort with the characteristics the King displays. Typically, the aspect of the King that causes discomfort is his sheer physical presence and power in the world— either because we feel that our power overwhelms others or because we feel ourselves to be powerless.

The challenge this King faces is to draw upon his positive qualities of power, rational awareness and the ability to stay grounded while monitoring his negative qualities of lack of emotion and insensitivity. The King tends to be drawn to physical manifestation and thus the Path of Service.

Queen of Pentacles

QUEEN of PENTACLES.

The Queen sits beneath a rose arbor on a throne decorated with ram's heads. She wears a red robe and a green cloak; she holds a yellow Pentacle in her lap. A rabbit frolics in the foreground; mountains and a stream are seen in the background.

The **Queen of Pentacles** combines the elements of earth (Pentacles) and water (Queens). The assignment of this card to the path from *Chesed* to *Malkuth* takes the joyous, outpouring energy of *Chesed* straight to physical manifestation in *Malkuth*.

The **Queen of Pentacles** represents an aspect that has many of the attributes of **The Empress**. She is an earth mother and a lover of nature—generous, reliable, dependable and nurturing. Her strong emotional nature manifests in physical ways such as cooking, care-taking and healing.

The mountains, the ram's heads, and the Queen's green cloak symbolize earth; the budding greenery and the rabbit symbolize the fertility that results from the combination of earth and water. The roses above her head represent the desire that fuels fertility.

As we discussed with regard to **The Empress**, the power of life and fertility is enormous; the **Queen of Pentacles** is similarly powerful. Learning to recognize, appreciate and become comfortable with the energy of the **Queen of Pentacles**—within and without—is part of the spiritual journey on all paths.

268

However, because female power is not highly valued in the world it often happens that both male and female aspirants suppress this aspect. Doing so may manifest as an aversion to this aspect in others. If we experience earth-mother individuals as distasteful, smothering and controlling, it may suggest that we have a similar distaste for this aspect within ourselves. Appreciating the value and importance of the **Queen of Pentacles** is an essential task for all aspirants.

This aspect is often found in aspirants who walk the Path of Service or Path of Devotion. The **Queen of Pentacles** may influence aspirants on other paths to select more earth-based practices. For example, a magician with a strong **Queen of Pentacles** aspect may lean toward shamanism rather than ceremonial magic.

Knight of Pentacles

KNIGHT of PENTACLES.

The Knight is mounted on a motionless black horse. He holds a yellow Pentacle in one hand. Tilled fields and trees are seen in the background.

The **Knight of Pentacles** unites the elements of earth (Pentacles) and air (Knights). The corresponding path passes from the *sephirah* of *Chesed*, representing mercy and kindness, to the *sephirah* of imagination, *Yesod*. The element of earth is symbolized by the greenery attached to the Knight's helm and the horse's head, as well as by the tilled fields and trees in the background.

The **Knight of Pentacles** is at a standstill. This comes about because the three major influences on this card—earth, air and imagination—produce an aspect of self that is frozen by, rather than active in, the physical world. This immobility rises from fears concerning real world consequences; such fears are created by the mind, magnified by the imagination and have their result in physical manifestation. The assigned path suggests that the Knight has a good heart and good intentions, but they progress no further than his *Yesod*ic imagination.

The **Knight of Pentacles** often thinks of his motionlessness as patience. He believes he possesses a steady, enduring energy which is far superior to short bursts of high energy. Indeed, every spiritual path demands endless patience and the ability to plod along to the end. Many a tortoise has succeeded where a rabbit has died of stress and exhaustion. However, the **Knight of Pentacles** fails to recognize that he is not blessed with patience, but afflicted by fear and the resulting inability to make a decision. His rapt gaze into the Pentacle suggests that he views it as a crystal ball that could tell him which direction would be safest.

We can recognize this aspect in ourselves or in fellow aspirants by the tendency to avoid commitment to a plan or goal. We often escape commitment by raising objections and creating obstacles under the guise of "thinking things through." All spiritual paths require us to deal with any **Knight of Pentacles** tendencies we may have. When we discover this aspect operating within ourselves, it's important to spend time discovering the source of our fears so that we may overcome them; then we have the opportunity to learn just how capable we really are.

Page of Pentacles

PAGE of PENTACLES.

The Page stands in a green field and stares deeply into the yellow Pentacle he holds in both hands. He wears a green tunic and a red hat. Flowers bloom at his feet. In the distance are trees and mountains.

The **Page of Pentacles** is a double earth card; both Pentacles and Pages are assigned to the element of earth. The path assignment, *Gevurah* to *Malkuth*, suggests a restrictive energy brought to earth. The element of earth is represented on the card by the Page's green cloak, as well as by the field, flowers and trees.

This well-grounded Page is patient as he serves out an apprenticeship on the path of his choice. The restrictive energy of the path assigned to this card represents the discipline required to master any particular field of endeavor. Restrictive energy feels uncomfortable; many of us interpret this uncomfortable feeling as a sign that we're headed in the wrong direction, impelling us to quit our endeavor instead of pursuing it to the end.

In spiritual life, depth is far more important than breadth. Anything, pursued long enough, has the potential to bring us to Initiation. As spiritual author Natalie Goldberg tells us, "In 1974 I began to do sitting meditation. From 1978 to 1984 I studied Zen formally with Dainin Katagiri Roshi (Roshi is a title for a Zen master) at the Minnesota Zen Center in Minneapolis. Whenever I went to see him and asked him a question about Buddhism, I had trouble under-standing the answer until he said, 'You know, like in writing when you...' When he referred to writing, I understood. About three years ago he said to me, 'Why do you come to sit meditation? Why don't you make writing your practice? If you go deep enough in writing, it will take you everyplace.'"5

If we go deep enough into anything, it will indeed take us every-place; but we have a tendency to not begin at all (like the **Knight of Pentacles**), to quit when things get difficult, or to spread ourselves too thin by sampling a little meditation, a little shamanism, a little prayer. We must learn to restrict our focus with **Page of Pentacles** patience and grounding. The Page could walk anywhere across the fields or vistas open to him, but he has chosen to restrict himself to the mystery before him.

Every spiritual path requires us to utilize our **Page of Pentacles** aspect by serving an apprenticeship. With patience and a narrow focus, we will be able to move deeply into our chosen practice.

King of Cups

KING of CUPS.

The King sits on a shell-shaped throne that appears to be floating on turbulent water. He holds a yellow Cup in one hand and a yellow scepter in the other. The King wears a blue robe, a yellow cape trimmed in red and an elaborate yellow crown with red decorations. His feet are shod in scaled armor and a fish pendant hangs from a chain around his neck. In the background we see a sailing ship and a fish leaping above the waves.

The **King of Cups** combines the elements of water (Cups) and fire (Kings). The card occupies the path from *Binah* to *Yesod*, connecting the Great Sea with the astral world ruled by the Moon. The Moon's gravity causes the tides in the sea; as we see in this card, the King's throne is floating on seas that are rough indeed. However, the King is secure on his throne, floating serenely upon this turbulent water. The card abounds with water symbols—the shape of the throne, fish necklace, color of the robe, scaly feet, etc.

The **King of Cups** unites will with emotion, representing that aspect of self that is aware of, and exercises control over, the internal emotional experience. His poise, like the throne pictured in the card, is a strong and powerful vehicle that allows him to ride above the stormy waters of his emotions.

When observed in others, the **King of Cups** may appear to have no emotions at all; but we must remember that he has learned to restrain his emotions, not eradicate them. Further, the experience gained while learning to master his own emotions has given him insight into the emotions of others. This insight may make him compassionate, but he may give in to the temptation to become manipulative.

Emotional poise and restraint is an important aspect of self on both the Path of Knowledge and the Mystic Path, both of which require strict emotional control. It is also important on the Path of Devotion, which demands a high level of control over the focus of its emotional content.

Queen of Cups

QUEEN of CUPS.

The Queen sits upon a throne elaborately carved with images of mer-babies. She is dressed in a sea-colored gown with a shell at her throat. An intricate crown sits on her head. She holds an elaborate yellow Cup, decorated with two angels and a cross. Scattered about her feet are colored rocks.

The **Queen of Cups** is a double water card; both Cups and Queens are symbolized by water. This card is assigned to the path from *Binah* to *Netzach*. *Binah* is called the Great Sea; *Netzach* is the *sephirah* of emotions, which corresponds to the element of water. The **Queen of Cups** is thus entirely a water being. The card's water symbols are the mer-babies, color of the robe, and her shell necklace.

This is the card of devotion. It is soft, feminine, intuitive and dreamy. The waters shown here are calm, unlike those upon which the **King of Cups** rides. The **Queen of Cups** represents an aspect of self that is tranquil, calm, patient, and intuitive. She is the guardian of religion and a quiet vessel for Divine waters. The Cup she holds appears to be a ciborium, a container for communion wafers, decorated with cherubim from the Ark of the Covenant. Her primary concern with the outer world is relationships; as water requires a

276

receptacle to hold it, so this Queen requires the receptacle of a relationship.

Externally, the **Queen of Cups** can be a nurturing, loving teacher. She is insightful and wise; her presence gives us such peace and joy that we may never want to leave her. However, the **Queen of Cups** has no balancing influences of earth, air or fire; thus, her emotions are not leavened by strong mind, body or awareness. As a result, she has a tendency to wallow in her own emotions and intuitions. Popular songs to the contrary, love isn't all there is. This is a person who loves her kids, but has trouble getting meals prepared; her home has enough chairs for everyone, but the utilities occasionally get turned off because she forgot to pay her bills.

People with a strong **Queen of Cups** aspect are usually found on the Path of Devotion and the Path of Service; alternately, the Queen may show up by establishing strong relationships with friends and family. In either case, the Queen serves us best when her watery attributes are consciously balanced by mind, body and will.

Knight of Cups

KNIGHT of CUPS.

Holding a yellow Cup before him, the Knight sits astride a white horse and prepares to ford a stream. The Knight's helmet and feet are winged; his tunic is decorated with red fish swimming through blue waves. The horse's bridle is decorated with blue waves.

The **Knight of Cups** unites water (Cups) with air (Knights), thus combining emotion and intellect. This card occupies the path from *Binah*, the Great Sea of the subconscious, to *Chesed*, the *sephirah* of mercy and loving-kindness. The **Knight of Cups** is the only Court Card to be part of the Lightning Flash described in Chapter One and shown in Figure 4. The card contains water symbols—red fish, watery bridle, stream—as well as the air symbol of the winged helm and feet.

The **Knight of Cups** is the messenger of communication, particularly the communication of emotions. The wings on helm and spurs symbolize the Greek messenger god, Mercury. The assigned path of *Keter* to *Malkuth* suggests that emotions can serve as the means of communication between the highest and lowest levels of awareness.

The **Knight of Cups** is that aspect of self that understands the language of emotions. The emotions we experience during dreams or in meditation are the **Knight of Cups** in action. We often ignore

278

these emotions because we're waiting for something more substantial—a voice or a vision—and fail to recognize that our emotion is the important messenger.

Emotion is also the primary means by which we communicate with others. We may exchange facts with one another, but a more powerful communication between human beings takes place on the emotional level. Observe that the **Knight of Cups** moves at a respectable and steady pace, holding his Cup steady so as not to spill its precious contents. Not for him the energetic frolicking of the **Knight of Wands**, the mad dash of the **Knight of Swords**, or the immobility of the **Knight of Pentacles**. Communication with others requires that the contents of our hearts be wisely and consciously brought forward.

The way we handle emotional communication with other people can provide insight into the way we handle emotional messages within ourselves. People who avoid emotional communication with others may also be deaf to emotional messages from and within themselves. The ability to receive and respond to such messages is an absolute prerequisite for advancement on the spiritual path. No matter how insightful our intellectual assessments, we must honor the journey, histories, and messages of our emotions in order to fully know ourselves. The skills of the **Knight of Cups** are to be cultivated on all spiritual paths.

Page of Cups

PAGE of CUPS.

The Page stands before a river, holding a yellow Cup from which a small blue fish peeks out. He is dressed in red leggings, orange boots, a red blouse and a blue tunic with red flowers on it. He wears a blue hat with a plume. The flowers on his tunic may have been intended to represent water lilies, though there is no great resemblance to those flowers.

The **Page of Cups** combines the elements of water (Cups) and earth (Pages). These elements are further reflected in this card's assignment to the path between the Great Sea of *Binah* and physical manifestation in *Malkuth*. The card's water symbols are the water lilies on the tunic, the fish in the cup and the river in the background.

Earth and water are often a happy mix; both are needed for growth. However, the fish in the Page's Cup suggests something else entirely. The appearance of the fish means that the water in the Cup isn't going to quench our thirst. The Page holds the Cup away from him and has his hand on his hip as if in exasperation; this aspect views his own emotions with disdain and keeps them at a distance. This Page possesses neither the control of the **King of Cups**, who has experienced his emotions and learned to master them, nor the overwhelming emotional content of the **Queen of Cups**. Instead, there is some part of him that fears his emotions or thinks that they are inappropriate. As a result, he keeps them at a distance.

A person with a small **Page of Cups** aspect may have just one or two parts of his life in which he refuses to participate emotionally. However, a person with a great deal of this energy may be emotionally frozen in many areas of life. We must consider how much of this Page we have within ourselves. Do we find ourselves bringing such Pages into our lives? If so, we should consider in what areas we ourselves may be emotionally frozen.

While it may seem that emotional disconnection is of value on the Path of the Mind and the Mystic Path, the inner wounds that have resulted in this disdain for the emotions will have to be resolved if these paths are to be walked to completion.

King of Swords

KING of SWORDS.

The King sits on a throne decorated with butterflies; he holds a Sword in his right hand. His crown is decorated with the face of a cherub. The trees in the background are jagged-looking, as if blown by a fierce wind. Birds fly high overhead and gray clouds gather in the background.

The **King of Swords** combines air (Swords) and fire (Kings). This card occupies the path from *Keter*, symbolizing will, to *Netzach*, the *sephirah* of the emotions. The element of air is shown in the card by the clouds, birds, butterflies and the winged angel.

Where the **King of Pentacles** looks down, the **King of Cups** looks to the side, and the **King of Wands** is seen in profile, this King looks directly at us. The **King of Swords** is a highly self-aware intellect, impartial and self-controlled. His superior and critical intellect allows him to maintain a clear head, no matter what the provocation. His gifts of intellect and self-awareness lead to scrupulous self-honesty. He does not flinch from the most excruciating self-examination, because he is far more interested in the truth than in pampering his feelings or ego. *Netzach* is the only emotional influence on this card, but it suggests that this wise King allows his emotional nature to help him govern his intellectual kingdom.

The unflinching character of this King can sometimes feel like criticism or judgment. However, the **King of Swords** intends not to hurt feelings but to remove roadblocks and correct faults. Those of us who avoid such teachers may find that we are not as honest with ourselves as we need to be. We may want to take a clear-eyed look at what we're trying to hide or protect.

Those on the Path of Service, the Path of Devotion, and the Path of the Mystic often feel that the resolute self-examination of the **King of Swords** is not necessary; however, this aspect is crucial on all spiritual paths to keep us from wandering off into fantasy, wishful thinking, or self-delusion.

Queen of Swords

QUEEN of SWORDS.

The Queen holds a Sword in her right hand; her left hand is extended and open, as if in welcome. Her cape is blue, decorated with white clouds. Both throne and crown are decorated with butterflies; the throne also shows a cherub's face. The trees and bird in the background are blown by the wind.

The **Queen of Swords** combines air (Swords) and water (Queens). This card is assigned to the path from *Keter* to *Gevurah*, suggesting restriction. The card's air symbols include the clouds, butterflies, cherub and wind.

This card's mix of intellect and emotion gives this Queen an intensively perceptive intelligence with an intuitive edge. Her understanding of both mind and emotion allows her to penetrate quickly into the heart of any matter. Her insight is so powerful it may seem she possesses psychic powers.

Unfortunately, the **Queen of Swords** has a tendency to exercise rigid control over not just her personal emotions, but over as much of her environment as possible. The Sword she holds is absolutely straight, suggesting rigidity; her mouth is grimly set. Despite the open hand she holds out, she is intolerant of weakness. Her need to control her environment causes her to feel strongly about rules and principles.

284

When seen in others, the **Queen of Swords** may appear overly strong and dominating; it is important to remember that, appearances notwithstanding, the weakness she despises is her own and the control she seeks is over her self. When we find ourselves disturbed by someone with a strong **Queen of Swords** aspect we may want to ask why we feel threatened; it may help to remember that her energy is truly not directed at us at all.

The **Queen of Swords'** control and her perceptive intelligence serve us well on all paths; even her rigidity may initially benefit us, as the discipline she imposes is important in the early stages. However, as we progress, this rigidity will need to be released.

Knight of Swords

KNIGHT of SWORDS.

The Knight brandishes his Sword high in the air as he charges, leaning forward over the saddle of his gray, wild-eyed horse. The Knight wears a feathered plume and a red cape. The horse's mane is jagged like the clouds above; the reins are decorated with the same birds that wheel in the sky. Birds, clouds and trees are blown about by a fierce wind.

Both Knights and the Suit of Wands are associated with the intellect and the element of air. This card is assigned to the path between *Keter*, symbolizing will or desire, and *Chesed*, which is mercy and compassion. The card's air symbols are the butterflies, feather, clouds and wind.

The **Knight of Swords** represents the unbridled power of the intellect. The mind, like its Sword symbol, likes to engage in battle. The **Knight of Swords** is frenetic and crazed, galloping as fast and hard as he can. With his quick, honed mind always unsheathed and ready, this Knight charges at the world, heedless of who or what might be in his way. The **Knight of Swords** represents sharpness of mind. But this may be intellect employed as a destructive force, used as a weapon rather than as a tool for discernment.

While the intellect's power is undeniable, we must remember that it isn't an all-purpose tool. A Sword may be good for cutting, but a Cup does a better job of holding water; a mind may be good for analyzing, but it's not good for holding emotion. The card's assignment to the path from *Keter* to *Chesed* suggests that the energy of this card—fast, sharp, destructive—must be softened by the energy of *Chesed*. Remembering that swordplay should be tempered by mercy will provide the necessary correction.

When seen externally, this aspect is a quick, sarcastic and often funny colleague. While laughing at the exhibition of verbal swordplay or admiring the keen, pointed criticism, we can lose sight of the inevitable consequences of warfare. A Sword can hurt; the damage it inflicts on others or on ourselves is not easily undone.

The razor-sharp, fast intellect of the **Knight of Swords** can be of benefit on the Path of Knowledge, where illusions and misapprehensions will fall quickly beneath his blade; but his tendency to cut and slice into others must be neutralized by the deliberate cultivation of compassion.

Page of Swords

PAGE of SWORDS.

The Page holds his Sword in both hands. He wears red leggings, red boots, a yellow blouse and a red tunic. Clouds gather behind him, birds are shown far overhead, and trees are blown by the wind.

The **Page of Swords** combines the element of air (Swords) and earth (Pages). The card occupies the path from *Keter*, symbolizing will or awareness, to *Hod*, symbolizing structure and the intellect; there is no balancing emotional influence found here. Air is symbolized by the clouds, birds and wind.

The **Page of Swords** is an aspect that employs the intellect inexpertly, unskilled in its art and unaccustomed to its weight. This Page waves his Sword in the air haphazardly and wildly, as if trying to get a feel for it.

An inability to focus the mind may, at first glance, look like deep spirituality; however, it is actually the sign of a weak and untrained mind. Those who are uncomfortable with the mind often disregard the need for training it. However, just as the heart must be taught to open, the body requires exercise, and awareness needs to be cultivated, so too the mind must be taught to focus, analyze and understand. To fully develop awareness on all levels, the mind must not be neglected.

If we find ourselves attracting weak-minded and unfocused people into our lives, it may indicate that we need to examine the strength of our own minds. We ourselves may need the training indicated.

This Page is a liability on all spiritual paths; however, it may be corrected if we applying ourselves to the discipline of the mind. Developing a sharp and focused mind will aid us in all aspects of our lives and on all spiritual paths.

King of Wands

KING of WANDS.

This stern, red-haired King does not sit comfortably on his throne. One hand is held tensely by his side and he leans slightly forward as if he's about to stand up. A salamander sits beside the throne; the high back of the throne is decorated with images of fire salamanders and lions.

Both Kings and the Suit of Wands are associated with the element of fire and the human will; thus, the **King of Wands** is a double fire card. This card is assigned to the path leading from *Chokmah* to *Yesod*. The influence of *Chokmah* suggests that mercy and compassion are necessary traits for the **King of Wands**; *Yesod* intimates that imagination is an important part of human desire and awareness. The element of fire is symbolized by the colors red and yellow, which are the predominant colors of all the Wand Court cards. Lions have been associated with fire since antiquity, as has the mythical fire salamander, which is born from, and is impervious to, flame.

There is no water or plant life shown—fire has burned up everything and only a desert remains. This suggests that the **King of Wands** has no regard for the concerns, pleasures, or distractions of the body, mind or heart. This King represents that part of us that wants to leave the plane of manifestation entirely. The Wand he holds is off the throne's platform, indicating that this King is ready to get up and go.

The **King of Wands** is strong-willed, energetic, charismatic, powerful and very advanced. The danger he faces is that the double fire energy may prove more powerful than the influences of *Chesed* and *Yesod*, burning out and overpowering these necessary influences of mercy and imagination as well as other aspects of the self. It may even burn itself out and reduce its powerful focus to ash; when this occurs, the King may then become the servant of superficial enthusiasms that come and go all too quickly.

Keeping this powerhouse energy appropriately muted when interacting with others can be a challenge for those with strong **King of Wands** aspects. The King's over-powering presence is the inevitable outcome of his strength. He is the enormous tree in the forest, casting such a long shadow that smaller trees get no sunshine. At his worst, this King knows he's hogging all the light, but his need to express himself is so strong that he cannot hold back. At his best, the **King of Wands** is able to keep quiet and actively help others to express themselves.

If we find ourselves attracting such Kings into our lives, we may wish to examine our relationship with our own power. It may be that we feel ourselves to be a small tree not deserving of sunshine.

The **King of Wands** aspect is helpful on the Path of the Mind and the Mystic Path. Those with strong **King of Wands** aspects tend to not be attracted to the Path of Service or the Path of Devotion.

Queen of Wands

QUEEN of WANDS.

The Queen holds a sunflower in one hand and a Wand in the other. Her throne is decorated with lions and sunflowers; the heads of two lions are carved into the throne itself. A black cat with sinister yellow eyes sits before the throne. In the far distance are three yellow mountain peaks.

The **Queen of Wands** combines two opposing elements—fire (Wands) and water (Queens). This card is assigned to the path from *Chokmah* to *Hod*. The **Queen of Wands** combines the power and force of *Chokmah* with the qualities of structure, mind and magic that are associated with *Hod*. The lions, sunflowers and the color yellow are all fire symbols, as befits a Wand Court Card.

The **Queen of Wands** is an aspect of self that is powerful, insightful and charismatic. Her calm and controlled demeanor tends to attract those who are out of balance in fire (desire, awareness) or water (emotion). As a result, she often finds herself to be the center of attention in a gathering. The lions on her throne face in opposite directions, indicating her ability to look at situations from both sides. Her capacity for spiritual awareness comes out of the calm that arises when water and fire quench each other's elemental nature. Though the **Queen of Wands** is as powerful and strong-willed as the

King of Wands, the Queen has more flexibility and possesses a calmer energy.

Unfortunately, the **Queen of Wands** may be tempted to use her power to pursue her own personal ends, instead of projects more appropriate to a higher order of being. She may meddle in the affairs of others or use her will magically in service of inferior goals. The black cat symbolizes this misuse of power.

The power and flexibility of the **Queen of Wands** is valuable on the Path of the Mind and the Mystic Path. Unlike the **King of Wands**, the Queen's more muted energy allows her to work well with and serve others; her fair judgment and spiritual awareness are also valuable assets on the Path of Service and the Path of Devotion.

Knight of Wands

KNIGHT of WANDS.

The Knight sits on a horse that is rearing up and out of control. He holds his Wand upright as if it were a lance. His armor is covered by a yellow surcoat emblazoned with salamanders. His horse is red, his gauntlets are red, and plumes of red sprout like fire from his helmet and the back of his surcoat. Three yellow mountain peaks stand in the background.

The **Knight of Wands** unites fire (Wands) with air (Knights). Together, fire and air are a highly combustible mixture, as implied by the high energy shown in this picture. This card is assigned to the path between *Chokmah* and *Gevurah*, suggesting that the high energy of fire, air and *Chokmah* may need to be controlled by the severity and restriction of *Gevurah*.

The Knight seems to be having difficulty controlling his mount. Though a great deal of energy is being displayed and expended, little actual progress is being made. The **Knight of Wands** represents an aspect that is struggling with the dissimilar goals of mind, symbolized by air, and will, symbolized by fire. Both mind and will are powerful, capricious creatures; neither easily relinquishes control to the other. It may seem unlikely for will and mind to be at odds, but it is actually quite common. The will reacts to desire on both conscious and subconscious levels; if these two levels desire different things, a battle ensues.

Seen externally, the **Knight of Wands** may appear as an aspirant who signs up for every class but attends none, who owns meditation cushions in every color but never meditates, and who possesses an extensive library of spiritual books but has never opened one up. What he thinks he wants to do, and what he actually does, don't match.

Aligning the desires of the will and the mind is important if we are to make progress, particularly on those paths represented by fire and air—the Path of the Mind and the Mystic Path.

Page of Wands

PAGE of WANDS.

The Page holds a Wand upright with two hands, staring at it intently as if trying to divine its purpose. His yellow tunic is decorated with fire salamanders, his hat sports a red feather, and the tops of his yellow boots look like flames against his red leggings. Three yellow mountain peaks occupy the background.

The **Page of Wands** combines fire (Wands) with earth (Pages). This card's assignment to the path from *Chokmah* to *Malkuth* gives us the impression of a high-level, expansive power brought to earth.

Wands and fire represent will, desire and awareness. Most of us have a pretty good idea of what desire is; though "will" is a little more esoteric, most of us can conjure up an idea of what a strong-willed person is like. The term "awareness," however, is far more difficult to apprehend.

The **Page of Wands** represents the discovery of awareness underlying mind, body and emotions, as well as learning how to use that awareness. Awareness is a powerful gool; it brings significant insights, heals wounds and helps us stay in balance. For some, this discovery comes early in the journey; for others, it remains theoretical for a long while.

In the early stages of the journey, awareness is a fragile flower. As earth extinguishes fire, it doesn't take much for awareness to be buried. This can happen in any number of ways—difficult life circumstances or physical pain, for example. Surprisingly, happy occasions can also result in loss of awareness. Falling in love or winning the lottery can effectively pull the aspirant's attention away from awareness and back into the physical or emotional worlds.

Remaining poised in our center, instead of swinging to the extremes of joy and despair, provides the best soil. The fragility of **Page of Wands** surfaces at some point on all spiritual paths and must be protected by mind, body and heart if it is to survive.

Chapter Ten Bibliography

1 Hulse, David Allen. *The Western Mysteries: An Encyclopedic Guide to the Sacred Languages & Magickal Systems of the World: The Key of It All, Book II.* St. Paul, MN: Llewellyn Publications, 2004, p. 333.

2 Waite, Arthur Edward. *The Pictorial Key to the Tarot.* Mineola, New York: Dover Publications, 2005, p. 112.

3 Waite, Arthur Edward. *The Pictorial Key to the Tarot.* Mineola, New York: Dover Publications, 2005, p. 206.

4 Warwick-Smith, Kate. *The Tarot Court Cards: Archetypal Patterns of Relationship in the Minor Arcana.* Rochester, VT: Destiny Books, 2003, pp. 77-78.

5 Goldberg, Natalie. *Writing Down the Bones: Freeing the Writer Within.* Boston, MA: Shambala Publications, Inc., 1986, p. 3.

Chapter Eleven

USING TAROT CARDS

Tarot cards are doorways into a higher way of thinking, feeling, and being in the world. They may also be used as subjects for meditation, as keys to unlock specific issues or problems, or as an initiatory system.

Tarot Cards as Meditations

There are many complex Tarot spreads that employ a large number of cards; the best-known Tarot spread is the Celtic Cross spread, which uses ten cards. However, when we use Tarot cards for spiritual guidance, complicated spreads are unnecessary and actually inhibit the working of our intuition. Beginners should start with just one card, then two and eventually three.

There are different ways of picking your cards. Generally, cards are chosen face-down, so that the selection is more or less random. Some people shuffle the deck and pick the top cards; others flip through the deck slowly, selecting cards that seem to "nudge" them and "ask" to be picked. Try different ways until you find what works for you.

Place the cards you've selected face-down in front of you. Become very quiet and centered. Turn the first card over. If it's upside-down, turn it right-side up. When using the cards for guidance or meditation, an upside-down image tends to inhibit the process. Now spend some time with this card. You might want to imagine that it is whispering to you, very quietly; you will have to become very still to hear it. What does this card have to teach you right now, at this point in your life? When you think you have heard what the card has to say, turn over the second card and repeat the process. When you have uncovered all three cards, see if you can create a unified message from the three cards, as if each of the three cards is an essential part of the message. You can use this book as a jumping-off point for the messages of the cards, but after you've used the cards for a while, you should expect to associate new meanings, perhaps very personal meanings, to the cards.

You may find a common element between the cards you've selected. For example, you might draw the **Queen of Pentacles, The Magician** and the **Three of Pentacles**. In comparing the pictures, you notice that all three cards have at least one Pentacle and also a rose. (In the **Three of Pentacles**, a rose design is built into the stone arch.) This might suggest that you pay particular attention to physical manifestation (Pentacles) and desire (roses).

Also, the placement of the three cards on the Tree can spur your intuition. For example, drawing **The Sun** (*Hod* to *Yesod*), **Temperance** (*Tifaret* to *Yesod*) and any of the Nine cards suggests paying particular attention to some aspect of *Yesod*. Perhaps there is an element of fantasy at work? Or perhaps a situation may be worked on an astral level before attempting to work it on the physical?

Sometimes one particular card will be silent—at this moment, it means nothing. Usually, the second or third card will clarify its meaning. For example, the **Three of Cups** usually signifies to me the basic structure of existence: birth, life and death. If it is partnered with the **Seven of Swords**, I look to see if I am struggling to accept one or more or these aspects of existence. However, if it shows up with **The Moon**, I might want to take a close look to see if I have woven some sort of fantasy around birth, life or death that I'm ready to release. If the **King of Wands** shows up with the **Three of Cups**, I might consider what the birth, life and death structure look like from a higher level of awareness.

The cards may also be viewed as a problem/solution statement. For example, if my three cards are the **Nine of Wands**, the **Five of Pentacles** and **Strength**, I can see that there are two "problem" cards and one "solution" card. The **Nine of Wands** and **Five of Pentacles** represent difficult times, spiritually and physically. Before proceeding further, I stop and reflect on how these difficulties are manifesting right now. Then I move on to the "solution" card, **Strength**; meditating on **Strength** can help me see what these difficulties can teach me and how to best deal with them.

It is important to remember that every card is the right card, representing a particular "take" on any situation, problem, event or time period. As a result, while each card may bring a slightly different aspect to light, no card can ever be wrong. Also, there is no incorrect interpretation of a card. Each card means something different to each person. Tarot is not a subject to be mastered; you don't get good grades for memorization or the ability to spit out what you've learned. It is intended to help you develop eyes to see and ears to hear; the only true measure of your success in working with Tarot is the degree to which it helps you attain that goal.

You may find it helpful to keep a journal of your meditations. Write down everything that comes to you, including ideas that you dismissed for any reason. It can be very informative to meditate on cards in the morning, write down what you think they mean to you, and then return to them in the evening. I am often amazed at how completely my understanding of the applicability of these cards to my life changes in just ten or twelve hours.

Sometimes having a question in mind helps to unlock the cards' messages. My favorite question is: What is happening right now? Other appropriate questions are: What aspect of self should I be looking at? What is keeping me locked into lower awareness right now? What have I forgotten? What should I keep in mind throughout this day?

Tarot Cards as
Keys for Specific Issues

If you're struggling with a particular problem or question, whether spiritual or mundane, Tarot cards can help you. If all you have is a vague feeling about what's wrong, communicating with the subconscious through Tarot cards can help you put your finger on what's bothering you. If you have a general idea of what the problem is, Tarot cards can help narrow the focus. If you have a pretty definite idea of what's wrong, Tarot cards can help you understand the problem on a deeper level, or on a level more suitable for a solution.

The Tarot cards will let you know if you've asked the wrong question or if you've asked it in the wrong way. If you ask a question and get a muddled response, it's usually an indication that the question isn't clear. It may also indicate that a more useful answer to the question exists but you need to ask the question differently or ask it from a different viewpoint. While it's easy to feel frustrated and immediately start asking more questions and flipping more cards, it's better to leave the cards alone and do something else for a while. The more frustrated you get, the less sense the Tarot cards will make. Settle down, clear your head and try looking at the question differently. If the question was asked from a personality level, consider asking from a Higher Self level—or vice versa. If the situation was viewed as a problem, try viewing it as a blessing or at least as a learning situation.

When you're feeling stuck on something, it can be useful to go through the deck and deliberately select a few cards that seem pertinent to the situation or question. It should be fairly easy to get a message from cards you've hand-picked. Once you feel you've mastered what these cards have to say, turn one of them face-down and choose another card at random to replace it. Starting from the familiar base of the hand-picked cards, the message of this new card may be incorporated into the mix with little difficulty. Then repeat the process, selecting another hand-picked card to turn face-down and replacing it with another randomly chosen card.

Advanced aspirants may wish to move into a meditative space, "invite" the appropriate cards to appear in awareness and then allow the meanings of the cards to become apparent. This method works best if there are clearly defined limits such as a maximum number of cards allowed and a clearly-framed question or situation. This is not recommended for aspirants still operating out of egoic consciousness, as there will be a tendency for fears and wishful thinking to color the results. Fears will generally manifest as the appearance of "scary" cards, such as Swords cards, **Death** or **The Devil**; wishful thinking brings "happy" cards such as **The Lovers, Ten of Cups**, **Six of Wands** or "important" cards such as **The Hierophant, The Magician, The Sun**, and **The World**.

The Court Cards may be used to identify personality traits other than those identified in this book. It can be useful to look through the Court Cards and see which cards seem to resonate with you. What aspects of yourself do you see in these cards? Do these aspects help or hinder you?

Tarot Cards as an Initiatory System

Another way of working with the Tarot cards is to go through all the cards, one at a time, slowly and thoroughly. Start with **The Fool** and work through the Major Arcana, then the Minor Arcana, and finally the Court Cards. Dedicate one full week to each card, using the following activities to deepen the experience. There are 78 cards, so recognize that this will take a year and a half. This may seem like a long time, but if you take this seriously, you may find you are a completely different person in a mere 18 months. Here's the weekly program:

1. Study the card visually. Learn every last detail of the card, down to the color of the sky and the background. It helps if we carry the card with us wherever we go, so that we can spend a few minutes with it while waiting in traffic or standing in line at the store. It's much more pleasant to spend that time gazing at a Tarot card than swearing at the driver in front of us or wondering why it is that we always pick the slowest cashier.

2. Meditate on the card several times during that week. Use the meditations in this book and write down your experience of them. Don't neglect these meditations throughout the week and then try to hurry up and get them all in on Friday. It's a far better practice to spread the meditations out over the week. One thing we tend to forget in our hurry-up culture is the importance of time—seedlings don't sprout overnight, no matter how much fertilizer we give them.

3. Consider the placement of the card on the Tree of Life. Draw the ten *sephirot* on a piece of paper and mark where the card fits on the Tree. What does this placement signify? Is there a place on the Tree that might be a better fit for our understanding of the card? Remember that there is nothing sacred about the card placements on the Tree.

4. Help the subconscious express itself through some form of creativity. Those who enjoy writing may wish to write a short story or poem about

this card. What is happening here? Who are you in this story? You may find that you are an animal, a tree, or part of the background. Why are you this figure or character? What are you here for? Is it pleasant or unpleasant? What emotions arise for you? If you are an artist, consider creating a picture, painting, sculpture or whatever you most enjoy that pertains to the card. How does your creation relate to the card? What aspect of the card does it reflect? Note your use of colors and composition—why these colors? Why is one part big and another part small, or one part dark and another part bright? Sometimes we don't recognize what our subconscious is expressing, so consider asking someone else to tell you what they see in this creation. There is no limit to what can be done creatively—write music, create a meal, wear certain clothes, make a mask, design jewelry, etc. And don't feel locked into any one art form: it's great to let different aspects of your creative genius express themselves.

5. Let dreams become part of the process. Before you go to sleep, ask your subconscious to communicate with you about the card you're studying. It may take a little time before your subconscious takes you seriously, but don't give up—the subconscious responds to persistence and repetition. Keeping paper and pen at your bedside, as well as a flashlight if there's a concern about waking up a bedmate, is important. Most Western Mystery Tradition adherents maintain a regular dream journal and periodically review their dreams to see what new insights arise.

6. Find Tarot cards in daily life. Once you become attuned to the cards, you'll find these archetypes everywhere. **The Hanged Man** appears as the person who has reached a new level of acceptance of life circumstances or is struggling to do so. What once appeared to be wanton destruction may now be seen as **The Tower**. Aspects of life that once seemed ugly and inappropriate may be seen as Auriel disguised as **The Devil**, challenging us to see through appearances. At the end of each day, look through the deck and see how many cards made an appearance in your day. You may find that some cards appear again and again.

7. Periodically, place the **Ten of Pentacles, Ten of Cups, Ten of Swords** and **Ten of Wands** side-by-side and consider how these four cards together represent a fully Initiated person. Over time, your understanding of the way in which the concepts represented by these four cards work together will deepen and develop.

Whether you choose to consult Tarot cards only when you are troubled, or commit to the long road of studying them for months or even years, they have much to offer. The cards might not tell you when you can expect fortune or love, but they can stimulate your thinking and fuel your meditations. They can remind you to keep your ego from interfering with personal development. They can shed light on the mysteries of awakening. More importantly, with self-honesty, patience and commitment, the wisdom hidden in their images and symbols can help you make steady progress on your spiritual journey, no matter how difficult the road or distant your ultimate goal of Initiation may appear.

Suggested Reading List

The books below may further your study of Kabbalah, Tarot and the Western Mystery Tradition.

Andrea, Raymund. *The Mystic Path*. San Jose, CA: Grand Lodge of the English Language Jurisdiction, 1999. Old-fashioned language, but highly recommended work from an often-overlooked source.

Andrea, Raymund. *The Technique of the Disciple*. San Jose, CA: Grand Lodge of the English Language Jurisdiction, 1999. Old-fashioned language, but highly recommended work from an often-overlooked source.

Andrea, Raymund. *The Technique of the Master*. Kingsport, TN: Kingsport Press, 1979. Old-fashioned language, but highly recommended work from an often-overlooked source.

Ashcroft-Nowicki, Dolores. *Illuminations: Mystical Meditations on the Hebrew Alphabet*. St. Paul, MN: Llewellyn Publications, 2003. Each Hebrew letter is given a prayer, a discussion of the letter, a series of meditations, a pathworking, a psalm and a ritual.

Ashcroft-Nowicki, Dolores and Brennan, J. H. *Magical Use of Thought Forms*. St. Paul, MN: Llewellyn Publications, 2002. Magical techniques such as observation, building desire, training the memory, etc.

Ashcroft-Nowicki, Dolores. *The Initiate's Book of Pathworkings*. York Beach, ME: Samuel Weiser, Inc., 1999. A wide variety of pathworkings—Egyptian, Grecian, Angelic, Fairy, etc.

Bentov, Itzhak. *A Brief Tour of Higher Consciousness: A Cosmic Book on the Mechanics of Creation*. Rochester, VT: Destiny Books, 2000. Imaginative work from a brilliant engineer and mystic.

Bentov, Itzhak. *Stalking the Wild Pendulum: On the Mechanics of Consciousness*. Rochester, VT: Destiny Books, 1988. Cult classic from the 1970s and best-known of Bentov's books;

Bonner, John. *Qabalah: A Magical Primer*. York Beach, ME: Weiser Books, 2002. Presents the subject from a Golden Dawn/Crowley viewpoint. Excellent overview of kabbalah for Western Mystery Tradition practitioners.

Case, Paul Foster. *Book of Tokens: Tarot Meditations.* Los Angeles, CA: Builders of the Adytum, 1968. Meditations on the Major Arcana, written by the greatest Tarot scholar of the mid-twentieth century.

Case, Paul Foster. *Tarot: A Key to the Wisdom of the Ages.* Richmond, VA: Macoy Publishing Company, 1947. Mini-version of the mail-order course developed by Case and now offered through Builders of the Adytum.

Case, Paul Foster. *The True and Invisible Rosicrucian Order.* York Beach, ME: Samuel Weiser, Inc., 1985. The first half of the book describes the symbolism and meaning of the principal documents of the Rosicrucian order. The second part explores a map of spiritual development based on the Tree of Life.

Chefitz, Mitchell. *The Seventh Telling: The Kabbalah of Moshe Katan.* New York, NY: St. Martin's Press, 2002. Fascinating fictional account of Kabbalist Moshe Katan's struggles with family and studies.

Chefitz, Mitchell. *The Thirty-Third Hour.* New York, NY: St. Martin's Press, 2002. Sequel to *The Seventh Telling*; the further adventures of Kabbalist Moshe Katan.

Christopher, Lyam Thomas. *Kabballah, Magic and the Great Work of Self-Transformation.* Self-paced course: light on Kabbalah, heavy on Golden Dawn magic.

Dedopulus, Tim. *Kabbalah: An Illustrated Introduction to the Esoteric Heart of Jewish Mysticism.* New York, NY: Gramercy Books, 2005. Attractive book with lots of photos, but not much information.

Decker, Depaulis and Dummett. *A Wicked Pack of Cards: The Origin of the Occult Tarot.* London: Gerald Duckworth & Co., 2002. Myth-debunking book on the history of Tarot. The authors are historians, not esotericists.

Eakins, Pamela. *Tarot of the Spirit.* York Beach, ME: Weiser Books, 1992. Lovely and intelligent earth-friendly Tarot deck and explanatory book by a practicing Kabbalist.

Epstein, Perle. *Kabbalah: The Way of the Jewish Mystic.* The history of Kabbalah traced through the lives of its participants; includes various practices.

Fine, Lawrence. *Safed Spirituality.* Ramsey, NJ: Paulist Press, 1984. Detailed, scholarly view of Kabbalists and practices of Safedic Kabbalism.

Fortune, Dion and Knight, Gareth. *An Introduction to Ritual Magic.* Loughborough, Leicestershire, UK: Thoth Publications, 2006. A series of lessons nicely supplemented with modern commentary by Gareth Knight.

Fortune, Dion. *Mystical Qabalah.* York Beach, Maine: Samuel Weiser, Inc., 2000. Classic work written in 1935; good overview of the Tree of Life and required reading for Western Mystery Tradition practitioners.

Fortune, Dion (commentary by Knight, Gareth). *Principles of Hermetic Philosophy.* Loughborough, UK: Thoth Publications, 1999. Contains at least as much Kabbalah as Hermetism; covers the Tree of Life and the Three Pillars as well as Hermetic principles.

Fortune, Dion. *Sane Occultism* and *Practical Occultism in Daily Life.* Wellingborough, Northhamptonshire, UK: The Aquarian Press, 1987. Two books in one, dealing with how occultism impacts—and is impacted by—mundane life.

Fortune, Dion. *The Cosmic Doctrine.* York Beach, ME: Red Wheel/ Weiser, LLC, 2000. Another Western Mystery Tradition classic; treat these concepts as symbolic rather than as astronomical facts.

Fortune, Dion. *Training and Work of an Initiate.* York Beach, Maine: Samuel Weiser, Inc., 2000. This is less about training and more about esoteric philosophy.

Frankiel, Tamar. *The Gift of Kabbalah: Discovering the Secrets of Heaven, Renewing Your Life on Earth.* Woodstock, VT: Jewish Lights Publishing, 2004. Excellent work on using Kabbalah for spiritual renewal. Highly recommended.

Goddard, David. *The Tower of Alchemy: An Advanced Guide to the Great Work.* York Beach, ME: Samuel Weiser, Inc., 1999. Interesting look at alchemy for personal transformation, with a little Tibetan Buddhism thrown in for good measure. Assumes some knowledge of Kabbalah and the Western Mystery Tradition.

Gray, William. "Patterns of Western Magic: A Psychological Appreciation" in Tart, C. (ed.) *Transpersonal Psychologies.* New York, NY: Harper San Francisco, 1992. Charles Tart is the only transpersonal psychologist to date who includes the western mystery tradition as a spiritual discipline. Gray's essay is an excellent contribution to the book.

Green, Marian. *The Path Through the Labyrinth: The Quest for Initiation into the Western Mystery Tradition.* Longmead, Shaftesbury, Dorset, UK: Element Books, 1988. Sensible guide to the Western Mystery Tradition that manages to be warm and whimsical, but not woo-woo.

Greenwell, Bonnie. *Energies of Transformation: A Guide to the Kundalini Process.* Saratoga, CA: Shakti River Press, 1990. Required reading for everyone on a spiritual path.

Grof, Stanislav and Grof, Christina (Eds.) *Spiritual Emergency: When Personal Transformation Becomes a Crisis.* New York, NY: Penguin Putnam Inc., 1989. Required reading for everyone on a spiritual path.

Halevi, Z'ev ben Shimon. *Introduction to Cabala: Tree of Life.* York Beach, ME: Samuel Weiser, Inc., 1991. Good introductory text from a modern and slightly New Age-y standpoint.

Halevi, Z'ev ben Shimon. *Kabbalah: Tradition of Hidden Knowledge.* New York, NY: Thames and Hudson, Inc., 1985. Beautiful photos; best as a companion text to his other book rather than as a stand-alone work.

Halevi, Z'ev ben Shimon. *Kabbalah and Exodus.* Boulder, Colorado: Shambala Publications, 1980. Examines the story of the Exodus as an allegory for spiritual growth. Great pre-Passover reading.

Halevi, Z'ev ben Shimon. *The Work of the Kabbalist.* York Beach, ME: Samuel Weiser, Inc., 1986. Easy to read modern work that explores the Tree from a psychological viewpoint.

Hall, Manly P. *Self-Unfoldment by Disciplines of Realization.* Los Angeles, CA: Philosophical Research Society, 1995. Worthwhile study of illumination.

Hall, Manly P. *The Secret Teachings of All Ages: An Encyclopedic Outline of Masonic, Hermetic, Qabbalistic and Rosicrucian Symbolical Philosophy.* Los Angeles, CA: Philosophical Research Society, 2000. This masterwork deserves a place of honor on every bookshelf.

Hoffman, Edward (Ed.). *Opening the Inner Gate.* Boston, MA: Shambhala, 1995. Collection of essays on Kabbalah and psychology from a variety of authors.

Hope, Murry. *The Psychology of Ritual.* Longmead, Shaftesbury, Dorset, UK: Element Books, 1988. Excellent discussion of how and why ritual works.

Hulse, David Allen. *The Key of It All: An Encyclopedic Guide to the Sacred Languages & Magickal Systems of the World. Book One: The Eastern Mysteries.* St. Paul, MN: Llewellyn Publications, 1996. Required sourcebook for all Western Mystery Tradition practitioners.

Hulse, David Allen. *The Western Mysteries: An Encyclopedic Guide to the Sacred Languages & Magickal Systems of the World: The Key of It All, Book II.* St. Paul, MN: Llewellyn Publications, 2004. Required sourcebook for all Western Mystery Tradition practitioners.

Kaplan, Aryeh. *Jewish Meditation.* New York, NY: Schocken Books, 1985. Easy to read overview, highly recommended.

Kaplan, Aryeh. *Meditation and Kabbalah.* Northvale, NJ: Jason Aronson, Inc., 1995. This is the advanced version of his Jewish Meditation, written from an orthodox viewpoint.

Kaplan, Aryeh (Trans.). *Sefer Yetzirah.* York Beach, Maine: Samuel Weiser, Inc., 1997. This is a popular modern translation of the ancient classic; Kaplan's excellent notes make it a worthwhile study.

Kaplan, Aryeh (Trans.) *The Bahir.* York Beach, Maine: Samuel Weiser, Inc., 1997. Kaplan's scholarship makes this an important addition to a Kabbalist's library; not a beginning text.

Kleigman, Isabel Radow. *Tarot and the Tree of Life.* Wheaton, IL: Quest Books. An unusual look at the Minor Arcana; worthwhile reading.

Kushner, Lawrence. *Sefer Otiyot: The Book of Letters: a Mystical Alef-bait.* Woodstock, VT: Jewish Lights Publishing, 2009. Calligraphy-style meditations on Hebrew letters. Beautiful little book for meditation.

Matt, Daniel. *The Essential Kabbalah.* New York, NY: Quality Paperback Book Club, 1995. Starter text from the number one *Zohar* scholar of our time.

Matt, Daniel (Trans.). *Zohar: The Book of Enlightenment.* Mahweh, NJ: Paulist Press, 1983. This is the mid-level *Zohar* text—make sure you use the notes in the back of the book.

Matt, Daniel (Trans.). *The Zohar, Volumes One through Five.* Stanford, CA: Stanford University Press. This is Matt's seminal work; not for beginners or the faint of heart.

Matthews, Caitlin and Matthews, John. *The Western Way: A Practical Guide to the Western Mystery Tradition. Volume 2, The Hermetic Tradition.* London, England: Arkana Paperbacks, 1986. Good overview of the various tributaries of the Western Mystery Tradition.

Motley, Evelyn. Exodus: *Through the Mystical Light of the Kabalah.* Decatur, GA: Booksurge, 2003. Christian Kabbalism: the Exodus is presented as a metaphor for spiritual advancement.

Novick, Leah. *On the Wings of the Shekhinah: Rediscovering Judaism's Divine Feminine.* Wheaton, IL: Quest Books, 2008. Kabbalah-light and feminism-heavy.

Regardie, Israel. *The Middle Pillar: The Balance Between Mind and Magic.* Woodbury, Minnesota: Llewellyn Publications, 2006. Regardie's classic text is a psychological/magical perspective on Kabbalah.

Scholem, Gershom. *Major Trends in Jewish Mysticism.* New York, NY: Schocken Books, 1995. Scholarly exploration of the development of Jewish mysticism from Merkabah in ancient times to Hasidism in eighteenth century. Bring your dictionary and take your time, but worth the effort.

Scholem, Gershom. *On the Kabbalah and Its Symbolism.* New York, NY: Schocken Books, 1996. Detailed look at Kabbalistic beliefs from the scholarly, rather than spiritual, viewpoint.

Scholem, Gershom. *Origins of the Kabbalah.* Princeton University Press, 1990. Scholarly exploration of development of Kabbalah.

Seidman, Richard. *The Oracle of Kabbalah.* New York, NY: Thomas Dunne Books, 2001. Lightweight little text offers meditations on Hebrew letters.

Three Initiates. *The Kybalion.* Chicago, Illinois: Yogi Publication Society, 1940. Dated, but still a classic and required reading for Western Mystery Tradition practitioners.

Underhill, Evelyn. *Mysticism: The Nature and Development of Spiritual Consciousness.* Oxford, UK: Oneworld Publications, 1999. Seminal text about Christian mysticism; well worth the time.

Waite, Arthur Edward. *The Holy Kabbalah.* New Hyde Park, NY: University Books, 1969. An English rendition of a French translation; interesting mainly for historic reasons.

Waite, Arthur Edward. *The Pictorial Key to the Tarot.* Mineola, New York: Dover Publications, 2005. Surprisingly uninspiring and dull work; interesting for historic reasons.

Wang, Robert. *The Qabalistic Tarot: A Textbook of Mystical Philosophy.* Canada: Marcus Aurelius Press, 2004. Required reading for Western Mystery Tradition practitioners.

Zimler, Richard. *The Last Kabbalist of Lisbon.* New York, NY: The Overlook Press, 2000. Gripping fictional account of Jews living in Portugal at the time of the Expulsion.

Complete Bibliography

Andrea, Raymund. *The Mystic Path*. San Jose, CA: Grand Lodge of the English Language Jurisdiction, 1999.

Andrea, Raymund. *The Technique of the Disciple*. San Jose, CA: Grand Lodge of the English Language Jurisdiction, 1999.

Andrea, Raymund. *The Technique of the Master*. Kingsport, TN: Kingsport Press, 1979.

Bentov, Itzhak. *A Brief Tour of Higher Consciousness: A Cosmic Book on the Mechanics of Creation*. Rochester, VT: Destiny Books, 2000.

Boyer, Ernest, Jr. *A Way in the World: Family Life as Spiritual Discipline*. San Francisco: Harper & Row, 1984.

Butler, W. E. *The Magician: His Training and Work*. North Hollywood, CA: Wilshire Book Company, 1969.

Case, Paul Foster. *Book of Tokens: Tarot Meditations*. Los Angeles, CA: Builders of the Adytum, 1968.

Case, Paul Foster. *Tarot: A Key to the Wisdom of the Ages*. Richmond, VA: Macoy Publishing Company, 1947.

Case, Paul Foster. *The True and Invisible Rosicrucian Order*. York Beach, ME: Samuel Weiser, Inc., 1985.

Cavalli, Thom. *Alchemical Psychology*. New York, NY: Penguin Putnam, Inc., 2002.

David-Neel, Alexandra and Youngdon, Lama. *The Secret Oral Teachings in Tibetan Buddhist Sects*. San Francisco, CA: City Lights Books, 1967.

Decker, Depaulis and Dummett. *A Wicked Pack of Cards: The Origin of the Occult Tarot*. London: Gerald Duckworth & Co., 2002.

Eakins, Pamela. *Tarot of the Spirit*. York Beach, ME: Weiser Books, 1992.

Elgin, Duane. "The Tao of Personal and Social Transformation" in R. Walsh and F. Vaughan (Eds) *Paths Beyond Ego: The Transpersonal Vision*. New York, NY: Penguin Putnam, Inc., 1993.

Epstein, Gerald. "What's Wrong with Freudianism: A Kabbalistic Perspective" in Hoffman, Edward (Ed.) *Opening the Inner Gate*, Boston, MA: Shambhala, 1995.

Fortune, Dion. *Applied Magic*. York Beach, ME: Samuel Weiser, Inc., 2000.

Fortune, Dion. *Aspects of Occultism*. York Beach, ME: Samuel Weiser, Inc., 2000.

Fortune, Dion. *Mystical Qabalah*. York Beach, Maine: Samuel Weiser, Inc., 2000.

Fortune, Dion (commentary by Knight, Gareth). *Principles of Hermetic Philosophy*. Loughborough, UK: Thoth Publications, 1999.

Fortune, Dion. *Sane Occultism and Practical Occultism in Daily Life*. Wellingborough, Northhamptonshire, UK: The Aquarian Press, 1987.

Fortune, Dion. *Training and Work of an Initiate*. York Beach, Maine: Samuel Weiser, Inc., 2000.

Fortune, Dion. *What Is Occultism?* York Beach, ME: Samuel Weiser, Inc., 2001.

Goldberg, Natalie. *Writing Down the Bones: Freeing the Writer Within*. Boston, MA: Shambala Publications, Inc., 1986.

Goddard, David. *The Tower of Alchemy: An Advanced Guide to the Great Work*. York Beach, ME: Samuel Weiser, Inc., 1999.

Grof, Stanislav and Grof, Christina (Eds.). *Spiritual Emergency: When Personal Transformation Becomes a Crisis*. New York, NY: Penguin Putnam Inc., 1989.

Halevi, Z'ev ben Shimon. *Kabbalah and Exodus*. Boulder, Colorado: Shambala Publications, 1980.

Hall, Manly P. *Self-Unfoldment by Disciplines of Realization*. Los Angeles, CA: Philosophical Research Society, 1995.

Hall, Manly P. *Spiritual Centers in Man*. Los Angeles, CA: Philosophical Research Society, 1999.

Hall, Manly P. *What the Ancient Wisdom Expects of Its Disciples*. Los Angeles, CA: Philosophical Research Society, 1982.

Hoeller, Stephen. *The Royal Road*. London, England: Arkana Paperbacks, 1986.

Hope, Murry. *The Psychology of Ritual*. Longmead, Shaftesbury, Dorset, UK: Element Books, 1988.

Hulse, David Allen. *The Western Mysteries: An Encyclopedic Guide to the Sacred Languages & Magickal Systems of the World: The Key of It All, Book II*. St. Paul, MN: Llewellyn Publications, 2004.

Johnson, Robert A. *Inner Work: Using Dreams & Active Imagination for Personal Growth*. San Francisco, CA: Harper & Row, 1986.

Jung, Carl. *Memories, Dreams, Reflections*. New York, NY: Random House, 1965.

Kaplan, Aryeh. *Meditation and Kabbalah*. Northvale, NJ: Jason Aronson, Inc., 1995.

Kaplan, Aryeh (Trans.). *Sefer Yetzirah*. York Beach, Maine: Samuel Weiser, Inc., 1997.

Kliegman, Isabel Radow. *Tarot and the Tree of Life: Finding Everyday Wisdom in the Minor Arcana*. Wheaton, ILL: Quest Books, 1997.

Levi, Éliphas. *Transcendental Magic*. (Waite, A. E., Trans.) York Beach, ME: Weiser Books, 2001.

Matt, Daniel (Trans.). *The Zohar, Volume Two*. Stanford, CA: Stanford University Press, 2004.

Matt, Daniel. *Zohar: Annotated & Explained*. Woodstock, VT: Skylight Paths Publishing, 2003.

Matthews, Caitlin and Matthews, John. *The Western Way: A Practical Guide to the Western Mystery Tradition. Volume 2, The Hermetic Tradition*. London, England: Arkana Paperbacks, 1986.

Moore, Thomas. *Care of the Soul: A Guide for Cultivating Depth and Sacredness in Everyday Life*. New York, NY: Harper Perennial, 1992.

Ouspensky, P.D. *A New Model of the Universe*. Mineola, NY: Dover Publications, 1997.

Perlmutter, Dawn and Koppman, Debra. *Reclaiming the Spiritual in Art: Contemporary Cross-Cultural Perspectives*. Albany, NY: State University of New York Press, 1999.

Regardie, Israel. *The Tree of Life: An Illustrated Study in Magic*. Woodbury, Minnesota: Llewellyn Publications, 2006.

Regardie, Israel. *The Middle Pillar: The Balance Between Mind and Magic*. Woodbury, Minnesota: Llewellyn Publications, 2006.

Roberts, Bernadette. *Path to No-Self*. Albany, NY: State University of New York Press, 1991.

Roberts, Bernadette. *What Is Self? A Study of the Spiritual Journey in Terms of Consciousness*. Boulder, CO: Sentient Publications, 2005.

Roscoe, Hugh. *Occultism and Christianity: A Restatement of Faith*. London, UK: Rider & Co., 2004.

Schnapper, Edith B. *The Inward Odyssey: The Concept of the Way in the Great Religions of the World*. London, UK: George Allen & Unwin, 1980.

Scholem, Gershom. *Major Trends in Jewish Mysticism*. New York, NY: Schocken Books, 1995.

Scholem, Gershom. *On the Kabbalah and Its Symbolism*. New York, NY: Schocken Books, 1996.

Scott, Cyril. *The Initiate in the New World*. York Beach, ME: Samuel Weiser, Inc, 1991.

Smith, Huston. *The World's Religions*. New York, NY: Harper Collins, 1991.

Tart, Charles (Ed.). *Transpersonal Psychologies*. New York, NY: Harper San Francisco, 1992.

Three Initiates. *The Kybalion*. Chicago, Illinois: Yogi Publication Society, 1940.

Troward, Thomas. *Edinburgh Lectures on Mental Science*. Charleston, South Carolina: BiblioBazaar, 2007.

Underhill, Evelyn. *Mysticism: The Nature and Development of Spiritual Consciousness*. Oxford, UK: Oneworld Publications, 1999.

Vivekananda, Swami. *What Religion Is*. New York, NY: Julia Press, 1962.

Waite, Arthur Edward. *The Pictorial Key to the Tarot*. Mineola, New York: Dover Publications, 2005.

Walsh, Roger. *Essential Spirituality: The 7 Central Practices to Awaken Heart and Mind*. New York, NY: John Wiley & Sons, 1999.

Walsh, R. and Vaughan, F. (Eds.). *Paths Beyond Ego*. New York, New York: Penguin Putnam, Inc., 1993.

Wang, Robert. *The Jungian Tarot and its Archetypal Imagery*. Canada: Marcus Aurelius Press, 2001.

Wang, Robert. *The Qabalistic Tarot: A Textbook of Mystical Philosophy*. Canada: Marcus Aurelius Press, 2004, p. 243.

Warwick-Smith, Kate. *The Tarot Court Cards: Archetypal Patterns of Relationship in the Minor Arcana*. Rochester, VT: Destiny Books, 2003.

Webb, Andrew. *The Occult Underground*. La Salle, IL: Open Court, 1974.

Whitcomb, Bill. *The Magician's Companion: A Practical & Encyclopedic Guide to Magical & Religious Symbolism.* Woodbury, MN: Llewellyn Publications, 2007.

NOTE: All Biblical quotes come from Etz Hayim, by The Rabbinical Assembly of the United Synagogue of Conservative Judaism, published by the Jewish Publication Society, New York, NY, 2001.

Lightning Source UK Ltd.
Milton Keynes UK
UKHW011332111119
353312UK00004B/1254/P